Event Impact Assessment:

Theory and Methods for Event Management and Tourism

Donald Getz, PhD.

(G) Goodfellow Publishers Ltd

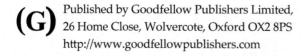

Published by Goodfellow Publishers Limited,
26 Home Close, Wolvercote, Oxford OX2 8PS
http://www.goodfellowpublishers.com

British Library Cataloguing in Publication Data: a catalogue
record for this title is available from the British Library.

Library of Congress Catalog Card Number: on file.

ISBN: 978-1-911635-03-1

The Events Management Theory and Methods Series

 Design and typesetting by P.K. McBride, www.macbride.org.uk

Cover design by Cylinder

Printed by Baker and Taylor, www.baker-taylor.com

Contents

List of Figures

Introduction to the Events Management Theory and Methods Series

Event management as a field of study and professional practice has its textbooks with plenty of models and advice, a body of knowledge (EMBOK), competency standards (MBECS) and professional associations with their codes of conduct. But to what extent is it truly an applied management field? In other words, where is the management theory in event management, how is it being used, and what are the practical applications?

Event tourism is a related field, one that is defined by the roles events play in tourism and economic development. The primary consideration has always been economic, although increasingly events and managed event portfolios meet more diverse goals for cities and countries. While the economic aspects have been well developed, especially economic impact assessment and forecasting, the application of management theory to event tourism has not received adequate attention.

In this book series we launch a process of examining the extent to which mainstream theory is being employed to develop event-specific theory, and to influence the practice of event management and event tourism. This is a very big task, as there are numerous possible theories, models and concepts, and virtually unlimited advice available on the management of firms, small and family businesses, government agencies and not-for-profits. Inevitably, we will have to be selective.

The starting point is theory. Scientific theory must both explain a phenomenon, and be able to predict what will happen. Experiments are the dominant form of classical theory development. But for management, predictive capabilities are usually lacking; it might be wiser to speak of theory in development, or theory fragments. It is often the process of theory development that marks research in management, including the testing of hypotheses and the formulation of propositions. Models, frameworks, concepts and sets of propositions are all part of this development.

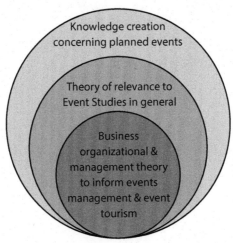

Knowledge creation concerning planned events

Theory of relevance to Event Studies in general

Business organizational & management theory to inform events management & event tourism

The diagram illustrates this approach. All knowledge creation has potential application to management, as does theory from any discipline or field. The critical factor for this series is how the theory and related methods can be applied. In the core of this diagram are management and business theories which are the most directly pertinent, and they are often derived from foundation disciplines.

All the books in this series will be relatively short, and similarly structured. They are designed to be used by teachers who need theoretical foundations and case studies for their classes, by students in need of reference works, by professionals wanting increased understanding alongside practical methods, and by agencies or associations that want their members and stakeholders to have access to a library of valuable resources. The nature of the series is that as it grows, components can be assembled by request. That is, users can order a book or collection of chapters to exactly suit their needs.

All the books will introduce the theory, show how it is being used in the events sector through a literature review, incorporate examples and case studies written by researchers and/or practitioners, and contain methods that can be used effectively in the real world. Online resources will include annotated bibliographies, additional resources, and for teachers an instructor's manual and set of power-point slides.

Preface To Event Impact Assessment

Aims of this book:

- ☐ To inform students and practitioners on impact assessment (IA) theory and methods, as applied to events and tourism.
- ☐ Develop professionalism for IA and evaluation in the event management field.
- ☐ Position impact assessment within sustainability and responsibility paradigms.
- ☐ Recommend goals, methods and measures for planning, evaluation and impact assessment pertaining to events and tourism.
- ☐ Encourage the adoption of standard methods and key performance indicators in evaluation and impact assessment in order to facilitate valid comparisons, benchmarking, reliable forecasts, transparency and accountability.
- ☐ Provide concepts and models that can be adapted to diverse situations.
- ☐ Connect readers to the research literature through use of Research Notes and provision of additional readings.

This book on impact assessment logically follows from the companion book *Event Evaluation: Theory and Methods for Event Management and Tourism.*

Organisation of this book

Three foundation chapters precede five thematic chapters on types of impacts. This first chapter explains the need for applying generic IA theory and methods to event management, encompassing consideration of event venues and tourism, then provides core concepts and definitions. Chapter two examines IA theory, including the conducting of impact assessments, and Chapter three explains measurement issues and generic methods that can be adapted to events and tourism.

The thematic chapters, four through eight, are based on the proposition that tourism and events are agents of change, resulting in social, cultural, built-environment, ecological and economic impacts. These are called the "objects" of impact assessment. The Economic Impacts chapter is longest, not because it is more important but because of the availability of so much material and the consequent need to ensure that readers understand the available methods and learn of additional, vital sources.

The impact "subjects" we consider are major categories of people or things that are likely to be changed by events and tourism, and we use seven categories that reflect major IA themes: individuals and families; groups and sub cultures; events and event organisations; businesses; communities and cities; tourist destinations, and politics and government. "Residents" are important in all of these categories.

In the Conclusions chapter there is a discussion of traditional Cost-Benefit Analysis (CBA) with emphasis on its limitations, and a suggested short-form using Key Impact Indicators. A description follows of my recommended approach to comprehensive IA and evaluation of impacts, the BACE model. It stands for Benefits and Costs Evaluation and is intended to be a planning framework within which all impacts can be compared and evaluated.

At the beginning of each chapter are Learning Objectives, and each of these can be readily reformulated as exam questions, in whole or in parts. Students are encouraged to prepare short answers for questions based on these learning objectives. At the end of each chapter are Study Questions more appropriate to essays, or possibly projects. Recommended Readings and Additional Sources are provided, all of which are cited within the text.

I have incorporated a lot of information in various chapters about Edinburgh, Scotland, as they are a leading event city internationally and have made available to the public a number of very useful planning and research reports (see www. EdinburgFestivalCity.com).

Acknowledgements

Special thanks to Rudi Hartmann, Department of Geography and Environmental Sciences, at the University of Colorado, Denver (see his case study in 6.6).

1 Basic Concepts and Definitions

Learning objectives

☐ Learn the meaning and nature of impacts and impact assessment (IA) applied to events and tourism, including categories and examples of evaluation and IA applied to events and tourism

☐ Know how impact assessment can be used for forecasting, post-event assessment, strategic policy decisions, and assessment of the impacts of conditions such as tourism in a given area

☐ Learn key definitions, including inputs, processes, outputs, outcomes, impacts and understand the variables affecting the definition and measurement of impacts

☐ Learn the nature and roles of mitigation, including prevention, reduction and compensation

☐ Be able to apply evaluation and impact assessment in many different event and tourism situations

☐ Recognize the importance of different value perspectives among the subjects and objects of impact assessment.

1.1 Introduction

It has never been more important to develop professionalism in the forecasting, measurement and evaluation of event and tourism impacts. While there has been widespread acceptance of the sustainability paradigm and principles of social responsibility, combined with serious public debate about the costs and benefits of events, venues and tourism, the problems seem to keep getting worse. The impacts of events and tourism have been studied extensively, yet evaluation and impact assessment have not been given the same attention, so theory and methods are relatively undeveloped (Brown et al., 2015). Hence the need for this book and its companion *Event Evaluation*.

There are generic principles and established methods available to guide professionals in Impact Assessment (IA) and evaluation, but in the realm of events and tourism we often witness poor methods and a deliberate lack of comprehensiveness, transparency and accountability for both political and selfish reasons.

As an introduction to some of the important issues, consider these scenarios relating to events and event tourism. There are four major types of IA discussed in this book and these scenarios introduce them.

1   **Forecasting**: During the feasibility assessment stage for bidding on a major event and building new venues the question of costs versus benefits inevitably generates debate. Proponents have made an effort to publicly stress all the benefits, in the hope that governments will provide funding, but opponents are asking "what are the costs? who gains and who will pay? what else can we do with the investment?" The only way forward is to conduct a full, objective impact assessment and make reliable forecasts, then evaluate the options.

2   **Post event**: Its over and the event organization is required to get its books audited and to evaluate its performance on a number of indicators pertaining to customer satisfaction, problems identified, and future prospects. However, this festival is designed and operated with social change as its primary goal. The organisers and supporters, including public culture and leisure agencies, believe they can be a powerful force in community development, fostering social integration and self-reliance through the creation of social capital. But have they articulated exactly what 'social capital' means, how events can play a role, and how the desired outcomes are to be measured? They need a Theory of Change expert and they have to integrate IA in their strategic planning. All stakeholders have to be involved.

3   **Retrospective**: Citizens are unhappy about the state of events and tourism in their community. There are many perceived negative impacts and some think that investment of public funds is benefitting only the business community. Here is a situation involving maximum complexity, as an IA will have to look backwards through the years to determine what has happened and why it happened, draw conclusions, then make recommendations for the future. The principles of social responsibility and environmental sustainability will certainly be brought into focus by various community and lobby groups. Serious political discourse is needed.

4   **Strategic**: The DMO (destination management or marketing organization) wants an aggressive strategy to employ events in marketing and economic development, but they realize they will have to collaborate with leisure, social and cultural agencies to cover all the interactions of goals and possible actions. Experts are brought in to work with the community and all the agencies to assess the potential impacts of various strategies. Politicians will eventually be asked to sort it all out and make an informed decision. Will they satisfy everyone?

This evolution of theory and method is a necessary accompaniment to the formalization of event and tourism studies at the university level, and to the professionalization of these sectors. It reflects the enormous resources invested in events, and the many impacts they have on society and the environment. It also reflects the many debates and conflicts that occur over costs, negative impacts, and irrational planning.

The legitimation of events, being a global acceptance of their roles in various government policies and industry and corporate strategies, has also forced attention on establishing more reliable and acceptable forms of evaluation and impact assessment. The estimation of impacts should be part of the process of determining the success, value or worth of events, event portfolios, and event tourism policies and strategies – but it is not the only needed input.

Comprehensiveness is essential. It makes little sense to learn that an event (or events in general) create new income for an area without also considering social, cultural and environmental impacts – both positives and negatives, and how important they are to residents and other stakeholders. The emergence of Triple-Bottom Line thinking, the Balanced Scorecard, Corporate Social Responsibility (CSR), Green Practices and Sustainable Event Standards reflects this imperative to consider all costs and benefits, plus the often more important question of distribution: who gains and who pays?

The approach taken in this and the companion book on *Event Evaluation* (Getz, 2018) reflects a paradigm shift in thinking about the purpose, nature and impacts of events and tourism – consistent with broader societal value shifts (Getz, 2009). Sustainability and social responsibility in tourism and events planning and management is a theme running through this book and the companion on evaluation, and impact assessment has to fit into these value perspectives. This 'sustainable and responsible' paradigm is not new, having evolved over the past several decades, but it has yet to be completely reflected in political decisions, nor is it always found in evaluation and impact assessment (IA) practice.

CSR is widely discussed in the business community, where this *Financial Times* definition fits:

> *"Movement aimed at encouraging companies to be more aware of the impact of their business on the rest of society, including their own stakeholders and the environment. Corporate social responsibility (CSR) is a business approach that contributes to sustainable development by delivering economic, social and environmental benefits for all stakeholders."*

Source: lexicon.ft.com/Term?term=corporate-social-responsibility--(CSR)

Other definitions readily found online include the notion of being ethical and producing overall benefits for society, and in is this regard it is similar to normative stakeholder theory. Businesses are encouraged to adopt CSR as a core concept and not merely engage in philanthropy. Many CSR definitions also mention sustainability, and this is defined later.

More a philosophy and idealistic set of outcomes than a code of practice, responsible tourism or events should follow these principles, according to

Harold Goodwin, author of the book *Responsible Tourism* (2012):

◆ Minimise negative economic, environmental, and social impacts

◆ Generate economic benefits for local people and enhances the well-being of host communities.

◆ Improve working conditions and career opportunities

◆ Involve residents in decisions that affect their lives and environment

◆ Make positive contributions to the conservation of natural and cultural heritage

◆ Provide more enjoyable experiences for tourists through more meaningful connections with local people, and a greater understanding of local cultural, social and environmental issues

◆ Provide access for physically challenged people

◆ Be culturally sensitive, engender respect between tourists and hosts, and build local pride and confidence

Source: http://haroldgoodwin.info/responsible-tourism/

Notice that these principles are mostly about the benefits desired, although minimizing negative impacts is the first one mentioned. The challenge for impact assessors and evaluators is to help implement these principles by providing the necessary theory, methods and measures.

There has been a huge amount published on tourism and event sustainability, including highly relevant books by Holmes et al. (*Events and Sustainability*, 2015), Jones (*Sustainable Event Management*, 3rd ed., 2018), and *Routledge Handbook of Tourism and Sustainability* (Hall, Gossling, and Scott, eds., 2015). One definition does not cover all perspectives on sustainability, but here is one from Holmes et al. (2015, p. 3):

> *"Sustainability is the goal of sustainable development. Sustainability suggests an equilibrium or condition of stability in which consumption and renewal of resources are in a balance that maintains conditions for human survival that can continue forever."*

In practice, sustainability is a process of becoming better, or continuous improvement, and not an end-state. It is clear that consumption and depletion of resources, use of fossil-fuels, and other forms of pollution are continuing unabated, and as a result climate change is to a degree irreversible. Since major principles of sustainable development are being ignored in many countries, and targets unmet, we can at least plan for incremental improvements.

Informing this book was a two-year research and development project in Sweden funded by BFUF, which is the research and development agency of the national tourism and hospitality industry. Its aim was to advance sustainability through improved evaluation and impact assessment in the sports sector, with the Swedish Sport Confederation as the client, but the project equally involved sports organisations, cities, destinations and events. The following quotes are from the final guidelines document, and reflect the issues revealed by participants. These are justifications for doing the project in Sweden, but are considered to be universal in their importance (Getz, 2015a):

"Input from many stakeholders revealed trends and issues, and in particular highlighted common problems with the current diversity of approaches to evaluation and impact forecasting/assessment. Collectively, these trends and issues provide justification for developing a standard approach as explained in these guidelines. The following are key trends and issues:

☐ *Growth* in sport events and event-tourism continues globally, as measured by the increasing numbers of events, their diversity, size and cost, and their overall significance.

☐ *Visibility*: Impacts are more evident, both positives and negatives, and often controversy occurs when governments subsidize and support major events. There are rising concerns about the sustainability of events and tourism, although this is usually reserved for the largest of events.

☐ *Legitimacy*: Events in general are now an expected part of modern life. Sport and other events are seen as legitimate tools in many policy fields, including tourism, economic and cultural development, social integration, health, and place marketing. People expect a variety of events in every city and region.

☐ *Competition* for international sport events has greatly increased, making it essential to continuously improve competence in the entire event management field. Countries with standard systems of forecasting, evaluating and reporting on costs and impacts should find competitive advantages.

☐ *Accountability and transparency*: demands have grown for accountability and transparency, from both politicians and the public. Politicians require a valid evaluation and impact forecasting/assessment process in order to gain confidence in the value of events. Too many 'black-box' impact assessments have confused the picture, and they have led to a lack of credibility.

☐ *Need for comparability:* Benchmarking and improved forecasting can only be obtained by *meta analysis* of many comparable evaluation results. Common methods, measures, reporting and terminology are needed.

☐ *Sustainability:* Events and event tourism should conform to Sweden's national sustainability policies and reflect the global brand of Sweden as a country leading in green practices and sustainable development. Accordingly, there is a need to define the meaning and ways of implementing sustainable development as applied to events and event tourism. As well, there is a desire among all stakeholders to justify events in terms other than economic impacts, leading to a triple-bottom-line approach that provides equal weight to social, cultural, environmental and economic factors.

☐ *Professionalism* is required in event evaluation and impact assessment, and this argues for a standard approach. It also necessitates ongoing research, education and training. Professionalism will help win bids and ensure sustainable, responsible events.

☐ *Flexibility*: Different criteria and measures are needed for local events aimed at residents versus large international events. Evaluation systems must take into account the various needs of residents, tourists and other stakeholders."

(Source: the Guidelines were written by Donald Getz and can be found online: http://www.svenskidrott.se/globalassets/svenskidrott/dokument/undersidor/centrum-for-idrottsevenemang/guideline-for-sport-event-evaluation-in-sweden.pdf)

1.2 Categories and examples of evaluation and impact assessment

Figure 1.1 provides a summary of evaluation and impact assessment categories and real-world applications. In the companion book *Event Evaluation* a graphic 'complexity model' is provided. This list is intended to reveal the progression, in general terms, from simple evaluation applications to more complex impact assessments, with complexity reflecting political concerns, the range of stakeholders involved, applicable theory, and methodological issues.

Figure 1.1: Categories and examples of evaluation and impact assessment

Categories	Examples
Data collection Comprehensive system to obtain data from all relevant sources Organisations need to implement knowledge management and decision support systems.	Visitor surveys; resident surveys; data from government agencies, suppliers, staff, volunteers, sponsors; internal audits and evaluations
Monitoring To observe and record, including trend analysis and environmental scanning	Trends in demand &supply; records generated by public authorities; energy & water consumption by events; waste generated & recycled; traffic flows linked to tourism; pedestrian movements on event sites
Comparisons and benchmarking Comparing conditions, performance and reasons for success with exemplars or competitors	Competitive SWOT analysis; information sharing within event associations or location-based networks such as marketing collaborations; formally managed event portfolios facilitating sharing and synergies
Formative evaluation To aid in planning and design	Needs assessments; demand forecasting; determining stakeholder preferences & potential support; testing programme ideas on target segments; attendee motivation research as an input to marketing and design
Problem solving Identifying and finding solutions to problems	Correcting onsite problems such as overcrowding; determining why advertising works or does not; rootcause analysis to evaluate possible causes of customer dissatisfaction
Decision support Any data collection, analysis or evaluation to support decisions	Obtaining visitor & other stakeholder feedback to decide on new programmes or a continuance of pricing structure; assessing likely penetration rate & demand for a proposed event; decision tree analysis to explore possible consequences of actions

Discrepancy identification and correction	Evaluating performance of staff & volunteers against job descriptions & standards
Evaluating performance and quality as defined by standards and as perceived by customers and other stakeholders	Evaluating customer satisfaction; importance & performance criteria
	Using service blueprinting and mapping (combined with experience evaluation) to maximise quality & safety
	Venues, programming & officiating according to the specifications of event owners
	Conforming to green or sustainability standards
Process evaluation	Ensuring the event, policy, strategy or marketing campaign is delivered as planned; fixing problems as they occur; heading off problems through monitoring and anticipation; taking appropriate action to keep programmes on track; collecting data and assembling evidence for future summative evaluation
Evaluating performance and quality while an event or programme is running	
Evaluating experience	Evaluation of the nature and perceived quality of event and tourism experiences, which is somewhat different from routine satisfaction and importanceperformance metrics; participant observation to gain insights; phenomenological research such as selfreporting during events or biometric monitoring; providing data for support of personal development impacts
Evaluating the experiences of attendees and all other event stakeholders	
Summative evaluation	Determining if the event attained its goals and if not, why
Post event: evaluating 'merit' (i.e., did event or project do what was intended) & 'worth' (a judgment, taking into account stakeholder value perspectives)	Learning how goals were realized
	Asking how can it be improved
Using logic models or theory of change models to plan actions (or transforming processes) with intended outcomes	
Goalfree evaluation	A method to avoid tunnel vision associated with goal attainment models, such as only examining economic impacts
Systematic evaluation of inputs, transforming processes, outputs and outcomes/impacts without reference to goals	Best for detecting externalities (costs not accounted for) and unintended effects
	Requires expert evaluators and stakeholder engagement
Evaluating organizational effectiveness and efficiency	Lack of resources and/or inadequate financial management is a frequent cause of failure
Effectiveness refers to goal attainment and efficiency to the obtaining and use of resources (e.g., Can we do more with less? Were resources wasted?)	Use triple bottom line logic or a balanced scorecard to evaluate overall effectiveness (the event compass is such a system, employing goal attainment and continuous improvement logic)
	Requires formal audits and ratio analysis
Forecasting project impacts	Predict the economic, environmental, and social/cultural impacts and when desirable implement mitigation actions
As part of feasibility studies for new events or venues, and evaluating event bids	Formally evaluate alternative actions or investments (which involves consideration of opportunity costs)

Postevent or post development IA Focusing on deviations from forecasts (if made) or a wideranging assessment of impacts at a given point in time	Economic impact assessments have dominated Unfortunately optimistic forecasts of the benefits of projects and events are often made but not followed up by post project impact assessments (for political or financial reasons) Deviations from forecasts should be simple to determine, whereas externalities and unintended outcomes require a goalfree approach
Strategic IA: evaluating potential impacts of policies, strategies or programmes Seldom attempted in the events and tourism sectors, this is a complex challenge for impact assessors and evaluators of the merit and worth of government and industry strategies, policies and programmes and the alternatives	What are the likely impacts of creating and managing a portfolio of events that stresses permanent, funded hallmark and iconic events versus a portfolio that emphasises bidding on onetime major and minor events? What are the relative costs and benefits of various methods of supporting cultural events: direct production and ownership? Subsidies and grants? Marketing only? Coordination only?
Comprehensive impact assessment of the 'state' of a system (i.e., city, destination, ecosystem) Looking back to determine how events and tourism have impacted an area or system; takes into account the original state, determines causes, and enables future scenarios	Combining social, cultural, environmental, & economic impact assessment to evaluate how tourism/events have affected an area/system requires expert researchers and evaluators and complete, multi-stakeholder input Long term, cumulative and synergistic impacts must be considered This type of IA seldom attempted – methods are undeveloped; few jurisdictions have full knowledge of their event populations; environmental forces such as competition & resource scarcity have to be considered; Sustainability criteria should be formulated to reflect multiple stakeholder perspectives
Evaluation of benefits and costs (BACE) Typical cost-benefit analysis is quantitative, employs mostly monetary metrics & fails to take into account externalities, distributional effects & sustainability criteria BACE stresses goal attainment (the desired benefits are stated up front) and is not limited to quantitative or monetary values; consider tangibles & intangibles separately; key impact indicators predetermined for each impact domain	Ideally all benefits and costs are evaluated in all impact assessments, but this is not the case Complexity is high This book provides key impact indicators to guide application of BACE
Proving cause and effect In the positivist paradigm, cause and effect can only be 'proven' through controlled experiments	There will always be uncertainty in predicting impacts for events and tourism, but employing logic models or theory of change models can be used to structure the collection and analysis of evidence and help develop theory When sufficient research, evaluation & IA studies are available, with reliable data from standard methods & measures, meta analysis can be used to boost confidence in forecasting impacts

Determining the worth or value of policies, events, portfolios of events, and tourism	'Worth' can only be determined through multi-stakeholder input, considering all possible goals and outcomes
'Worth' is open to interpretation, considering many possible value perspectives	This will be very complex for portfolios of events because each event is an asset with intended outcomes contributing to overall return on investment or goals
In political terms, asking what an event/tourism is worth is equivalent to justifying intervention	Portfolios managed for different purposes (e.g., social, cultural, economic development) can share goals and indicators at some level, opportunity costs, externalities and the distribution of costs and benefits must all be included
Long term, cumulative impact assessment and sustainability	The need is to make events and tourism positive forces for sustainable cities and environments
Similar to evaluating the impacts of events and tourism on the state of an area or system, but requires a permanent system of planning, IA and evaluation	
Currently this is not done, and appropriate theory and methods are not available	

The starting point is data collection and monitoring, without which little analysis can be done. Problem-solving and supporting decisions with evidence probably encompasses most of the evaluation projects done within events and tourism. Goal-attainment evaluations are the norm in other fields and have given rise to professionalism in programme evaluation.

At the extreme end of the complexity spectrum is long-term, cumulative impact assessment, especially within a sustainability paradigm. Increasingly cities and destination develop portfolios of events for multiple purposes (Ziakas, 2013, 2014, 2018) and the populations of events (Andersson, Getz & Mykletun, 2013; Getz and Andersson, 2016) have grown largely without control or quantification. Little is known about how event portfolios are managed over time, or about how whole populations of events respond to environmental forces.

Along these lines, Tanner et al. (2018) developed a set of indicators for evaluating the performance of events in the context of public subsidies. A cost-benefit analysis employing their indicators would enable stakeholders to consider the worth of individual events. Their indicators: size of the event; economic value; touristic value and image; innovative strength; value of networking (local cooperation and exchange); value of participation and social exchange, and relative ecological burden.

The treatment of events as 'assets' within a portfolio, and their evaluation in the context of risk and value was the subject of a paper by Andersson et al. (2017). Asset value van be quantified, as done in financial portfolios, or events can be value intrinsically as creators of welfare of public good.

1.2.1 The matter of scale or scope

Another perspective on complexity is to look at evaluation and IA at different scales, from projects to cities to regions and nations. Hall and Lew (2009, p. 81) had this to say about tourism impacts:

"We note that historically tourism impacts have only been studied at a local level and there has often been a failure to appreciate that impacts occur at all stages of the tourist trip rather than at just the eventual destination. The failure to account for impacts at the national and global scale is regarded as particularly important given the significance of economic and cultural globalization as a process influencing and influenced by tourism."

Later we introduce the concept of 'within-scope' for calculating economic impacts, meaning the area(s) for which the economic contribution will be forecast or estimated.

1.2.2 IA for mega events

Usually we think of World's Fairs, the Olympics and World Cup, but other events can be so huge, so expensive to hold, and with such substantial impacts that they can be called 'mega'. Indeed, any planned event of the types discussed in this book (see, in particular, Section 8.4) can raise capacity issues and be interpreted as being of the size or significance that they are deemed to be the maximum that can be accommodated. In the context of LAC (Limits of Acceptable Change), limits on size, cost, or operations can be imposed by stakeholders through consensus building, or by regulators. With the scale and cost of events continuing to rise, questions must be asked about what is appropriate, affordable and sustainable. McGillivray and Turner (2018), in their book *Event Bidding*, critically discuss the reasons for bidding, mega event impacts, and growing resistance to the pro-development powers that have sustained the trend to bigger and costlier events.

Impact assessment for mega events is categorically different from that pertaining to small and single events, or event portfolios. Mega events have the potential to initiate major changes, that is to be shocks to the system, and across all types of impacts. Complexity is very high for mega-event IA because of the enormous costs, the politics, and the lobbying of elite groups. It is certain that intense media scrutiny and pubic debate will occur, right from the first idea being raised by a proponent, through feasibility studies, bidding, the event as it unfolds, and for a long time afterwards when the legacy is monitored.

Dawson and Jons (2018) discussed the nature of mega events and their legacy, and developed a model to guide impact assessment. They combined the five research dimensions outlined by Preuss (called a 'legacy cube') with theory on leveraging benefits, network theory (discussed later in this book). Their model consists of five rings (time, space, intention, agency and evaluation) and each encompasses specific considerations. 'Time' includes legacy considerations, while 'intention' includes intended, unintended, and planned but not realized impacts. 'Evaluation' encompasses impacts judged to be positive, negative or neutral.

In each of the five chapters of this book devoted to social, cultural, built-environment, ecological and economic impacts there is a short section on mega events and what makes the impacts and the IA process different. This theme is of interest and concern to everyone, to inform students and practitioners of the issues, and to contrast mega events with the more everyday tasks of evaluation and impact assessment.

1.3 Evaluation, impacts and impact assessment defined

Figure 1.2 lists basic definitions. Within the logic of systems modelling, inputs such as money and skill are transformed by various processes into desired outputs. Events can be conceptualized as instruments of change, and the desired outputs are normally expressed as goals: for example attendance, generating revenue, satisfying customers and other stakeholders – things that can be immediately measured during and after events. The terms 'outcomes' and 'impacts' in this book are defined as longer-term or system-altering changes that can be attributed to an event or events and tourism, such as economic, social and cultural transformations. Impacts are sometimes desired, related to policies and goals, and sometimes unintended. The companion book *Event Evaluation* deals mainly with the outputs, while this book is more oriented to the longer-term impacts, but there is considerable overlap.

Figure 1.2: Key definitions

Evaluation: (a) The process of establishing the merit and/or worth of events or tourism, or some element of them, where 'merit' means it is performing as intended and 'worth' is based on value perspectives and consideration of alternatives. **Programme evaluation** is a generic term that refers to evaluation and impact assessment of policies and programmes rather than specific events or projects.

(b) Evaluation is also a technical process directed at identifying and solving management problems and aiding in decision-making.

Inputs: The resources required and committed (monetary, natural, human, organizational, etc.) to an event or project; various forms of **capital** can be invested as inputs to creating events and developing tourism; information and expertise are critical inputs.

Processes: actions taken that are intended to generate outputs and outcomes.

Transforming processes: Many events and development projects are intended to change the state of something (e.g., the economy, politics, social structure, living conditions, personal development, etc.); events can be created or viewed as transforming processes, or media for change

Outputs: A measure of what is intended to be produced by events and tourism, usually in quantitative terms, such as profit, money raised for causes, attendance, customer and stakeholder satisfaction, visitor spending and direct economic contribution; these can be immediately measured and evaluated by evaluators, but can also be considered impacts for the purposes of IA.

Impacts (often used synonymously with **outcomes**): changes in the state of something, generated by external stimuli; impacts/outcomes are usually considered to be longer-term in nature, and include both desired, negative, or unintended costs and impacts; the term **legacy** is often used to describe permanent or long-term outcomes.

1.3.1 Impact variables

One object can forcibly 'impact' another, like a hammer striking a nail. Any number of variables, listed in Figure 1.3, might be of importance when defining impacts, determining the scope of the assessment, or in their measurement. The questions asked in the figure, and the accompanying comments, provide a set of heuristics that can be used in impact assessment, but with caution. See the definition below:

Heuristic: "any approach to problem solving, learning, or discovery that employs a practical method, not guaranteed to be optimal, perfect, logical, or rational, but instead sufficient for reaching an immediate goal. Where finding an optimal solution is impossible or impractical, heuristic methods can be used to speed up the process of finding a satisfactory solution. Heuristics can be mental shortcuts that ease the cognitive load of making a decision. Examples that employ heuristics include using a rule of thumb, an educated guess, an intuitive judgment, a guesstimate, stereotyping, profiling, or common sense." (Wikipedia)

Figure 1.3: Impact variables and some key questions to ask (heuristics for IA)

Direct/Indirect
Q: Are the impacts direct or indirect?
Direct impact will include the desired outputs (such as attendance, satisfaction, profit) and observable environmental damage; indirect impacts might arise sometime later, or as a ripple effect, such as the results of successful events in generating increased civic pride and institutional networking leading to community development. Indirect and cumulative impacts are best detected through multi-stakeholder engagement in IA.
Temporal
Q: When do impacts occur?
They can occur at the planning stage, at the time of construction, during events, and post-event. Logically, post-event/project impacts are easier to detect and measure - compared to forecasts.
Q: Are impacts short or long term? permanent? periodic? reversible?
Permanent impact will often be considered a higher priority than one that is forecast to be short-term and reversible.
Q: Are the impacts cumulative, and can we predict the ultimate effects of actions?
Cumulative IA is very complex and requires extraordinary planning and measurement (as discussed later).

Spatial
Q: Exactly where are impacts felt? Are they stable or dynamic?
Local effects might be easier to mitigate than wider impacts; but determine if local impacts might spread geographically, such as with pollution.

Severity
Q: How are different perceptions of severity to be evaluated?
As with risk management, impacts can be ranked (e.g., minimal and acceptable through to substantial and unacceptable) but appropriate metrics are needed; disagreements over perceived severity are likely to occur and so compromise might be required.
Q: Is there a possible cascading effect that could lead to increased severity?
A minor negative effect might expand over time, so monitoring is required. Again, multi-stakeholder engagement will help.

Risk
Q: How certain are trend and impact forecasts?
There can be no absolute certainty about the future, so contingency plans are always required; repeating forecasts periodically is desirable.
Q: What is the probability and potential severity of risks?
Just as in risk management, IA can utilize a grid to compare probability with potential certainty in determining priorities for mitigation, or to decide upon whether or not to proceed with a project.
Q: Should the precautionary principle be applied?
If uncertain about probability, but potential cost or negative impact severity is high, it might be best to wait for more information, or to cancel the event/project.

Mitigation
Q: Can the forecast impacts be prevented?
Prevention is generally the best option, but cancellation is often resisted by proponents of events and development – this leads to debates over mitigation.
Q: Can observed and forecast negative impacts be mitigated?
If not, re-think the entire event or project – is it really necessary? What are the alternatives?
Q: Is compensation to be provided? Is it acceptable to the affected parties?
The potential cost of compensation has to be factored into decisions: Sometimes it will be rejected by those affected, as they will argue for cancellation.
Q: How will we monitor the changes and the mitigation efforts, and how will that evidence shape future actions?
IA should be accompanied by mechanisms for ongoing monitoring, and multi-stakeholder identification of impacts.

Real or perceived?
Q: Are impacts demonstrably real, or perceived?
Q: Is the impact positive or negative? Important or minor? Who determines this?
IA planners will have to consider if 'proof' is necessary, or if the perceptions of stakeholders are sufficient evidence. Particularly in social/cultural IA the voices of stakeholders should be given prominence as sources of credible evidence.

Real or perceived? (Cont.)
Q: Under what conditions will impacts be felt and/or measureable?
Sometimes impacts will be too subtle or slow to evolve to permit detection or measurement, as in cultural change; in these cases the fears or issues raised by residents and other stakeholders have to be considered valid.

Who or what is impacted?
Q: Can the impacted speak for themselves? Who speaks for the environment or for a cultural group?
In general, residents and other stakeholders have spokespersons or lobby groups to speak for them. If not, extra steps are required to obtain valid input.
Q: What are the distributional patterns of impacts (i.e., who wins, who pays or loses?)
This is often the most important question, and it can be expected that the voices of those expecting to gain will be loudest.

Flexibility
Q: What can be done to enhance positive outcomes?
It's not always about costs and negative impacts. IA can lead to plans for maximising benefits.
Q: What are the alternatives to proposed actions?
There are always alternatives! Opportunity costs must be considered, as events and venues require investment that could be directed elsewhere, to achieve the same goals.

There are other important terms used when referring to impacts. In Figure 1.4 'primary and secondary impacts' are differentiated, then the term 'cumulative'. A system in 'equilibrium' is self-correcting. 'Feedback' is another term from systems thinking, and it can be 'positive' (i.e., reinforcing of a force or trend) or 'negative (resisting or negating the force or trend). Often used in the context of climate change, the concept of a 'tipping point' is relevant when thinking about impacts, as is 'cascade' effects. The concept of 'cumulative impacts' is discussed in greater detail in Chapter 2, alongside 'synergies', 'feedback' and 'tipping points'.

Figure 1.4: Additional concepts and definitions

Primary impacts (or first-order impacts): direct consequences of a project or condition

Secondary impacts (or second-order impacts): indirect impacts that are manifested over time; think of a chain reaction or cascading impacts, such as a new venue creates jobs in the short term but also attracts new events in the long run.

Impact chain (or path): the links between primary impacts (or first order impacts) and secondary impacts. The chain or path can also refer to links between social change processes, such as in-migration, and effects on the community or its environment and economy.

Cumulative impacts are generally long-term in nature and arise from the synergistic, or interactive effects of multiple actions

Equilibrium: a state in which opposing forces are in balance, such as might occur when supply and demand are in balance and the event sector is not static (i.e., no growth or shrinkage).

Feedback: we use this term to describe any information about operations and impacts that can be employed in evaluation and planning.

Positive feedback: in a system like a business or event, positive feedback is reinforcing - that is, the impacts are magnified; an example might be the increase in stakeholder satisfaction that comes from participation in events and leads to more events and more community development

Negative feedback: outputs or impacts that tend to return the force or trend to its original state, thereby maintaining equilibrium; an example might be resident dissatisfaction with event tourism, resulting in political pressure to not bid on major events or to suspend event portfolio growth.

Tipping point: "A critical moment in a complex situation in which a small influence or development produces a sudden large or irreversible change." (Thefreedictionary.com)

Impact chain (or path): the links between primary impacts (or first order impacts) and secondary impacts. The chain or path can also refer to links between social change processes, such as in-migration, and effects on the community or its environment and economy.

Cascade effect (or cascading impacts):
"A cascade effect is an inevitable and sometimes unforeseen chain of events due to an act affecting a system. If there is a possibility that the cascade effect will have a negative impact on the system, it is possible to analyze the effects with a consequence/impact analysis. Cascade effects are commonly visualised in tree structures, also called event trees." (Wikipedia)

1.3.2 Impact Assessment (IA) defined

Most countries have environmental impact legislation, and some have integrated social impacts into this process. This is how the International Association of Impact Assessment (IAIA) defines it:

"Impact Assessment *(IA) simply defined is the process of identifying the future consequences of a current or proposed action. The 'impact' is the difference between what would happen with the action and what would happen without it."*

(Source: www.iaia.org)

Note that 'current action' could refer to any form of development, including events or tourism in general, but mostly we see this kind of forward-looking IA applied to major proposed developments and mega events. For our purposes, however, it is too narrow to only define or use impact assessment methods when forecasting. Figure 1.5 illustrates the four main applications of IA discussed in this book, and it is worth noting that hardly any attention has been given in the literature to the strategic and retrospective types.

Figure 1.5: Four applications of IA for events and tourism

Forecasting impacts
What impacts will occur if we take a specific action?

Post-event IA
What were the demonstrable outputs and impacts of a planned
event or a tourism project?

IA of events/tourism on the economy, society or environment
What have been the overall impacts of events and/or tourism on the
economy, society or environment?

Strategic impact assessment
What are the probable impacts of alternative policies, strategies
or programmes?

1.3.3 Mitigation

Mitigation can encompass a wide range of policies and actions to prevent,
reduce, or compensate for costs and negative impacts. Two definitions are provided in Figure 1.6.

Figure 1.6: Mitigation defined

European Union Directive 2011/92/EU:
Mitigation is…
"measures envisaged in order to avoid, reduce and, if possible, remedy significant
adverse effects."

…………

United States Council on Environmental Quality (1980).
"…any activity that includes:
(a) Avoiding the impact altogether by not taking a certain action or parts of an
action.
(b) Minimizing impacts by limiting the degree or magnitude of the action and its
implementation.
(c) Rectifying the impact by repairing, rehabilitating, or restoring the affected environment.
(d) Reducing or eliminating the impact over time by preservation and mainte-
nance operations during the life of the action.
(e) Compensating for the impact by replacing or providing substitute resources
or environments."

The term 'over-tourism' is increasingly heard in places where events and tourism are causing residents and lobby groups to challenge development and marketing. They want mitigation actions, such as negative marketing (e.g., "please stay away from here") or development freezes. In some cities "no more events" might become a common refrain. In reaction to terror attacks and mass shootings, cities are erecting barriers and putting tougher security requirements in place – both to prevent incidents, if possible, and to otherwise minimise consequences. Carbon offsetting, often in the form of planting trees, is an effort to mitigate the effects of travel on air pollution and climate change. Mitigation might also consist of re-directing traffic away from sensitive ecosystems or specific communities in cities. There are numerous possibilities.

We cannot cancel or replace tourism, it is all-pervasive, and there are so many events held that it is unreasonable to think the events sector could be eliminated. What can be done is a change in policy, regulations, strategy, marketing and investment – based on sound evidence.

Compensation is often thought of as the last resort. It might result from a lawsuit (indeed, we can see an accelerating trend to sue governments and organisations), an attempt to pacify complainants, or a confession that mistakes were made. If mitigation actions do not work, the affected persons might deserve some financial compensation. But for environmental damage, who is to be compensated – the wildlife? It might be reasonable to suggest that restoration of habitat or planting trees elsewhere (after damage is done) is reasonable, but that will be disputed.

1.4 The objects and subjects of impact assessment

Armbrecht & Andersson (2016) discussed the *objects* and *subjects* of event studies. The *objects* are impacts, usually thought of in a triple-bottom-line context as being social/cultural, environmental and economic, while the subjects are those groups or things being impacted. Regarding *subjects*, the editors of *The Value of Events* suggested the following (p.7):

"*The dimension spanning from the Individual to the Society accommodates a large number of stakeholders and stakeholder groups as subjects of analysis in the sense that they are affected and might have different perspectives on value. The local industry and particularly the local tourism industry is, for example, the typical subject of a standard economic impact analysis.*"

Events, venues and tourism are all agents of change, either intentionally or inadvertently, and in this book the focus is placed on assessing the impacts (or outcomes) of events, venues and tourism on five objects. The five thematic chapters (4-8), consider the objects of IA, being social, cultural, built environment, ecological and economic impacts (see Figure 1.7). These were not arbitrarily selected, as they represent an expanded triple-bottom-line approach with *social* and *cultural* given separate treatment, and *environmental* impacts divided into *ecological* and *built* environment. These cover the full range of impacts as found in the academic literature and in most practical applications of IA, but of course they can be subdivided and categorised differently. In each of the five chapters many specific types of impacts are identified and citations provided.

The *subjects* of IA are those people, groups, organisations or things that are impacted. The categories and sub-divisions of impact subjects are open to preference and convenience, but also to logic. In this book a uniform framework with eight categories has been adopted, based on the premise that these cover a full spectrum from the individual and family to society as a whole, or the nation, and reflect the majority of topics covered in the events and tourism literature.

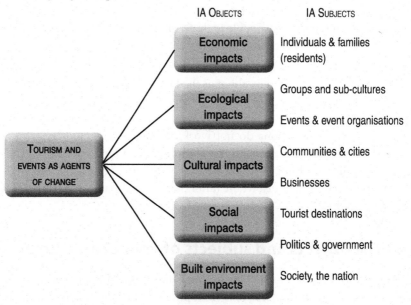

Figure 1.7: The subjects and objects of impact assessment

An additional consideration is the approach taken in this book to express indicators of impacts as goals. This not only reflects what usually happens in practice, with events and organisations or governments setting goals for desired benefits, as well as for costs or negative effects to avoid, but also demonstrates how impact assessment and evaluation are integral parts of strategic planning. For example, in the chapter on social impacts we examine how individuals and social groups (or sub-cultures) can be affected by events and event tourism, and then present appropriate goals, methods and measures for social planning, evaluation and impact assessment.

Some of these combinations of objects and subjects are minor, at least in terms of what knowledge is available, while others are dominant themes in the literature. If we look only at what has been published, then economic impacts on destinations probably has the largest content, while ecological impacts on individuals the least. A brief overview of the eight subjects is now provided.

1.4.1 Impacts on residents (individuals, families, groups and sub-cultures)

It should never be expected that the residents of any community, city or nation will be affected uniformly, nor will they perceive impacts (benefits and costs) in the same way. A dominant theoretical perspective in the events and tourism literature is that of Social Exchange Theory (reviewed in Deery and Jago, 2010) which suggests that in most cases people who benefit will perceive impacts more positively, and hold attitudes more favourable to the development of events, venues and tourism.

Residents are often the first to feel impacts, and they cannot possibly be ignored in any impact assessment or evaluation. Different value perspectives have to be considered, including those who value events intrinsically for the good they do, and those inclined to require extrinsic and quantitative measurement of benefits. Individuals and families are our starting point in all the discussions of impact subjects, but the effects of events and tourism on families has been less researched. Individuals are also frequently examined as spectators, attendees, and participants, and so we examine the impacts of event experiences on people. Groups and sub-cultures are the other category of residents being examined, but here the emphasis is on social and cultural identity.

1.4.2 Events and event organisations

It might seem strange to include events and event organisations as subjects of IA, but it is evident that events influence the organisations that support or produce them; events affect each other (for an organisational ecology perspective, see Andersson and Getz, 2016); and every event held has the potential to impact a venue. Perhaps more importantly is the consideration that events and organisations use impact assessment and evaluation to determine if they are achieving their goals, and to directly influence strategic planning.

1.4.3 Impacts on businesses and tourism destinations

All business activity can be impacted by events, venues and tourism, but the focus will usually be on those businesses that supply events, and those that benefit from tourism. Corporations that produce or use events for their purposes are a factor, as they expect direct returns on their investment, and the leveraging of events is supposed to benefit the business sector in general. At the destination level, both government and the business sector are generally involved in DMOs and in formulating event-tourism strategies. Destinations have somewhat unique event-related concerns related to image, positioning, reputation and branding, dealing with seasonality of demand, attracting preferred tourist segments and generating an economic impact. Goals for these impacts are often shared (explicitly or implicitly) with residents who are supposed to see the benefits, and with development-oriented government agencies. Destination authorities must also be good corporate citizens and practice sustainable development, however conflicting objectives arise in attempts to achieve multiple aims and to please both members and residents.

1.4.5 Impacts on communities, cities, politics and government

Hall (2012) discussed the politics and political economy of events, focussing on the exercise of power, the allocation of resources, and resolution of conflict. Applied to events and tourism, key questions relate to how and why they are supported by governments, and under what conditions. 'Public good' has to be created, but it can be in many forms: social and cultural capital formation, employment, tourism development, liveable cities or environmental protection. In return, events and tourism can influence politics and government decisions, in part linked to media coverage, resident reactions and the results of professional impact assessment and policy evaluations. We consider these issues at the community level (community action and development being political in nature), within the category 'politics and government', and at the level of the whole nation.

1.4.6 Assessing impacts of multiple events and managed portfolios

Complexity increases greatly when assessing the impacts of multiple events are the task. In a retrospective IA, the interactions and cumulative impacts of many events might have to be analysed, and it is quite likely they did not have comparable goals, documentation or evaluations. For managed portfolios there should at least be a strategy to regularly consult stakeholders, and the portfolio managers should implement standardized methods and measures so that trends can be monitored.

Richards and Palmer (2010), in the book *Eventful Cities,* looked at several multi-event studies, including some that measured impacts at intervals, and noted that impacts change over time. Edinburgh has done impressive periodic assessments of its festivals, and some results are presented later in this book. Those assessments have increasingly taken a triple-bottom-line approach, adding social, cultural and environmental indicators to the original economic assessment.

Portfolios require a different approach, with the basic assumption that there is a strategy, goals and indicators. In the book *Event Tourism* (Getz, 2013, pp. 348-351), a model is presented that shows the difference between single-event and portfolio evaluation, stressing the premise that in a portfolio events are assets that must contribute to the overall value and sustainability of the whole. Capacity building becomes a primary concern, with each event and the entire portfolio expected to contribute to growth in the destination or city's achievement of desired benefits, all the while improving efficiency and the evaluation system. In narrowly defined portfolios there might be a focus on economic or social goals, but increasingly cities are having to bring all the stakeholders together to set comprehensive goals and decide upon the goals and indicators that satisfy all parties.

Because this book series will include a title on *Event Portfolios*, the discussion in this book will not be detailed. But all the points made on interactions, cumulative impacts, synergies and benefits/cost evaluation apply to portfolios.

1.4.7 IA and value perspectives

Can impact assessment and evaluation ever be value-free? Professionalism should mean that IAs are value-free, objective, and thorough, but even when the task is assigned to professionals (internally, or consultants) there will always be political considerations reflecting differing ideologies and value perspectives. Many value perspectives have been identified in the companion book *Event Evaluation*, and there is no need to repeat them here. When residents and other stakeholders are consulted the differences will become apparent, and some positions taken on issues will be irreconcilable. This is a fact of life, and professionals have to find ways of coping with the pressures. Probably the worst situation possible is when proponents of pubic expenditure on events, venues and tourism are the ones that make the impact forecasts and do the evaluations.

Study questions

1   Provide a question and answer for each of the Learning Objectives. This should be done for all the chapters.

2   Discuss the political considerations involved in each of the four main types of IA: forecasting, post event, retrospective and strategic. Find examples from the events or tourism sectors.

Recommended additional readings and sources

Getz, D. (2018). *Event Evaluation: Theory and Methods for Event Management and Tourism*. Oxford: Goodfellow Publishers.

Goodwin, H. (2012, 2d.ed.). *Responsible Tourism: Using Tourism for Sustainable Development*. Oxford: Goodfellow Publishers.

Hall, C. & Lew, A. (2009). *Understanding and Managing Tourism Impacts: An Integrated Approach*. London: Routledge.

International Association for Impact Assessment (www.IAIA.org)

Edinburgh Festival City (https://www.edinburghfestivalcity.com/about/documents/156-research-reports) to download various reports.

2 Theory

Learning objectives

☐ Understand the Outcomes System model and its relevance to impact assessment, including the use of indicators.

☐ Be able to employ both Logic and Theory of Change models in evaluation and impact assessment, and know how to integrate them in strategic planning.

☐ Learn the nature of evidence and the types applicable to IA for events and tourism.

☐ Understand the Forces-Stressors-State-Impact-Response (FPSIR) Model and its importance in impact assessment.

☐ Know the meaning and nature of impact interactions and cumulative impacts, with reference to synergies, cascade effects, feedback, risk and uncertainty, and tipping points.

☐ Be able to adapt theory on Limits of Acceptable Change (LAC) to impact assessment, including the related concepts of thresholds, standards, capacity, and the precautionary principle.

2.1 Introduction

Outcomes theory incorporates a systems approach to planning, and builds evaluation and impact assessment into the management process. It corresponds with the approach taken in the companion book *Event Evaluation* and particularly with the Event Compass as a comprehensive approach to planning and evaluation. To put it into IA practice, a logic model or theory of change model is required.

The nature of evidence is then considered. It is of critical importance when it comes to measurement and the use of indicators, as the question of "what constitutes acceptable evidence?" will frequently arise in the undertaking and interpretation of impact assessments.

The forces-pressures-state-impacts-response model (FPSIR) is then presented. It provides a cyclical framework in which specific types of impact can be addressed by examining general forces and more specific trends that lead to pressures on the environment, economy or society. Specific impacts can then be viewed within a context that examines causes, followed by consideration of how people and systems respond to impacts.

The chapter ends with another planning model, Limits of Acceptable Change, which introduces several interrelated concepts that impact assessors need to be familiar with: capacity; tipping points; cumulative impacts; risk and uncertainty; precautionary principle.

Why planning models? Evaluation and impact assessment are seldom if ever conducted without reference to plans, strategies or policies. The results have to be used in practice, plus some contribution to theory is always possible. When goals are specified and indicators determined in advance, evaluators and impact assessors know what they are looking for.

2.2 Outcomes theory

According to Wikipedia: "Outcomes theory provides the conceptual basis for thinking about, and working with outcomes systems of any type. An outcomes system is any system that: identifies; prioritizes; measures; attributes; or hold parties to account for outcomes of any type in any area." In other words, events are an outcome system and their organisers and supporters are accountable for those outcomes. In the business world, outcomes theory is more about strategic planning and managing change for improved productivity and profit, whereas in the realm of events and event tourism it is usually about creating and demonstrating public good. All organisations employ some methods of accountability and evaluation, with impact assessment being part of the process.

Duignan's (2009) Outcomes System Diagram has been adapted for our context (see Figure 2.1). It identifies seven different building blocks of outcomes systems. Some comments have been added for relevance to our discussion of IA for event and tourism impacts. The 'outcomes model' specifies the desired outcomes or impacts and the steps that lead to them, and this requires a logic or theory of change model. Outcomes models, as discussed in this book, are based either on theory that enables prediction of impacts, or logic models that employ previous evidence (if any) to suggest the process to follow. Priorities for action are specified, and these follow from goals.

Indicators are essential to operationalise such a system. Duignan's 'controllable indicators' are those that provide proof that outcomes have been caused by the event, project or tourism. Of course, what constitutes 'proof' is a big question in evaluation and IA, and the acceptable evidence and related methods have to be agreed upon in advance. Specification of these indicators will depend on some prior theory or understanding based on experience, for example to answer the question: "How will we know that the event/project/tourism created social capital?" A simpler question to answer would be: "what are the event's economic impacts?", as indicators can be readily identified (e.g., use visitor surveys to measure new money brought into the in-scope area, attributable to the event).

'Not necessarily controllable indicators' can also be important for evaluation and IA, but there are believed to be confounding variables such as outside forces. These indicators can also be used as evidence of success or goal attainment or impacts caused by the event or project, but there also can be additional causal factors, known or unknown.

Evaluation can be of two basic types: the first is 'performance improvement' and can be called technical evaluation related to decision making and problem solving – the focus of the companion book *Event Evaluation*. The second is 'impact evaluation attributing change', which has the purpose of making claims about whether or not goals have been attained and what cause the outcomes. Duignan identified a third type called 'economic and comparative evaluation', in which financial measures such as profit/loss or return on investment for different plans, strategies or interventions are directly compared. This is typical of economic impact assessment that puts monetary values on benefits and costs of alternative actions.

Finally, the model incorporates 'contracting, accountability and performance management arrangements'. These can be contracts, such as between events and their grant givers and sponsors that specify goals, evaluation and impact assessment methods and measures. Agreement will also almost always be needed among key stakeholders on what constitutes sufficient evidence of outcomes.

OUTCOMES MODEL
Logic models or theory of change models that specify high-level desired outcomes (i.e., priorities) and actions necessary to attain them. Use theory or past experience that suggests how to attain goals.

CONTRACTING, ACCOUNTABILITY AND PERFORMANCE MANAGEMENT ARRANGEMENTS

Stakeholders must agree on goals, methods and measures for IA and evaluation.

CONTROLLABLE INDICATORS
(Key Impact Indicators that show outcomes have been caused by the event or project)

NOT NECESSARILY CONTROLLABLE INDICATORS
(these also suggest goal attainment, but might be partly or wholly due to uncontrollable external forces.

What evidence of goal attainment (outcomes) will be acceptable?

PERFORMANCE IMPROVEMENT EVALUATION -e.g. service and programme quality	IMPACT EVALUATION ATTRIBUTING CHANGE (The IA process)	ECONOMIC & COMPARATIVE EVALUATION (e.g., Comparing ROI of alternatives)

Adapted from: Duignan, P. "Using outcomes theory to solve important conceptual and practical problems in evaluation, monitoring and performance management systems." *American Evaluation Association Conference*, Orlando, Florida, 11–14 November 2009.

Figure 2.1: Outcomes System Model Adapted From Duignan

2.3 Logic and theory of change models

If there is theory to support a claim that X will cause Y, then planners of events and tourism can be reasonably assured they will achieve their goals. But that is generally not the case; we do not have theories that are both explanatory and predictive. We do have lots of experience to draw on, and we have theory fragments that can be incorporated into our planning and evaluation through the tools of 'logic models' and 'theory of change models', as developed by Weiss (1972; 1995).

In the Duignan outcomes model it is necessary to specify both the priority outcomes and actions necessary to achieve them. Logic models are most appropriate for goals-oriented evaluation, whereas theory of change (TOC) models are specifically intended for use by those either seeking to make fundamental changes in the state of society or the economy, or at least to generate longer-term impacts. Figure 2.2 is from the *Event Evaluation* book and it intentionally separates the kind of outputs that an event normally wants to evaluate (e.g., attendance, revenue, customer satisfaction) from desired changes or impacts that are more in the realm of impact assessment. For event tourism, a process illustrated along the bottom of the diagram, the overall aims of the strategy or policy are for cumulative impacts that create public good – economic and community development, and improved destination competiveness.

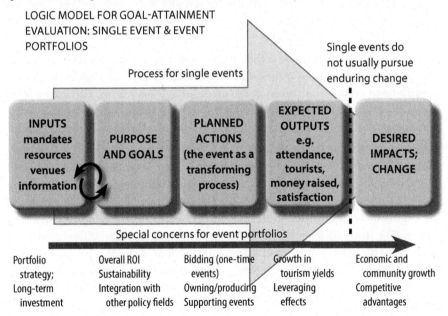

Figure 2.2: Logic model for event and tourism evaluation and impact assessment

All logic models aim to direct planning towards attainment of goals by specifying the actions necessary to achieve them, and alongside this process to reveal assumptions and uncertainties. There has to be an underlying theory that supports the causal chain (i.e., theory that explains why X leads to, or causes Y), but that can take the form of propositions derived from previous experience, or understanding gained from what others have reported in the literature.

The logic can also take the form of suppositions (some would call this wishful thinking), meaning the planners hope an event or development will lead to social-capital formation or community development, in which case the whole project or event is really an experiment, and the evaluators will be contributing to theory development. It has to be repeated that this is a goals-oriented approach to planning, meaning the impact assessors and evaluators have to also consciously avoid tunnel vision.

Edinburgh

A logic model was collaboratively developed for the 2011 impact study of 12 festivals by BOP Consulting, with the aims of updating an earlier impact assessment from 2004/05 and expanding its scope beyond economic impacts. In the BOP model inputs were defined as "sustainable festival organisations" – a generalisation that subsumes all their management functions and event production activities. There were four output categories, namely: "outreach events; public events; participative workshops, and industry events, training & networking". In this logic model, therefore, outputs are not just festivals but other measureable activities of the organisations, and that is different from a logic model that specifies the goals of a particular event.

Inherent in this logic model is the intention, and belief, that the festival organisations can create certain outputs directly (such as cultural experiences), and contribute to broader outcomes in the medium to longer term. Edinburgh festivals are working collaboratively, and with external stakeholders, to attain environmental, economic, social and cultural benefits for the city and for Scotland.

Commissioned by Festivals Edinburgh, the 2018 report by BOP Consulting entitled *Edinburgh Festivals The Network Effect: The role of the Edinburgh Festivals in the national culture and events sectors* developed twin logic models for examining the wider impacts of Edinburgh's festivals on Scotland. These employed an 'inputs-activities-outputs-outcomes-impact' path, with the inputs consisting of funding from all sources, resources from partners, stakeholders and staff, and creativity from Scottish and International talent. Activities for creative and cultural impact included the delivery of events and programmes, networking, importing talent while showcasing Scottish talent, and employing staff and volunteers.

The measureable outputs were defined in quantitative terms: events produced and audiences reached, jobs created in the wider economy, Scottish performers, artists and speakers receiving profile and platforms, and networking activities.

Outcomes were defined as follows: Edinburgh recognised globally as worlds' leading festival city; Scotland's creative talent gains profile and opportunity; the festivals facilitate and support sectoral development, and formal and informal education and training opportunities.

Finally, impacts included increased confidence and pride, enrichment of the cultural ecosystem, and gains for Scottish artists and companies. As suggested by this logic model, Scotland has a very broad, long-term goal of national significance that guides the definition of outputs and outcomes for planned events.

2.3.1 Designing the TOC model and related IA process

Theory of Change models were invented to guide interventions that have the specific aim of causing, or contributing to longer-term impacts. Here is one definition:

> *"Theory of change is essentially a comprehensive description and illustration of how and why a desired change is expected to happen in a particular context... It does this by first identifying the desired long-term goals and then works back from these to identify all the conditions (outcomes) that must be in place (and how these relate to one another causally) for the goals to occur... This leads to better planning, in that activities are linked to a detailed understanding of how change actually happens. It also leads to be better evaluation, as it is possible to measure progress towards the achievement of longer-term goals that goes beyond the identification of program outputs."*

Source: http://www.theoryofchange.org/what-is-theory-of-change/

There is a TOC organization (see their website: www.theoryofchange.org/) that advocates a model, and has software. Here are the basic principles of TOC as they define it:

> *-It is a causal framework of how and why a change process will happen in a particular context.*

> *-Rather than projecting outcomes from your activities, TOC reverses that process by focusing FIRST on WHAT OUTCOME you are seeking (your goal) then thoroughly considering all preconditions necessary.*

> *-Interventions and Activities are then based on your outcomes framework. (So you know why you are doing them!)*

> *-It is a system with built-in Indicators so that you know you are on track ove time.*

> *-It is a process that makes assumptions explicit and identifies rationales for all preconditions and interventions (activities).*

> *-It is both a "process" and a "product."*

Events and their stakeholders have to ask themselves this question: "What makes us think that holding an event (or creating an event portfolio), and all the surrounding activities plus publicity, will cause or contribute to our goals?" This forces planners to consider their assumptions, and more importantly the evidence available to support their actions.

In addition to considering the logic, or plausibility of the model, planners have to assess feasibility. Do they have the resources, skills and time to achieve the desired impacts? If not, something has to be modified. Then indicators of progress and goal attainment must be specified, and tested (in practice or through critique) to ensure they do in fact measure what is intended (this is the 'validity' problem as discussed in Chapter 3).

Steps are described below, and the example being developed pertains to a very difficult social impact question – 'social integration' (also see the related treatment of 'social capital' in Chapter 4).

Step 1: Outcomes specified

TOC models require that planners work backwards from a clear statement of what outcomes or impacts are intended. Outcomes have to be stated as conditions or end-states – something tangible. If a festival or a portfolio of events is intended to foster 'social integration', what exactly does that mean? Here is one definition, from Study.com:

> "In sociology, the concept of social integration refers to a situation where minority groups come together or are incorporated into mainstream society. Though, we should note, this doesn't mean in a forceful way. Social integration also refers to a process of largely agreeing on a shared system of meaning, language, culture, and the like. This doesn't mean there aren't any differences, but that we kind of agree to live together and, at least to an extent, feel part of a larger community. Increased social integration helps reduce conflict in society, and it can help us feel more connected to our community."

(Source: study.com/academy/lesson/social-integration-definition-theory.html)

Theory on how to achieve social integration through events is lacking, but advice is available under the heading of 'social leveraging' as put forward by Chalip (2006; see the research note).

If we assume that social integration is not something that can easily be created, then a number of Key Impact Indicators of social integration as a process are required. Here are a few suggestions, the first two being generic and the next three specific to what festivals and other events will hopefully contribute:

♦ Hate-crimes in the city/community are reduced or eliminated

♦ Quality of life increases for all residents and groups (e.g, as measured by surveys and census data that consider happiness, health, economic opportunities and incomes, and perceived progress)

♦ Representatives of all cultures actively collaborate in producing the event

◆   The number of event volunteers from each group increases each year

◆   Target groups (e.g., recent immigrants, small minorities, people in need) are satisfied with the ways in which events help meet their particular goals

Outputs such as "increased attendance and participation by minority groups" are relatively easy to measure, but it is only a process indicator and does not validly measure the concept of social integration. Picking the best indicators requires a lot of thought.

Laing and Mair (2015) explored 'social inclusion', a related concept, and suggested that bringing people together could be facilitated in by festival organisers through providing opportunities for local participation, learning new skills, and access to education about social justice. A narrow focus on event attendees is inadequate, they claimed, and outreach to the entire community is required.

Research Note

Chalip, L. (2006). Towards social leverage of sport events. *Journal of Sport & Tourism, 11*(2), 109-127.

Abstract: Despite the predominant policy focus on event economic impact, event organisers and host community residents are calling for attention to be paid to the social value of events. Anthropological work on events demonstrates that their celebratory nature engenders a liminoid space that can foster social value, particularly through a sense of communitas. In order to enable and amplify liminality and communitas, event organisers and host community planners should foster social interaction and prompt a feeling of celebration by enabling sociability among event visitors, creating event-related social events, facilitating informal social opportunities, producing ancillary events, and theming widely. The resulting narratives, symbols, meanings, and affect can then be leveraged to address social issues, build networks, and empower community action. These may be furthered when the arts are used to complement sport, and when commercial elements support social leverage. Future research should explore and examine the strategic and tactical bases for social leverage.

Step 2: Preconditions and causal pathways specified

This is the step that requires underpinning theory and careful attention to logic and evidence. Every intended impact has to be addressed in this way: "We want to achieve Z, so we first need to put in place X and Y". Thus every 'causal pathway' describes a process by which it is expected that interventions will work as planned. Evaluators and impact assessors will examine every goal and its causal pathway to determine what worked or did not, and the reasons.

Planners have to explain the logical pathway for attaining each goal. Also, is there a logical sequence of outcomes? For example, it might be that volunteers have to be recruited and trained first, and therefore that outcome actually becomes a precondition for the others.

Step 3: Interventions (activities), leading to the relevant outcome(s)

Not all events are conceived as agents of change, but they are interventions. Unfortunately, some organizers of events are satisfied with NOT specifying outcomes, and others will merely specify very basic (and not necessarily explicit) goals like satisfying guests and other key stakeholders, and staying financially viable. Event-tourism on the other hand, is instrumentalist by nature, as it always serves to generate business income, create jobs, or achieve marketing and development goals. See the earlier Edinburgh example for how they define interventions.

Step 4: Assumptions

Logic and/or theory might not answer all our questions about the causal pathways – we might have to make assumptions, and they have to be explicit. Another type of assumption is the taken-for-granted kind, such as "we assume the industry will respond to higher demand by expanding capacity and/or raising prices". These kinds of assumptions have to be grounded in real-world evidence.

Step 5: Rationale

The rationales for the causal pathway, and for each assumption and precondition, have to be made explicit. No 'black boxes' are allowed in which the assumptions and algorithms are invisible.

Step 6: Indicators

Success, or attainment of goals, has to be measured. The metrics must be specified for all planned outcomes. Where precise, quantifiable metrics are unavailable or unwanted we need surrogate indicators.

I use the term Key Impact Indicators because planners and evaluators have many measures and indicators to choose from and they have to pick the ones that are practical and convincing. When there is no agreement on precise measures of success or goal attainment, then there must at least be agreement on what 'evidence' will be assembled and how it will be evaluated.

Step 7: Narrative

A diagram might not be sufficient to explain the logic model or the evaluation process, so a full narrative is desirable. Constructing the narrative in concert with the graphic model will probably be a good way to get stakeholders talking the same language, and hopefully agreeing on the process. If consensus is not attained, the process or the event might have to be re-conceptualized.

2.3.2 TOC Illustrated

Figure 2.3 is a very simple illustration of the logic and steps in designing a TOC model. The starting point is specification of outcomes or impacts, those intended longer-term or permanent changes that require social or economic action. Indicators are needed to operationalize the construct we call 'social integration', and a few examples are listed. They will overlap with other social/cultural goals such as community development (through capacity building and self-determination) or economic development to provide more job and entrepreneurial opportunities for immigrants. Unless the target groups agree to the goals and indicators, 'success' will be impossible to declare.

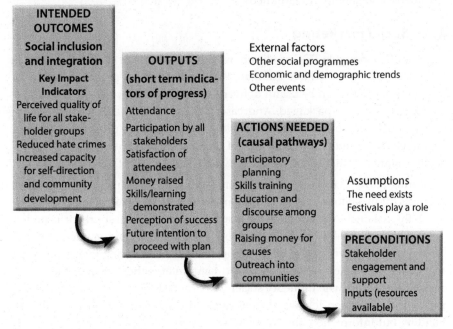

Figure 2.3: Theory of Change model

Certain assumptions accompany these kinds of policy decisions, mainly that intervention is needed and will be supported by the affected stakeholders – in this case multiple communities or social/cultural groups that have the desire and will to strive for integration, with events being facilitators. Festivals and events cannot hope to achieve such lofty goals on their own. As well, external forces and trends have to be taken into account, as nothing happens in isolation. There might be a cluster of social and economic programmes available, a context within which the event organisers and supporters must work collaboratively.

Outputs, or short-term indicators of progress, are specified in this example. Normal event evaluation will deal with these, as they reflect the operation and perceived success of the event. Obviously if the festival fails to attract and satisfy the target groups, there will be little hope of facilitating social integration.

Actions are to be arranged in causal pathways, such as "participatory planning and production of the festival will build trust, establish ongoing collaboration mechanisms, and build capacity for future production of this festival and other projects".

Impact assessors will determine if the desired changes are achieved, along with careful examination of the causal pathways that have been formulated on the basis of some theory or experiences. This assessment will form part of (and perhaps the major part) of an evaluation of the event and related programmes. The same people might be involved with IA and evaluation of 'merit' (did the event achieve its goals?) and 'worth' (a determination that the programme/event is valuable and should be continued).

2.3.3 Social marketing

Many of the possible TOC applications in the events sector can be described as 'social marketing' (Kotler and Zaltman, 1971), with events as agents of change. At a minimum, events can be useful delivery vehicles within which social marketing messages can be packaged. Andreasen (1994, 110) defined social marketing as "the adaptation of traditional marketing technologies to programs designed to influence the voluntary behaviour of target audiences to improve their personal welfare and that of the society of which they are a part."

Jutbring (2018, 2) discussed events that were used to 'frame' issues or act as catalysts for behaviour change, pertaining to the following aims: foster environmentally sustainable behaviours; the inspiration effect where sport participation is to encourage healthy activity; promote vegetarianism and gender equality. He referred to 'downstream' interventions aimed at countering perceived negative behaviours, like smoking; and 'upstream' interventions targeted at policy makers and others who influence society. At events, for example, the anti-smoking or pro-vegetarian lobbies can engage in downstream social marketing by handing out information and showing videos, while the event itself promotes these causes in a positive light by offering a smoke-free and meat-free experience. Active lobbying of politicians to change the law by using events to promote causes is upstream social marketing.

One can immediately see that social marketing at, and through events embodies principles of CSR (corporate social responsibility) and can be directly linked to sustainability or green practices. Theory of Change applies because clear goals are expressed and desired outcomes have to be evaluated. However, social marketing is usually conceived as a long-term, sustained campaign to foster awareness, alter attitudes and ultimately change behaviours - so how can a single event contribute? Obviously if the event is periodic there can be multiple efforts, and if the campaign reaches many events (targeted to specific audiences) better results can be expected. For any one event, therefore, limited expectations will be the norm when it comes to impact assessment.

Jutbring's research led to several conclusions regarding social marketing through events, starting with the desirability of stakeholder collaboration for wider and longer-term effort. The event experience itself can be designed as a social-marketing medium, including theming, consumption options, exposure to new ideas and desired behaviours, messages from sponsors, experts or celebrities, facilitated interactions that reinforce desired behaviours, and emotional engagements. Securing favourable publicity through media management is a path to "upstream" marketing, as media are influential and decision-makers will likely pay attention to coverage. All of these design features are actions to incorporate into TOC models.

2.4 The meaning and nature of evidence

The dictionary meanings of 'evidence' do not provide us with a firm answer to the inevitable question arising in evaluation and IA, being "do we have proof, or at last sufficient evidence?" Here are two paraphrased dictionary definitions:

Evidence is....

a) what we employ to demonstrate clearly that a project or event causes identifiable outputs and impacts

b) what we employ to confirm or refute a theory, assertion of belief, or something proclaimed to be a fact (as in: is there clear evidence to prove that mega events are good for the economy? do we know for certain that festivals generate social capital? does learning theory provide us with the means to ensure that conference/meeting attendees will learn what they need to know?)

In a courtroom there will be arguments about evidence, with claims and counter claims about what has been proven. Many positivists believe there is only one kind of evidence, and that is to employ experiments to demonstrate cause and effect; this methodology entails the confirmation or refutation of hypotheses. But in applied fields, evaluators and impact assessors are seldom able to employ experiments and will often have little or no theory to draw upon. Evidence will consist of whatever is agreed upon to permit drawing conclusions or making decisions. Evidence in such situations is a social contract, agreed to by stakeholders. In the absence of such agreement there is a real risk that conclusions will not be accepted.

Miller and Fredericks (2003) emphasized that 'data' are not evidence. They asked (p. 21) "How can or does qualitative data become evidence for a claim? Or to use the language from confirmation theory, are there 'good reasons' to believe that qualitative research findings are evidence?" The answer is that 'evidence' is what we agree upon, and that will often be a range of indicators believed to validly demonstrate a concept like social inclusion or social capital.

What kinds of evidence will be acceptable in a given evaluation or IA context? Figure 2.4 should assist in the process of deciding upon what data to collect, how to conduct analyses, and what, in the end, will be acceptable to draw conclusions and make decisions. Again, this is most likely to be a social contract among stakeholders. Note the inherent differences between qualitative and quantitative methods, and consider the main evaluation and research paradigms, namely positivism, interpretive and critical/emancipatory that are explained in the book Event Evaluation.

Figure 2.4: Types of evidence and related data and possible applications

General categories of evidence	Specific types of data & Possible applications
Voices: what people say is often the most important form of evidence when it comes to evaluation and impact assessment for events and tourism - but can all voices be considered of equal weight? what are the biases and limitations?	**Personal opinions and attitudes**: Respondents to surveys or interviewers can express opinions on event/trip satisfaction, quality, future intentions, and attitudes towards events and tourism.
	Expert opinion is testimony based on theory, accepted practice, or context-specific research and analysis (such as "experts concluded that traditional marketing was ineffective"). Simulations and econometric models are part of the arsenal of "experts", but in themselves are always open to criticism for their inherent assumptions, or the quality of data available.
	Judgment can be accepted as evidence, either by experts comparing sport/artistic performance to specifications/standards, or by consumers as in "people's choice" awards for the best wine/food.
	Consultations: Providing information, leading discussions and obtaining input from individuals and groups (e.g., residents, stakeholders) is a method for gathering important evidence. This can include opinions, attitudes, tacit and implicit knowledge about how events, tourism or development is changing or expected to change their lives.
	Political opinions or ideology can be used as evidence of societal values and divisions that can influence reaction to proposed events or venues
	Media content: Content analysis might reveal evidence of what is important in a given community, or how opinions are shaped.
Actions: what people do is evidence of what is important	**Consumer behaviour** is evidence of supply and demand interactions or other economic and market forces, such as falling demand in response to price/cost increases.
	Institutional arrangements can be evidence of what is valued in society (e.g., the importance attached to education, religion, certain traditions) and of social/cultural capital as reflected in festivals and arts/cultural networks.
	Political action: Policies, programmes and investments are evidence of underlying ideology and priorities related to development or creating public good through events and venues.

Actions (cont.)	Community actions such as producing events can be evidence of community development (e.g., by demonstrating self-sufficiency, social integration, networking and innovation).
	Action by social worlds and sub-cultures: Their events can be interpreted as evidence of values, goals such as legitimacy-seeking, and preferred experiences.
	Demonstrate, protest, riot: More extreme actions are evidence of serious issues, unresolved conflict, or perceived lack of political/institutional legitimacy.
Observation What we can see, or testimony from a 'witness'. A witness in legal terms usually gives testimony under oath.	Systematic observation: Researchers can yield evidence of crowd behaviour, responses to programming stimuli, and the effects of controls. Participant observation (or ethnography): In-depth evidence based on personal involvement can be important, as in the nature of the event experience or the nature of host-guest relations in a community. Netnography: Evaluators can employ non-intrusive content analysis or interactions with others online (in blogs, chat rooms etc.) to obtain evidence of involvement, social world influences, or the effects of experiences as described by contributors.
Money/economic data -in business and economics money talks!	Profit and ROI are evidence of business success or competitive strengths. Growth in jobs, income or domestic product (GDP) is often used as evidence of successful economic policy.
Experimentation -with randomized control groups; quasi and field experiments	Theory of Change models can be considered experiments but evidence builds slowly, through replication and critical review. In quasi and field experiments reliability and validity problems abound because of 'messy' real-world conditions (i.e. many intervening variables).
Meta-Analysis: from meta analysis there can be critical reviews and higher certainty in forecasting, plus theory development to guide planning and evaluation/IA	Meta analysis can only be achieved if many research projects and experiments utilize the same methods and measures, OR there are many conclusions considered to be highly reliable and valid.

Not all evidence will be perceived to be equal. In the medical and pharmaceutical worlds, where life and death questions are the norm, observational studies and expert opinion rank at the bottom of their list of acceptable evidence! Of medium value are experimental studies, preferably the kind involving randomized control groups, where 'proof' of cause and effect, plus theory development, are the aims. The highest level of evidence comes from critical appraisal, which includes meta-analysis of many studies, and systematic reviews leading to evidence-based practice guidelines.

In the applied management fields we cannot adhere to this ideal hierarchy of evidence. For evaluation and impact assessment, other standards have to be developed, and one set of guidelines will not suit all situations. There are occasions when the voices of residents or key stakeholders will be considered supreme, given the precautionary principle or adherence to social responsibility values, and other times when only hard economic data will suffice. Remember, evidence is a social contract.

2.4.1 Explicit, implicit and tacit knowledge

Residents and other stakeholders likely to be impacted are potential experts; they can know what will affect them, and how, or at least they can express legitimate concerns.

Some probing might be required to first elicit *'explicit knowledge'*, meaning the facts and sources of information that already exist but have to be collected, codified and analysed. Then there is *'implicit knowledge'*, or the 'know-how' people and groups accumulate that might be difficult to pass on to others in words or documents. For example, a community might know how to respond to a stimulus or a crisis because they have done it before, but it is not a formal plan. Implicit knowledge might not come to light unless individuals and groups join a formal consultation process or begin to collaborate within a network. It might be necessary for IA projects to organize such networks.

Tacit knowledge is the kind that is personal and difficult to transfer. It is sometimes a 'taken for granted' way people have of doing things, usually based on considerable experience, or an unconscious adaptation of behaviour to the environment – again, in response to external stimuli. When asked "why do you do it that way?" or "how do you know that?", the respondent might not be able to explain it – that is tacit knowledge. Whole groups, such as aboriginal people, might possess a wealth of implicit and tacit knowledge that can help forecast impacts or suggest how to cope with the consequences of development.

2.4.2 Reliability and validity

In statistics, *'reliability'* refers to the ability of researchers to obtain the same results through repeated measurements. It also means we can trust something, or someone is dependable, and that definition is more relevant in the context of a discussion of evidence. How trustworthy are the perceptions of witnesses? Can we depend on public consultations to give us an accurate picture of impacts in the community? Will our indicators produce reliable measurements so that we have enough confidence in them to draw conclusions about the impacts of events and tourism?

'Validity' refers to how well our measures and indicators reveal the truth, for example is there theory or evidence from previous research that suggests our

measures and indicators do what is required of them? There is little use trying to measure economic impacts with the perceptions of uninformed people, for example (although their answers might be interesting for other purposes). Do we really know how to measure social capital? Is the ecological footprint a valid measure of ecological impacts?

When it comes to evidence, we are not talking about *'internal validity'* because that refers to the proof of cause and effect – that is something for random experimentation.

'External validity' refers to the generalizability of results, but this is usually only applicable for experimentation. If we want to claim that the results of our impact assessment or evaluation are applicable elsewhere, or to the world in general, we will have to provide the kind of evidence that comes from meta-analysis of many comparable projects.

'Construct validity' is important, as it refers to the operationalization of a construct such as social capital. Can we develop practical tests that are supported by social-capital theory? If you do not have a lot of confidence in the construct itself (perhaps you think social capital does not really exist as an important social phenomenon, or it has been poorly defined) then you cannot have valid measures of it.

Consider this quote from the Wikipedia article on validity:

"In logic, and therefore as the term is applied to any epistemological claim, validity refers to the consistency of an argument flowing from the premises to the conclusion; as such, the truth of the claim in logic is not only reliant on validity. Rather, argumentative claim is true if and only if it is both valid and sound. This means the argument flows without contradiction from the premises or the conclusion, and all of the premises and the conclusion correspond to known facts."

Here is the key to logic and theory of change models: the argument that events or event-tourism will cause certain changes to occur, with measureable impacts/outcomes, must flow from the initial premise (which is either based on a theory or a premise that is backed by evidence) without contradiction. The logic has to be explained and unchallenged. Otherwise these models do not work. Think of it this way: if our goal is to have events and event-tourism generate or contribute to any outcome/impact, we have to explain the logic of the initial premise and the pathways that show how our actions (the event and its programme and related activities) should lead to the desired or expected consequences. Then impact assessment will show how valid and logical our models are.

2.5 The forces-pressure-state-impact-response model (FPSIR)

Driving forces (see Figure 2.5) are fundamental agents of change. A common acronym for forces is PEST – referring to Political, Economic, Socio-Cultural, and Technological. Forces give rise to changes and we usually can see these and document the related trends. A major trend has been the global legitimation of events as instruments of policy and corporate strategy, giving rise to substantial and continuous growth in the number, diversity, size and significance of events.

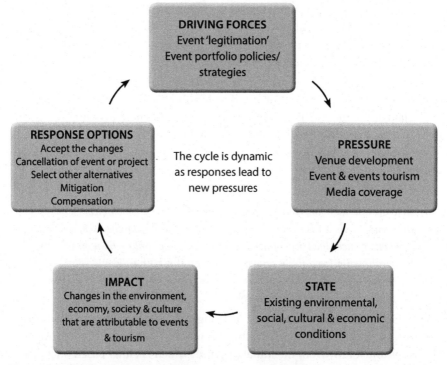

Figure 2.5: The Forces-Pressure-State-Impact-Response model

Within IA the relevant driving forces must reflect the context, such as economic, social and political trends within a given city that lead to its particular mix of events and venues. Technological forces tend to be global in scope, but there might be local or national conditions to consider. In the diagram, event portfolio development is the major force, and this reflects underlying policies for place marketing, economic development and social-cultural improvements. The force of strategically creating and managing a portfolio of events leads to pressures.

Pressure refers to the ways in which events, venues and tourism put pressure on the environment, society and the economy. Remember that we conceptualize planned events as agents of change. These pressures cover the full spectrum of possible causes of impacts, including event venue development, event production and activities (e.g., investment, consumption of food and beverages, marketing, energy use by events, waste generation, crowds, celebration), event tourism (generating carbon emissions, demand for services), and even media coverage of events and tourism can have an impact. Some pressures are rather obvious, such as the link between events, tourism and increased automobile and air traffic, while others more subtle and open to interpretation, such as the role of media coverage of events in influencing resident attitudes.

The *state* of environment, society, culture and the economy is always dynamic, and if we do not have data on existing conditions and trends we cannot readily forecast potential impacts. If the impact assessment is looking back at what the cumulative effects of events and tourism have been, then we have a real challenge in determining what might have happened in the absence of events and tourism. A post-event impact assessment should ideally be able to compare new conditions with what existed before the event.

Impact: In IA we are looking for changes attributable to the pressures imposed by events, venues and tourism. We need appropriate and legitimate evidence to support claims about causes and effects, as 'undisputed proof' is rarely possible. To get the evidence, we need key impact indicators, as there is little use saying (for example) that tourism generates carbon emissions and contributes to climate change if we cannot measure the amount of car versus bus travel generated by an event, then use a carbon calculator to estimate total emissions.

Some researchers stop at this point, being only interested in determining what impacts are caused by events and tourism; indeed, much of the available literature is of that type. But for IA and evaluation we need to know more: what are the appropriate responses, from cancellation to compensation, and how do these responses affect the system? The process is cyclical, obviously because human responses to most pressures and impacts are constantly evolving and thereby changing the underlying forces. In portfolio management, for example, constant monitoring of the event population and its health, along with measures of return on investment, leads managers to continuously alter the mix. The management principle of risk reduction is important, and this means diversification of event types, target segments, season and location (Andersson et al., 2017).

Torres-Delgado and Palomeque (2014) have used the FPSIR model in developing indicators for sustainable tourism. Indicators were recommended for each stage (forces, pressures, state, impacts and responses) then in a TBL approach for sociocultural, economic and environmental impacts. Every event, city and destination can do this to achieve personalized impact assessments, and this logic is followed in the ensuing chapters of this book.

Research Note

Torres-Delgado, A. & Palomeque, F. (2014). Measuring sustainable tourism at the municipal level. *Annals of Tourism Research, 49,* 122–137.

Abstract: The objective of this research is to provide a scientifically sound, applicable method for studying tourism sustainability at the local level. This is done by developing an indicator system based on an initial literature search that serves to compile a preliminary list of indicators, which are then verified and scientifically validated by conducting a Delphi survey. This process is used to develop a consensual indicator system that is adapted to the tourism sector and includes 26 indicators of social, economic and environmental sustainability. To ensure the applicability of the system, indicator values are then calculated for 20 tourism municipalities in Catalonia (Spain). The results confirm the proposed system is an effective tool for planning and managing tourism at municipal level.

2.6 Cumulative impacts

One event can cause impacts, but what about many events and tourism over a long period of time? They are, taken together, bound to have a major effect, especially on small communities and sensitive environments, but sometimes on whole cities and nations. We have little evidence of the cumulative impacts of events because the necessary research is very challenging.

One of the difficulties in measuring and evaluating long-term, cumulative impacts is taking into account 'synergistic effects'. Synergy can be defined as interactions that produce a combined effect greater than the sum of separate effects. The interactions of events with each other and with other forms of tourism and development are often invisible and confusing. What, for example, does a large and growing population of events and related venues do for the host community in terms of economic prosperity, social integration, and ecological sustainability? We simply do not know, although we can take informed guesses and develop pertinent scenarios.

Synergies occur when two or more effects interact to create something greater than the mere sum of the parts. For example, if you combine voluntarism at events with community-based planning you might hope to get the synergistic effect of increased self-reliance or a community-development process that can continue on its own. Expressed this way it is a social goal and sets in motion an evaluation/IA process. Synergies can also be bad, as in attracting protestors who interact poorly with event organisers, police, residents and tourists, which leads to an outbreak of violence, injuries, counter-protests and years-long legal proceedings to sort out the mess.

Another consideration is that of *cascade effects* or *cascading impacts*, being the chain of events, or the ripple effect, whereby action leads to a change that triggers another, and so on – until disaster strikes or finally we wake up to a new problem. Climate change is one of these effects, being the sum total (through numerous synergistic effects and feedback mechanisms) of centuries of interventions in the planet's ecosystem, until at some point everyone agrees it is a serious problem and must be fixed.

Positive feedback means any response to change that reinforces the direction or magnitude of that change, such as global warming causing an annual diminishment of polar sea ice which in turn speeds up warming. A positive feedback mechanism pertinent to events is that of 'legitimation', being the global acceptance of events as instruments of policy and strategy, as that process has led to continuous growth. Considering the opposite force, one possible kind of *negative feedback* mechanism is this: as event populations soar, each event becomes less able to secure resources and capture demand, thereby leading to more failures, fewer start-ups, and some degree of homeostasis. This is one aspect of 'organisational ecology' theory as discussed in Getz and Andersson (2016).

Climatologists also theorize about '*tipping points*' beyond which change becomes irreversible, or impacts become impossible to prevent, or disaster occurs. We can foresee the day when climate change and its many negative impacts and imposed costs might halt growth, but can we identify or hypothesise tipping points related to the impacts of events and tourism on a city or region? Again, we have little evidence to draw upon. Suppose an event continues to disrupt the community until, one day, the residents mobilize and lobby their politicians to cancel the event or impose new regulations (we have seen this scenario played out in various cities). What exactly was the tipping point? Was it the tenth time traffic congestion surrounding the event caused severe delays, or perhaps the most recent report of crime associated with the tourists attracted? Tipping points of these kinds are difficult to forecast, and in the events and tourism sectors it might be that a gradual 'slipping' is more likely than a 'tipping'.

Here is a definition of cumulative impact assessment by the IAIA:

The process of (a) analyzing the potential impacts and risks of proposed developments in the context of the potential effects of other human activities and natural environmental and social external drivers on the chosen [valued component] over time, and (b) proposing concrete measures to avoid, reduce, or mitigate such cumulative impacts and risks to the extent possible.

Cumulative effects are typically the result of incremental changes to the environment caused by multiple human activities and natural processes. For example, wildlife habitat fragmentation has many possible causes such as road building, clearing native vegetation for land development, and water diversion projects. However, cumulative effects can also result from repetitive actions such as cyclical or

episodic discharges of liquid waste or sewage into a water body or many wells tap-
ping and depleting an aquifer. There are many different types of cumulative effects
including additive, interactive, and synergistic, and they manifest in different ways
whereby the ability of the valued component (VC) to absorb or adapt to the effect
is ultimately exceeded. Ideally, CEA leads to decisions that maintain VC resil-
iency. (Source: http://www.iaia.org/uploads/pdf/Fastips_16%20Cumulative%20
Effects%20Assessment_1.pdf)

We need definitions of two terms introduced above:

♦   *Additive impacts:* are an assembly of separate impacts; IA often uses a matrix
    to identify all possible impacts that might arise from a project and its com-
    ponents.

♦   *Interactive impacts:* sometimes impacts interact and together create a new
    impact, raising the possibility of cascading and synergistic effects.

2.7 Limits of acceptable change (LAC) and related concepts

Although LAC is a planning system mostly used in parks and protected areas,
(Stankey et al., 1985) it contains a number of principles of use to event and tourism evaluators and impact assessors. As noted by McCool (2013) it is a decision-making framework based on goals, indicators and standards. The key LAC
principle is that decision making should focus on the appropriateness or accept-
ability of actions and impacts. Consider these propositions that are put forward
to stimulate thoughts about limits:

♦   Events and tourism inevitably have some impact on the community, the
    environment, the economy and society.

♦   The character and amount of impacts at some point becomes unacceptable
    to at least some stakeholders, reflecting different perceptions and value per-
    spectives.

♦   Also inevitable is that debate will occur about what impacts are important,
    how severe they are, whom they affect, and what can and should be done
    about them.

♦   Development of venues, and producing events, may conflict with other
    values such as preservation of heritage and ecosystems, but there might
    also be overlapping or compatible goals cutting across all perspectives.

♦   Planners, decision makers, and event producers are generally required to
    maintain change within a certain level of acceptability or appropriateness;
    this level will likely vary or oscillate, and will be imposed by some combina-
    tion of politics, regulations, and pursuit of sustainable development.

The following are LAC concepts that can be applicable to IA in general.

2.7.1 Thresholds

A threshold is a point in time or a condition (usually identified by monitoring key indicators) beyond which change should not be allowed to continue, or an impact considered acceptable. For example, what is a given community's 'threshold of tolerance' for increased traffic, noise, or disruption of normal life? How much change can a culture accept without losing its core values? When does pollution become so serious as to become a public health threat? There is a clear conceptual link to 'tipping points'.

2.7.2 Standards

In LAC 'standards' are set to ensure that desirable conditions are maintained and/or acceptable changes not exceeded, but this is more challenging than it sounds. What are the desired conditions within environmental, ecological, cultural, social and economic domains? Who decides? In community-based planning the community or residents decide, and that will be a political process. Standards can take a number of forms:

♦ *No change:* standards can be based on indicators of the current 'state' of the community or environment, being conditions that should not be allowed to change. For example, all existing open space and wildlife habitat are to be protected, traffic and noise levels will not be allowed to increase, or housing supply is not to be diminished.

♦ *Maxima and minima:* standards can take the form of defining the maximum tolerable (e.g., the maximum decibels allowed from a music concert at a distance of 500 metres/yards between 6 pm and midnight); a minimum standard could be set for the number of events to be held in a venue or a community, reflecting the goals of animating public spaces and fostering social integration.

♦ *Acceptable Rate of Change:* sometimes it is the rate of change that is the perceived problem, as with development that is occurring too fast for the community to adapt, or for services to be provided. Standards can be set to regulate growth, as in a policy that no more than five events are produced or added in a year, with a maximum increase of 5,000 visitors/attendance.

♦ *Mitigation:* When a new event venue is built there will likely be a sudden increase in events, traffic and potential disruption to the community, but negative impacts can be mitigated. Standards can be set for the provision of infrastructure and services required to ensure new developments have minimal negative effects.

2.7.3 Capacity

Capacity has several pertinent applications. Most venue capacities (e.g., numbers of people permitted at one time) are fixed by health or fire authorities, in order to prevent disasters. It is also a design concept, taking into account an optimal experience for users, and might take the form of fixed seating (with some or no standing room) or recommended standards for event planners. Setting the capacity of open spaces is more difficult, especially when crowds are part of the atmosphere, as at concerts. Crowd safety and ability to evacuate are critical considerations, and many jurisdictions have applicable regulations that must be met.

◆ *Limits:* There might be circumstances when it is considered that a given venue, site or community cannot – or should not – be subjected to too much pressure or change. What can be limited? The number and size of events is a primary target for those worried about capacity, but it might be more a question of location – not permitting events in protected or sensitive environments or too close to residential areas. Note that limits are restrictions on growth, or numbers and size, and these might be enforced by reference to standards.

2.7.4 Precautionary principle

This is a fundamental principle of risk management and sustainable development, but is often ignored:

The precautionary principle (or precautionary approach) to risk management states that if an action or policy has a suspected risk of causing harm to the public, or to the environment, in the absence of scientific consensus (that the action or policy is not harmful), the burden of proof that it is not harmful falls on those taking that action.

Source: https://en.wikipedia.org/wiki/Precautionary_principle

Fennell (2014, p. 514) discussed the precautionary principle in the context of tourism, pointing to many cases of disregard for environmental quality and how that, in turn, negatively affects tourism. Six basic concepts are associated with this principle:

◆ Preventive anticipation (i.e., Always looking at potential impacts)

◆ Safeguarding ecological space

◆ Adoption of restraints that are not unduly expensive

◆ Duty of care; putting the onus of proof on proponents of change

◆ Recognising intrinsic rights for nature/non-human entities

◆ Paying for past ecological debt.

The reasons why this principle is frequently resisted or ignored are several:

1   Many impacts, especially cumulative and long-term impacts, cannot reliably be predicted, and indeed are not adequately understood; the required burden of proof that actions are NOT harmful is therefore often impossible to provide

2   Many forms of development and daily life in the modern world are going to cause changes with known negative consequences, and yet society is, in the short term at least, powerless to stop them (e.g., using non-renewable energy, generating emissions and waste, cutting down or burning forests, overusing groundwater – the list is endless)

3   Somebody will gain, regardless of the consequences, and influence is often exerted to gain advantages for the few at the expense of the many – or with reckless disregard for the environment

We simply do not know enough, nor are evaluation systems in place to give us the answers to fully implement the precautionary principle. The more evaluation and risk management we do, the more preventative can be our planning.

2.8 Theories, concepts and models in this book

Theories of impacts have been discussed in this chapter, plus theories applicable to impact assessment. Throughout the book are discussions of other theories, and of concepts and models that have some theoretical significance, and Figure 2.6 provides a reference for these, and the locations by chapter and section.

Figure 2.6: Theories, concepts and models

Corporate Social Responsibility (CSR) (Chapter 1; 1.1)
A guiding set of principles for the planning and management of events, venues and tourism; IA should be transparent, comprehensive with full public accountability; professional evaluation and IA to respect human rights and place priority on the people affected by projects.
Responsible Tourism (1.1)
Principles to guide event-tourism planning and development; can provide standards by which to judge impacts.
Sustainability; Greening (1.1; 7.2)
Principles to guide event operations, and event-tourism planning and development; can provide standards by which to judge impacts.
Values; Evaluation; Worth; Merit (1.3; 4.5; 8.2; 8.3)
There are many different perspectives on value to consider when doing evaluation and IA; 'worth' requires a value judgement, while 'merit' refers to how well goals are met; the results of IA should inform evaluation of worth and merit.
Impacts (2.6)
Impact and outcome are used synonymously in this book, distinct from outputs; impacts are long-term or permanent changes in a system; many variables affect impacts (temporal, spatial, etc.); special consideration is given to synergies and cumulative impacts.
Systems Theory /Systems Thinking (see also: Outcomes Theory) (1.3)
Incorporates the concepts of equilibrium, and feedback; impact assessors and evaluators must think systematically about inputs, transforming processes and outputs/outcomes; organisations should incorporate an evaluation and IA system like the Event Compass or Balanced Scorecard.

Event portfolios (1.4)

Complexity increases greatly when the interactive, long-term impacts of event portfolios are to be considered in IA and evaluation; in portfolios, events are 'assets' that must contribute to overall goal attainment and/or return on investment.

Outcomes theory (2.2)

A model that stresses the need for indicators in performance evaluation and impact assessment; a basis for logic and theory of change models.

Logic models (2.3)

Useful in planning and evaluation; set goals and work out how to achieve them; provide indicators of goal attainment.

Theory of Change models (2.3)

Specifically designed for changing systems or social marketing; valid pathways have to be developed for achieving desired changes; TOC should be based on a theoretical foundation, or experience that suggest causal pathways but they can be conceived as experiments in themselves.

Social integration and inclusion (2.3)

Often cited as goals for planned events, these are complex social theories; use of TOC models is required.

Social marketing (2.3)

Any form of action or communication intended to increase awareness, and change attitudes and behaviour; events are often conceived as agents of change or provide suitable platforms for social marketing.

Evidence (2.4)

What constitutes evidence, and the legitimacy it is assigned, are important considerations in all IAs and evaluation; often this is a political decision subject to multi-stakeholder input (i.e., a social contract).

Knowledge (2.4; 5.4)

Traditional, tacit and implicit knowledge can supplement factual evidence gained through research and analysis.

Reliability and validity (2.4)

Reliability can mean both replication of findings (relevant to random sampling) and trustworthiness; validity refers to how well our measures and indicators reflect the theories or constructs under analysis; Logic and TOC models must carefully consider validity.

Forces-Pressures-State-Impacts-Response model (FPSIR) (2.5; 7.5)

A circular model that indicates how our responses to impacts affects the forces and pressures that cause them; a starting point for thinking about the underlying causes of trends and the state of a system.

Limits of Acceptable Change (LAC) (2.7; 5.5)

A planning model for natural areas, with implications for planning and IA; consideration of capacity, thresholds and limits might be part of the event planning process, or discussion of these concepts might be generated by an impact assessment

Precautionary principle (2.7)

A principle central to sustainable development; if we cannot predict impacts, or risks are considered to be too high, action/investment/development should not proceed

Social capital (4.2; 4.6)

A goal and purported benefit of events aiming to change society in a positive way; method and indicators for its assessment are provided.

Place: identity, attachment, meaning (4.2; 6.4)
Events can contribute to the identity of places (related to place marketing and image) and the meanings and attachment people have to or about a place.

Social Exchange theory (4.2)
The theory that when people perceive benefits they will be more positive in their attitudes towards events and tourism.

Transformation (4.3)
(a) The theory that experiences can transform people in terms of identity or self development; (b) in a systems approach inputs are transformed into desired outputs.

Identity: personal and social (4.3)
Experiences and engagement with events can contribute to personal and social identity formation and reinforcement.

Quality of Life (4.3)
Various measures can be used to determine if events and tourism contribute to improved qaulity, such as satisfaction, family togetherness, engagement with events.

Personal development (4.3)
A motivation for developing event travel careers or participating in various leisure pursuits, it can mean different things such as increased knowledge/learning, fitness, or feelings of self worth.

Communitas (4.3)
Turner's theory that belonging and sharing as equals are elements of liminal or ritualistic experiences.

Inspiration (demonstration) effect (4.3)
Sometimes used as a justification for events, the theory (largely unproven) is that engagement with sport leads to increased participation or physical activity.

Authenticity (5.2)
Objective authenticity refers to the truthfulness of something or the accuracy of a recreation, where tourism can threaten cultural authenticity through commodification; *existential authenticity* refers to the perceived meanings of an experience, unique to individuals.

Social worlds (5.3)
Unruh's theory about why and how people form associations and identity through participation in special interests.

Event setting spectrum 7(.3)
Events in nature have different impacts than event in venues; there is a spectrum of variables that influence IA.

Ecological footprint (7.5)
A concept related to sustainability that applies a measure of how much events or tourism consume and contribute to depletion of resources.

Equity; distribution effects (8.1-3; 9.3)
Equity principles should apply to all forms of impact assessment; the distribution of costs and benefits can be more important than simple measurement of impacts.

Benefits and Costs Evaluation (BACE) (9.3)
The BACE planning model suggests how IA should start with desired benefits, consider all costs and negatives, and incorporate equity principles.

Study questions

1 Explain the Outcomes System Model of Duignan and how it informs Theory of Change models.

2 Illustrate a TOC process to show how it is to be integrated in strategic planning and how it shapes impact assessment.

3 Discuss the difference between 'proof' and 'evidence' in the context of event impact assessment. What types of evidence do you think will be most convincing when it comes to a political decision on whether or not to bid on a mega event?

4 The FPSIR model is a starting point for thinking about event and tourism impacts. Use the elements of this model to demonstrate how a new arena might impact residents of a city.

5 For a large, diverse managed portfolio of events in a tourist destination, explain how you would plan to assess cumulative impacts. In particular, what are the long-term risks?

6 When key impact indicators are established, should they include limits or capacity? Discuss this in the context of LAC theory.

Recommended additional readings and sources:

IAIA's quarterly journal: Impact Assessment and Project Appraisal

IAIA: Cumulative Effects Assessment

(http://www.iaia.org/uploads/pdf/Fastips_16%20Cumulative%20Effects%20 Assessment_1.pdf)

Theory of Change (http://www.theoryofchange.org/)

3 Impact Assessment Process, Measures and Methods

Learning objectives

☐ Know how to plan and implement an impact assessment

☐ Understand the uses and difference between the four process models: forecasting impacts, strategic, retrospective and post-event

☐ Be able to select and use appropriate impact methods and measures, and determine key impact questions and indicators for different IA applications

☐ Learn the variables that influence impact measurement: magnitude or severity; duration; spatial patterns; direct or indirect effects

☐ Know what methods are available for IA, and when to use them. In particular: Leopold matrix, rapid impact assessment, network diagrams, field and quasi experiments, trend analysis, scenarios, mapping, decision trees, simulation models, calculators, and visualizations

3.1 Introduction

We start with four planning or process models: one for forecasting impacts (the kind usually required by legislation for major projects); one for post-event or post-development IA; one of retrospective assessments of the impacts of events and tourism on a given state of the economy, environment or society; and another for strategic impact assessment (for policies, programmes and strategies). Figure 3.1 compares these models, with the ten steps in the forecasting model being the benchmark.

Then a range of generic methods or tools are presented, all of which can be adapted for many possible applications. Most basic is the IA Matrix, generally used to break down a project into its components and identify possible impacts of each. Other generic methods include flowcharts, checklists, mapping, decision trees, scenarios, consultations, forecasting with simulations, and trend analysis. Logic and TOC models have been explained in the previous chapter. Additional methods are discussed in the ensuing chapters, more pertinent to social, cultural, ecological, built-environment or economic impacts.

3.2 The IA planning process: four models

There are four models to consider, reflecting four major applications of IA compared in Figure 3.1. The steps outlined in the ensuing sub-section are the reference point for the comparisons.

3.2.1 Steps in the IA Process (Forecasting Impacts)

This model is the most generic, with many of its issues and elements being applicable to the other processes. This process must incorporate one or more forecasting methods, as discussed later in the chapter, or be tied to the Theory of Change Model with underpinning logic or theory. Compare these steps to the TOC model in Chapter 2.

Step 1: Initiation

Forecasting is typically done when there is a legal requirement to predict the impacts of proposed major developments, but also as part of feasibility studies for mega events and expensive investments in venues. These types of IA can influence decisions to bid or invest, or not, and of course to shape the nature of the event/project and decide upon mitigation actions.

A detailed specification of the event, project or change is desirable, but there might be uncertainty and alternatives to consider. Who is calling for the IA, or why is it required will influence how the IA is done, and its parameters. This could be highly political, responding to lobbying or stakeholder demands, so the mandate has to be determined and resources committed; a timeline has to be specified.

Step 2: Screening

If legal requirements have to be met, then a formal process will have to be followed, otherwise there will likely be flexibility in the process design and contents. In a formal IA there might be a requirement to establish a steering committee or a chain of responsibility, and who gets involved.

Step 3: Scoping

This refers to determining the size and parameters of the IA project. An IA might be restricted to economic, social or environmental impacts, or comprehensive. If stakeholders have a say in this determination, the scope is probably going to be wide. The objects and subjects of IA can be determined at this stage (e.g., a narrow economic impact study looking only at local business benefits, versus a full TBL study for the entire community and its environment).

Setting *Key Evaluation Questions* (KEQ) or *Critical Impact Issues* will help determine priorities and limits. This leads to the question: "What evidence will be provided, and how will it be used in reaching decisions?"

Step 4: Technical work

The technical work has to begin with a thorough analysis of the proposed event or project. An advisory panel might be useful at this stage, consisting of people with the necessary expertise to advise on the process. An initial question is: "What is there in the proposal that will likely change existing conditions or have a new impact?" A *baseline* will be established, being the existing conditions (or state) that might be affected by the proposal. In a narrow study this could be limited to economic conditions, but in a full TBL study the baseline conditions are very wide. Field work and original research might be required, complemented by reviewing existing data. Stakeholder input will be needed.

This is where a variety of generic methods can be employed, as described later in this chapter, plus methods specific to events and tourism as discussed in subsequent chapters. IA usually includes a matrix to identify elements of the proposal that might cause different types of impact.

Strictly speaking, IA and feasibility studies have different aims, but they can be combined. It seems foolish to determine potential impacts and not raise the question of whether the project is actually feasible in technical terms, as well as being financially viable, and desirable in terms of stakeholder preferences.

Assessment of alternatives is a feature of many IAs. This type of analysis compares alternative developments or policies as to impacts and eventually reaches a conclusion on which one is best, if any. Opening the process to public input probably will result in suggested alternatives (including "don't do it!"). Decision trees are discussed later, being adaptable to this purpose.

Step 5: Public and stakeholder consultations

There is no logical reason why consultations should not begin, perhaps informally, as soon as an event or project is suggested. Indeed, early input, media coverage or lobbying might lead to the decision to undertake an IA. A narrow IA process will consult only the key stakeholders, but this could be a difficult political issue. In stakeholder theory the question of 'legitimacy' always arises, being the determination of who has a claim to be heard or actively engaged in the process (Larson et al., 2015). In a broad IA, gaining legitimacy will require open public consultations augmented by targeted consultations with those who are deemed to be critical because of their knowledge, their power, or their probability of being impacted. Convening a citizens' advisory body might be desirable, especially where there is no established mechanism for pubic input. Methods include: open pubic forums; focus groups; general resident and specific stakeholder surveys, as discussed later.

Step 6: Forecasts

Impact forecasts have to be made, but uncertainty and risk almost always enter the picture so the assessors must answer the question "What is the probability of impacts occurring from the event or project?" Forecasting methods are discussed later.

Step 7: Mitigation

Most IAs will not be complete without detailed consideration of mitigation, including: prevention/avoidance actions; reduction of severity of negative impacts or costs; maximising desired impacts, and compensation. Note the similarity to risk management, which also includes the potential need for insurance. In some instances mitigation of negatives and costs might be impossible, leading to a recommendation to cancel. Other options include: recommend modifying the proposal; giving consideration to an alternative; doing more research and analysis to fill gaps and reduce uncertainty.

Step 8: Reporting and consultations

The results are generally first presented to the client or responsible regulatory body, but the public and other key stakeholders also need to be advised. It will not be unusual to find that IA reports generate controversy and necessitate additional research and analysis – or more consultation. However, when stakeholders say "we were not consulted properly" they might in fact mean "we do not like it and will continue to oppose or at least delay it". That is often the political reality, however illogical.

Step 9: Decisions

In politically charged environments, usually where there are both vocal and active opponents and proponents of a project or event, a decision might be deferred or the whole process halted until emotions cool. Arising from a decision to proceed, with mitigation possibly included, an action plan has to be formulated. This might become a legal or contractual process, requiring developers or organisers to meet specific conditions.

Step 10: Monitoring and feedback

Someone has to monitor the implementation. In some cases citizen panels are charged with monitoring impacts in order to ensure the conditions of approval are fully met. Where problems arise, there has to be a procedure for reporting these to authorities and ensuring that action is taken.

Figure 3.1: Four IA planning processes compared

Type 1: FORECASTING	Type 2: STRATEGIC	Type 3: POST-EVENT	Type 4: RETROSPECTIVE
Forecasting impacts in advance of an event or development; may be part of feasibility study	Evaluation of alternative policies, programmes or strategies by government agencies or private companies	Impacts assessed after the event (or project)	Evaluate how events/tourism have changed the "state" of the economy, environment or society
1: Initiation: often a legal requirement for major projects including mega events	Initiation: is there a problem, or a new idea suggesting change?	Might be required by stakeholders with power (i.e., sponsors, grant givers); should be part of strategic planning	Generally not mandated, but might arise from perceived problems; can be part of continuous learning
2: Screening: is the process specified or flexible? Need for a steering committee? Transparency and accountability have to be built in	Generally done internally when the consequences of alternative actions have to be evaluated. Might be part of continuous learning process.	Events seldom have the skills or resources to do post-event IA. Mega events often elect to not do comprehensive post-event IA	A good starting point is the Forces-Pressure-State-Impact-Response model
3: Scoping: the exact nature of the IA: e.g., comprehensive or just economic? Set Key Evaluation Questions	The scope and KEQs depend upon the nature of the alternatives considered	Economic impact IAs have dominated; triple impact assessment methods are developing	Stakeholders will have to be involved in establishing the scope and setting KEQs
4: Begin Technical Work: Assemble the team; establish the baseline; determine appropriate analytical methods	Identical, but for corporations there is likely a bigger emphasis on comparing costs and potential ROI; government can co-opt technical people	Consultants might be required, but black-box models are to be avoided!	Historical trends have to be assessed from the baseline requiring a lot of trend data
5: Consultations with Stakeholders: for events and tourism this should start with potentially affected residents; consultations can run throughout the entire project	Might be avoided for political reasons, or integrated into the process to ensure legitimacy; corporate stakeholders will include "customers" rather than "citizens"	Resident perceptions of impacts are a critical input; attitudes should also be measured; other stakeholders will have important insights and opinions	Stakeholders should be able to contribute data and insights on the baseline, trends and changes

6: Forecast impacts: make forecasts of likely impacts and specify risks & uncertainty; are there possible interactive or cumulative impacts?	Similar methodologies, but broader in scope	Use of logic or TOC models provides the framework for obtaining evidence and in which intended impacts can be attributed to the actions taken; unintended impacts and externalities must also be identified	Not forecasting, but deduction: what has happened and why? what were the role of events and tourism in causing changes?
7: Mitigation Considered: prevention, reduction, compensation	Similar to Type 1	Implications for the future are drawn	Implications for the future are drawn
8: Reporting & Consultations: recommendations should accompany conclusions; stakeholders need to evaluate the methods and the conclusions	Internal considerations might be all that is required, unless the aim was to engage the public and specific stakeholders	Event or project management will have to decide how much to make public	Everyone will want to review the conclusions and recommendations before new strategy or policy is made
9: Decisions: The prime decision is to proceed or not, then to implement mitigation.	A choice will be made from the alternatives considered	Decisions are always required before moving forwards; periodic events can be modified; bidding agencies can change their criteria; facility operators can adapt	There might be no decision necessary, or it could be to modify a strategy or policy.
10: Monitoring & Feedback: Mitigation has to be evaluated; externalities and unintended impacts must be discerned; a committee of residents/stakeholders might be assigned this task	Monitoring procedures and indicators should be established before new actions are taken	There might be the possibility for mitigating negative impacts; changes to periodic events are possible, as are changes to the operations of facilities	There might be the possibility for mitigating negative impacts; an option is to set new future-oriented policies (e.g. for sustainable development)

3.2.2: Strategic Impact Assessment

Wikipedia's article on impact assessment provides a rationale for this kind of strategic IA, although framed for policy makers:

♦ "Informing policy makers about potential economic, social, and environmental ramifications

♦ Improving transparency so that contributions to sustainability and "better regulation" are disclosed and special interest lobbying is discouraged

♦ Increasing public participation in order to reflect a range of considerations, thereby improving the legitimacy of policies

♦ Clarifying how public policy helps achieve its goals and priorities through policy indicators

♦ Contributing to continuous learning in policy development by identifying causalities that inform ex-post review of policies."

The same basic IA questions and inputs are required as those outlined above, but when trying to forecast the impacts of a policy, strategy or programme initiative or change there are additional questions to ask: "Why is the change or initiative needed or desired? Is there evidence of problems that should be fixed, or is it based on new ideas that have to be tested?" This will set the tone of the IA, and the ultimate use of conclusions, but the process might be the same. For example, if there are known negative impacts related to events and tourism, based on media coverage or stakeholder/resident input, then there is a clear need to address those specifics. If there are new ideas, perhaps to invest more in event portfolio management or more intense event bidding, then these options will have to be compared to the status quo and other possibilities that might arise in pursuit of the same goals.

3.2.3 Retrospective IA planning process

This is quite a different process because the idea is to look back at what has already happened and determine the impacts of some past actions, naturally occurring trends, policies, strategies, or decisions made. A typical starting point would be: "What are the benefits and costs of event tourism in our community/destination?" or "What have been the impacts of creating and managing our event portfolio?"

Development and management of event portfolios implies that there is at least an assumption that events in general have had a positive impact, but can that be demonstrated to the satisfaction of all stakeholders? At some point in time it is likely that all proponents of events in a given jurisdiction will be asked to demonstrate the public good and to identify and deal with costs and benefits. This is one reason why a retrospective IA can be critical.

Although quite different in intent from the forecasting of impacts, the retrospective model incorporates many of the same elements. Consultations are needed, a baseline (the 'before' situation) has to be established, research and analysis can be similar. But the outcome of this process is very different, as decisions are not required to approve or modify a proposal, rather some change might be made in policy, strategy, regulation or investment.

Determining retroactively what has happened, and the causes, will always involve ambiguity because of multiple forces and trends affecting the events and tourism sectors. One way to narrow the analysis is to limit the scope of the study to a short period of time. There might be a logical starting point, such as the construction of a major venue, the holding of a mega event, the establishment of a bidding agency, or perhaps a change in policy, leading to this critical IA question: "what has happened since that date, and why?"

Alternative explanations as to why outcomes might have occurred have to be analysed, asking "is it logical, or is there evidence to suggest that outcomes are attributable to the actions under review?" This can also include the null hypothesis (i.e., to be disproved logically and through evidence) that an event or development caused specific changes.

Whether looking back in time or making forecasts, we need baseline data about the state of the system being investigated. Here are some standard baseline data points:

♦ *Nature and ecology*: soil properties, geological characteristics, topography, drainage and watershed properties, biodiversity (types of flora and fauna, species richness, species distribution), types of ecosystems, endangered species, protected and sensitive areas, pollution, land use patterns

♦ *Social and cultural*: population, migration, demography, social structure, archaeological and/or religious sites, cultural and social institutions, the arts, discrimination or exclusion, festivals and celebrations

♦ *Economic*: unemployment, local and world economic conditions, developmental capabilities, tourism volumes and segments, investments made or promised

♦ *Built environment*: land use, infrastructure, heritage sites and buildings, traffic patterns, noise, public services, living standards, housing quantity and quality, affordability

'Benchmarking' can also be an important part of the retrospective IA. Similar to the concept of a control group when conducting experiments (but obviously not rigorous, and results are not generalizable) a comparison to other places can shed light on impacts. A community with limited tourism or events can be compared systematically to one with considerable development and many apparent impacts.

3.2.4 Post-event IA

Many organisations require plans, budgets, and post-event evaluations in order to qualify for assistance. The post-event evaluation might include basic data such as attendance and a financial accounting, or more difficult-to-provide analysis of impacts. The process ideally starts with planning, setting goals, selecting key impact indicators, and putting in place a permanent, comprehensive evaluation system – the kind that defines a learning organisation. Without goals and indicators a post-event assessment can be too wide and complex to even attempt. If a system like the Event Compass is used (see the companion book *Event Evaluation* for details) one option is to sequentially do post-event evaluations and/or impact assessments on the eight main dimensions: social/cultural impact, economic impact, environmental impact, and the five dimensions of organisational management.

The goal-attainment approach is suitable for evaluation, but unless there is a theory of change model in place (or implicit) there will be no guidance for impact assessment. A goals-free evaluation can be attempted, but it is very challenging. The TOC approach ensures that impact assessors know what desired changes to look for, and the actions assumed or believed to generate those impacts.

3.2.5 Edinburgh Festival impact studies

Edinburgh is a city known for its festivals, and their impacts have been studied repeatedly, starting with ground breaking research by Vaughan (1971) on the Edinburgh Festival. Multi-event assessments have been reported by Scotinform Ltd. (1991), SQW Economic Development Consultants (2005), and BOP Consulting (2011 a/b; 2016 a/b; 2018). Selective findings are reported later in this book.

According to VisitScotland's 2015 visitor survey (cited in BOP Consulting 2018, p.8), "Edinburgh's Festivals each year deliver over 3,000 events, reaching audiences of more than 4.5 million and creating the equivalent of approximately 6,000 full time jobs. 32% of the 14 million+ annual visitors to Scotland are motivated by the nation's cultural and heritage offer, in which the Festivals play a defining role."

There are special considerations in doing multi-event impact assessments, not the least of which is the attribution of tourist demand to particular events when people attend more than one. If the aim of the IA is to determine individual event impacts then it is necessary to find out exactly which event was instrumental in making the visitor's decision to travel, or allocating proportions of visitor spending to a number of events according to their perceived importance in motivating the tourist trip.

But that is not as important as determining the relative contributions of events to the city's event portfolio. Results of surveys of Edinburgh's festivals (BOP Consulting, 2011) revealed that there were huge differences in the drawing power for overnight tourists from outside Scotland, and therefore in spending. For the Military Tattoo, in 2010, fully 71.3% of sampled Tattoo visitors were in this category, compared to only 3.7% of Imaginate Festival visitors. Hogmanay at 57.9%, and the Fringe at 44.6% were the other two major tourist events. The International Festival, the city's traditional, high-culture festival, maintained its international status with 31.7% .

Photo 3.1: Edinburgh festival crowds - success or over-tourism?

Photo 3.2: Performers at Edinburgh Fringe - consider impacts on culture, and on the artists

Photo 3.3: Edinburgh's brand is shaped by its festivals and events; meaning is given to places by virtue of how they are animated

3.3 Measurement issues and metrics

Whenever possible, evaluators and impact assessors want to take accurate, quantifiable measurements. This should be possible for many of the baseline conditions (i.e., the state of the economy, environment or society), for event and project activities (i.e., actual developments, traffic, noise, erosion, waste, energy consumption, etc.) and for outputs (i.e., hard facts like attendance, costs, revenues, satisfaction). The most important of these direct measures can be called '*Key Impact Indicators*'.

But direct, quantifiable measures of impacts are not always available, and sometimes we have to use 'surrogate indicators' that we believe are associated with the impact being studied. For example, we might use the indicator 'institutional networks created' as a measure of social capital formation. For sustainability we will have to use a number of measures, both direct indicators like energy consumption, and indirect or surrogate indicators like the ecological footprint (which in itself is a collection of indicators). Any of these can be designated as key impact indicators.

'*Incommensurability*' is the lack of a uniform measure for all types of impacts. This is a crucial concern when monetary values are not suitable or available for all outcomes. Economic impacts require monetary measures, but what about social and cultural outcomes – how are they to be measured? Andersson & Lundberg (2013) have attempted to deal with incommensurability by employing monetary values for use and non-use values ascribed to events, and for environmental impacts (see 4.5.2 for details), and in some cases this total monetary cost-benefit analysis is useful.

Systems like the Event Compass have been developed to counter incommensurability by focusing on degrees of goal attainment rather than a common measure of impact. As explained in *Event Evaluation*, the Event Compass compares three impact dimensions (socio/cultural, environmental and economic) and five internal management functions on the degree to which goals are being attained. Within these dimensions a variety of direct measures and other indicators can be used, but they are not directly compared. Economic impacts can employ monetary metrics, while social impact assessment can use perceptions, attitudes, and surrogate measures like satisfaction or perceived quality of life.

3.3.1 Indicators

The importance of indicators has been discussed above, and here is a simple definition:

Indicator: a sign that shows the condition or existence of something

With this definition in mind, resident satisfaction and safety measures can become indicators of wellbeing, a concept with multiple dimensions, or indicators of the effects of events and tourism on a city. And pollution can become an indicator of how well events are doing to eliminate dependence on fossil fuels and contribute to sustainability.

The concept of Key Impact Indicator is similar to key performance indicators, but instead of being relevant to achieving success in an organisation, and therefore being useful in performance evaluation, KIIs are essential in impact assessment as a way to focus our IA efforts on what is really important.

The selection of indicators and KIIs should reflect a number of criteria:

◆ *Relevance*: do they meet the users' needs and priorities? will the indicators be used in decision-making?

◆ *Comprehensiveness*: there is a need for measures covering all aspects of social, cultural, environmental and economic impacts as well as the performance of internal management functions; it is also important to avoid bias towards reporting positive results only, so we need indicators of costs, problems and unintended outcomes

◆ *Practicality*: all events and organizations should be able to collect the desired information and report findings in the same way; standardization leads to enhanced forecasting and theory development

◆ *Clarity*: everyone should be able to understand the indicator, how it was obtained and why it is important

◆ *Verifiability*: measurements should be verifiable by external auditors.

Effectiveness indicators measure the degree of goal attainment, and *efficiency* indicators are concerned with the use of resources. In the Event Compass and other evaluation systems you will have both. In performance evaluation, goal-attainment indicators usually pertain to targets reached, such as achieving a high percentage of satisfied customers or reducing waste, while in impact assessment goal attainment indicators attempt to measure longer-term or permanent changes such as "fostering social capital through creating trust and establishing inter-group networks". Efficiency indicators include the usual ratios employed in financial audits, including return on investment, or measures of how much output is generated by a given level of input. All organisations want to achieve their goals and improve their efficiency.

3.3.2 Variables for metrics

What exactly is being measured? In Chapter 1 we discussed impact variables, each of which influences what has to be measured in IA. Re-visit Figure 1.4 with a view to identifying actual measures (metrics) for each of them. Examples are:

♦ *Magnitude or severity:* e.g., minor damage to a waterway caused by erosion, versus complete destruction of a wildlife habitat; minor occasional noise exceeding decibel standards versus continuous, excessively loud music affecting entire neighbourhoods; the degree and probability of risk and uncertainty must be determined; will damage be irreversible?

♦ *Frequency and duration:* e.g., temporary traffic congestion during construction versus permanent increases in disruptive traffic arising from a major new venue; short-term air pollution attributable to fireworks versus ongoing, unhealthy smog caused by cumulative developments and resultant traffic; timing can be important, such as beginning a major development project during peak wildlife migration periods; will the impacts be interactive and cumulative?

♦ *Spatial:* e.g., negative environmental impacts confined to the immediate event site versus widespread damage to the watershed caused by multiple venues and events; social impacts on one residential area versus permanent demographic changes affecting an entire city or destination attributable to new employment and in-migration.

♦ *Direct or indirect:* e.g., direct impact on those employed by events and tourism versus the secondary impacts arising from multiplier effects on the economy; direct land-use impacts on the urban landscape by new facilities versus the indirect affects caused by resultant increases in event tourism, such as altered distribution of retail businesses.

♦ *Who or what is impacted?* e.g., measuring impacts on people and ecological processes with hard data versus abstract concepts such as social integration or sustainable development; determining if the impact is occurring on wildlife or an entire ecosystem with accumulating, harmful effects on humans.

3.4 IA methods

Many types of research and analysis can be employed in IA (see Veal and Burton, 2014 for generic methods), so we have to start with some generic methods that can be used in the main stages of impact assessment. These are methods for conducting IAs, not to be confused with the theoretical frameworks or models discussed previously which provide insights on the nature of impacts and impact assessment.

Figure 3.2 provides a list of methods discussed in this book, with suggested applications. The chapter references are indicated.

Figure 3.2: Methods discussed in this book

Matrices (e.g., Leopold Matrix) (Ch.3 (3.4)
A good starting point for all IA applications; more detailed matrices can reflect analysis of probability, magnitude, etc.

Rapid Impact Assessment (RIA) (3.4)
For a quick, pre-IA or when resources or circumstances do not permit a full IA

Network diagrams (3.4)
Useful in all IAs, network diagrams plot the flow of pressures and impacts; compatible with critical paths/scheduling

Field and quasi experiments (3.4)
e.g., comparing test results before and after the event; these are practical methods, but without the ability to prove cause and effect or to generalize results

Trend analysis, time series, longitudinal research (3.4)
Particularly suitable for retrospective IAs to reveal changes attributable to events or tourism; can be combined with forecasting by way of trend extrapolation

Scenarios (3.4)
Not strictly a forecasting method, but useful in considering potential impacts or how to achieve desired future states; used in strategic IAs for considering alternatives

Mapping (3.4)
All IAs can employ maps as forms of analysis or visualization for consultations

Decision trees (3.4)
Used for comparing the impacts of alternatives and aiding in decision making; can incorporate probabilities for anticipated outcomes

Simulation models (3.4)
Quantitative forecasting tools, especially for ecological impacts and climate change; within economic impact calculators "sensitivity analysis" can be performed, which is a type of simulation

Carbon calculators (3.4)
Carbon calculators are available online, but their valid use requires reliable data on travel modes, distances and purposes

Visualisations (3.4; 5.4)
Cognitive mind mapping is particularly valuable in social and cultural IA; mind mapping can be used in all consultations to explore impacts

Ecological footprint calculators (3.4; 7.5)
Complex in formulation, and not available for most regions; a short form can be compiled from different ecological impact indicators including carbon emissions

Resident surveys (impact perception, attitudes, use and non-use values) 4.5)
Consultations are always required and a survey of residents is a primary tool for input; can be modified to obtain tourist input on use values, attitudes towards regulations, or perceptions of impacts.

Socio-cultural data analysis (4.5)
Census and other available data can establish baseline conditions and aid in trend analysis/fore-
casting.

Case studies (4.5)
Theory can be developed through systematic comparisons or meta-analysis of case studies; comparisons can assist in identifying possible impacts

Ethnographic (participant observation) (4.5)
Participation in events, or as a tourist, provides insights useful in IA and evaluation; residents of
communities will have insights on all forms of impact.

Measuring social capital (4.6)
Theory and indicators are provided for measuring social capital.

Impacts of cultural engagement (5.5)
Theory and indicators are provided for use in assessing potential impacts of engagement with
culture and cultural events.

Longitudinal research (6.5)
Not practical for most IA projects, but necessary for monitoring impacts (see also trend analysis)
and mitigation efforts.

Media impact (6.5)
Concepts (image, reputation, branding, positioning) and indicators are provided for assessing the
impacts of media coverage.

Cost-Benefit Analysis (8.3)
A traditional, but narrow method for analysing costs and benefits of a project; difficulties abound in
comparing tangibles and intangibles; a short-form CBA is provided.

Direct economic contribution (DEC) (8.3; 8.5)
Direct economic contribution calculators are available; in forecasting IAs they require separate and
reliable forecasts of visitor numbers, spending, etc.; a procedure for estimating post-event DEC is
specified.

3.4.1 Matrices

An early task in IA is to describe the event or project in detail and then imagine
(or forecast) what impacts might occur, and this can be done through a technique such as the Leopold Matrix (Leopold et al., 1971). In the original version,
designed for environmental impact assessments, the matrix has two axes: existing characteristics and conditions of the environment (i.e., physical and chemical
characteristics, biological conditions, cultural factors, ecological relationships);
and proposed actions which may cause environmental impact (i.e., modification

of regime, land transformation and construction, resource extraction, process-ing, land alteration, resource renewal, change in traffic, waste emplacement and treatment, chemical treatment, and accidents). Used as a starting point, a matrix is like a checklist to shape more detailed impact assessment. The information has to come from past experience, case studies and comparisons, theory, or consul-tations. If a logic or theory of change model was prepared, that also provides a starting point.

Within each cell of the matrix there can be nothing more than an X or check-mark indicating a likely impact, for example that traffic associated with an event will impact on the peace, quiet and normal movements of neighbours. But much more information can be provided, including probability of occurring (e.g., in percentage terms, or perhaps high, medium low probability), measures of direc-tion (positive or negative; perhaps neutral or unknown), magnitude (size of area or number of people affected; one or more ecosystems impacted; short or long-term duration), and importance (in political or economic terms, or as perceived by stakeholders).

Some of the information and forecasts will be subjective and open to debate. When considering magnitude of impacts, technical assessments should prevail in some areas of concern, and perceptions of stakeholders in others. Other elabo-rations to the matrix can be a judgment as to severity (raising the question: will mitigation work?) and distribution effects (who gains and who pays?). It might not be possible to indicate all of these on a single matrix, but they can be inputs to the designation of 'importance'.

A matrix is also adaptable to post-event or retrospective IA, in which case it is a summary of what is believed to have happened together with conclusions about magnitude and importance.

In Figure 3.3 across the top are the main types of IA being examined in subse-quent chapters. The matrix could, however, be developed for only one of these, as in social impact assessment or economic IA. Down the left-side column are major components that are deemed likely to generate impacts. The list of com-ponents can be as detailed as necessary, and therefore quite long, but only three are shown in this example.

In Figure 3.3 five types of information are suggested in the cells: probability of occurrence (in some cases this can be quantified), perceived direction (positive or negative), magnitude of potential impact, risk (relates to both uncertainty and the damage that could be done) and, if available, the predictions of simulation models or calculators. Actual composition of the matrix should involve experts in IA and key stakeholders, and should be linked to their goals for the event.

Figure 3.3: Sample IA matrix for event impact forecasting (showing optional types of information that can be included in each cell)

Components of the event	Social impacts	Cultural impacts	Economic impacts	Built environment impacts	Impacts on nature & ecological processes
Tourism and vehicular traffic caused by the event	Probability: Traffic congestion in residential areas is: -Certain to occur -High probability -Low probability -Will not occur	Perceived direction of impact: positive or negative? on a scale of 1-10	Magnitude: The cost of mitigation is estimated to be...	Risk: Failure to mitigate traffic could lead to serious accidents and injuries	Simulation: Carbon emissions to increase by (estimate)
Noise caused by traffic and on-site activities; music in particular	Probability: -decibel limits can be set, but negative resident reaction is almost certain	Perceived direction of impact: All increases in noise will be perceived as a negative	Magnitude: Compared to existing levels the increase in economic contribution will be: -minor -moderate -significant	Risk: Noise levels could increase beyond expectations if the city population grows faster than forecast	Simulation: increased noise will impact negatively on wildlife breeding potential
Consumption of food and beverages as a contributor to waste and ecological footprint	Probability unknown: need for social marketing to inform and persuade residents and visitors	Perceived direction of impact: Unknown: need to consult cultural groups	Magnitude: The cost to the event of meeting green standards is....	Risk: -waste reduction might not alleviate the need for more landfill sites	Simulation: controls of the supply chain can result in X decrease in packaging waste

3.4.2 Rapid Impact Assessment

RIA can be any number of approaches to obtaining a quick assessment, usually by a team. This can be done in advance of a detailed IA, or in place of a full assessment where there is insufficient time, a lack of resources, or a perceived absence of need. Whether or not the RIA should be informed by stakeholder input is a good question, because full consultations will tend to slow it down. On the other hand, can a team of 'experts' really be expected to rapidly come up with conclusions that will gain legitimacy? Some inputs will be needed, but deciding on the scope of research and consultations is part of the RIA process.

A sample RIA method is provided in Figure 3.3. What makes it 'rapid' is the use of a checklist or a set of key evaluation questions (or key impact indicators) to focus the assessment, and if desired a scoring system to provide quantitative analysis. To answer the questions there is a need for indicators, or else expert judgment is substituted for metrics. This particular RIA approach is derived from the Rapid Health Impact Assessment Tool (2013) developed by the London Healthy Urban Development Unit of the National Health Service.

Assuming a new event is proposed for a small town, what are likely to be the main impacts – both positive and negative? Is mitigation indicated, and in what forms? Is the balance of probable impacts positive or negative, and what is the recommendation? Drawing on experience and/or theory, the RIA team develops a set of questions and indicators. This can also be done as a checklist, derived from the detailed tables of objects and subjects contained in ensuing chapters of this book.

Figure 3.4 provides a very short list to illustrate the method, and could easily be expanded with some preliminary scoping and selected consultations in the community. The Key Questions can easily be subdivided and many indicators employed. 'Relevance' requires judgment as to the issues, goals and 'state' of the local economy, society and environment. 'Types of available evidence' is a crucial consideration, and in order to be 'rapid' the assessors need the help of local officials and groups, reference to available studies and comparables, and some form of stakeholder input.

The assessors make judgments as to what the potential impacts might be. This could be quantified in a number of ways: by assigning probabilities (as in the later discussion of decision trees) or developing a scoring system based on any of the previously discussed impact variables (e.g., magnitude, scale, duration). Finally, mitigation recommendations should accompany the assessment. Note that alternatives are not being considered, nor are detailed feasibility items like costs. Much is sacrificed when doing RIAs.

Figure 3.4: Illustration of a Rapid Impact Assessment

Key questions & indicators	Relevance	Types of available evidence	Judgment on potential impact	Mitigation
What will be the tourism impact? -projected demand by tourists -estimated direct economic contribution	Attracting tourists is one goal; it is highly likely that special-interest visitors will make the trip	Obtain data on other events in the same area from impact studies and tourism statistics.	Economic impacts will be modest, but important, as the event will be in the slow-demand season; image benefits should be realized	Grow the economic benefits by a targeted marketing campaign and providing all-inclusive weekend packages.
What will be the environmental impact on the site and immediate area? -site and venue capacity -potential impact on sensitive wildlife habitats	There are sensitive habitats in the area, with water quantity and quality being critical concerns; mitigation will be necessary	-estimated site capacity (for safety, parking, experience) -direct input from local conservation officials -management of the site and venues are ISO certified	Probability of damage is moderate and can be managed	-limits should be set on attendance -certain activities should be prevented (e.g., no entry to sensitive areas; fire ban; water rationing)
Can the proposed event be successful? -existing volunteer commitment -local organizational capacity -potential local sponsorship and grants	A relevant question given a history of many festival/event failures in the region	Conduct interviews with event organisers, local government agencies, local clubs and teams, community associations, and businesses	Probability of success is moderate to high	Test the proposed event with smaller versions before committing to major investment
Will residents benefit directly from the event? -traffic and noise implications -employment and training opportunities -leisure/entertainment available in the area -businesses that can benefit -legacy: plans for use of any surplus revenue; improvements to site and venues	A key issue: is this proposed event a community initiative or to be imposed on the community?	Resident and other stake-holder surveys might take too long, but a community forum and several focus groups should be feasible	Resident benefits are considered to be conditional on the planning, managing and leveraging of the event	-need for business leveraging to ensure local suppliers benefit -shuttle-bus service recommended to avoid congestion & noise within town -prepare a legacy plan to specify longer-term benefits for residents and businesses -early engagement and buy-in of volunteers and businesses is essential

3.4.3 Network diagrams

Usually network diagrams accompany a project plan, together with a critical path, and that is where the impact assessors can begin their own diagram and schedule. In many jurisdictions the actual IA process will be prescribed by regulations so that proponents of a project (e.g., event bidders or venue builders) will have to show exactly how and when the project is to be developed or the event produced, AND the impact assessment completed. But that is just one application.

A matrix provides a static overview of potential impacts, and that is a good starting point, but it fails to indicate how a dynamic project or a periodic event can lead to impacts in stages, to cumulative impacts, and to possible unknowns. Can the information in the matrix be converted to a network diagram linking the various elements of the project/event to the potential impacts? In what sequence might they occur is an important question. Do social, ecological and economic impacts begin as soon as construction starts, or in phases? Where and when should consultations take place to obtain input on forecasting impacts? A network diagram can aid in visualizing the sequence and inter-connections of change processes, and that can determine what research to do, when consultations should be made, and the nature of a permanent monitoring process.

This technique can be very complex or the diagram kept to a simple mind map, depending on resources available and the nature of the IA. For a periodic event, each time it is produced there will be impacts, and that sets the schedule for consultations and data collection. For a one-time mega event, planning begins years in advance and forecasting of impacts has to accompany the feasibility study.

3.4.4 Field and quasi experiments

Randomized experiments, using interventions and control groups, are the gold standard for IA and evaluation – they aim to prove cause and effect. But they are difficult and rarely attempted for events and tourism. Two reported examples of field experiments are that of Levy et al. (2011) and Malek et al. (2018). Levy compared results from four bus tours to determine the effects of managerially-facilitated consumer-to-consumer interaction on satisfaction and enjoyment, and Malek studied the effects of technology on meeting-attendee outcomes using different platforms (face to face, online, and online with moderator) by convening a simulated meeting and comparing results with those from an actual meeting.

In real-life situations there might be uncontrollable factors at work, so results are usually not definitive or generalizable. Whether or not field experiments provide acceptable evidence of impacts is a matter for decision-makers.

Pre and post-experience tests

In pre-and post testing the purpose is to determine changes attributable to an experimental treatment or intervention, which could be a trip or time spent at an event. A simple pre and post-testing procedure will provide potentially valuable evidence but without proving cause and effect.

An example can be the testing of the hypothesis that a travel or event experience will change participants' attitudes towards the host population. However, if the results are different the researcher is still left with the question of what exactly caused the change. In true IA we have to be able to attribute the change to something more vague than "travel broadens one's horizons". Adding a comparative group (one with no event or travel experience) can add insight, but will not prove anything.

3.4.5 Case studies, comparisons and benchmarking

Simple comparisons (meaning there is no control group) are usually possible; for example, comparing economic and social conditions among residents of one community with another, but this has to assume that differences are attributable to an intervention such as the presence of events, or level of tourism. Results will be open to interpretation but might yield important insights on observed impacts. Cities at different stages of tourism development can be compared on residents' perceptions of impacts and attitudes towards events or tourism to gain insights on how levels and types of development cause impacts over time.

Case studies of how events have caused various impacts have been reported in the literature, but inferring that results apply elsewhere is always risky. At best these case studies can suggest issues to examine, relevant methods and possible measures. Many case studies (using cross-case analysis) are better than one. Over time, theory can be developed that can shape TOC models and inform management strategies.

Benchmarking can yield insights on impacts if the comparison generates deeper understanding of how policies and actions (like investment in venues, number and types of events, or marketing) lead to impacts. Benchmarking requires the full cooperation of a partner, such as another event or tourist organisation or city. Deep insights into impacts and management are required in order to have any confidence in the gained understanding of impacts and impact assessment.

3.4.6 Trend analysis

Usually pertinent trend data are available from the census, DMOs, and various government agencies; these include demographics, unemployment rates, crime, housing supply and cost, seasonality of demand for accommodation, or wildlife numbers and distribution. These can be useful in many IA projects, but trends in themselves do not indicate underlying causes or forces; that is a separate question. We also want to know responses to trends, such as how events have been used strategically to combat seasonality of tourism demand, and then we want to know if the strategy affected the trend.

Time-series designs (or 'before and after') involve examination of changes in trends that are believed to be attributable to an intervention at a point in time, such as an event or venue development. For example, what was the trend in business start-ups and turnover before a major investment, and did it then change after completion of the project? The changes might indicate causes and effect but certainly do not prove it, as other factors might be involved, such as international economic conditions.

Time-series analysis is more suited for IA related to a one-time event or new venue than for periodic events that might have cumulative impacts. And the impacts of event portfolios over time will be even more difficult to discern. Nevertheless, if we look back at trends in an indicator such as seasonality of demand, or resident attitudes towards events, and we do not see positive changes, then perhaps the strategy or the interventions did not work. More analysis will then be needed.

Trend data should ideally be available for all key impact indicators, such as demographics being available from the census. Measurements of resident perceptions of impacts and their attitudes towards events can be part of omnibus surveys that collect data on many issues. Tourism agencies collect data on demand and supply. Impact assessors might have to search to find out where appropriate data are located and how (or if) they can be used.

3.4.7 Scenarios

Scenarios are designed to provide a look at possible futures, and are therefor appropriate for impact forecasting projects with a high degree of uncertainty. Yeoman et al. (2015) in the book *The Future of Events and Festivals*, discuss prediction versus what-if scenarios and provide a number of scenarios to explore possible futures.

If there is no clear chain of impacts (as in a logic or theory of change model), creating two or more scenarios can help identify what might happen, sometimes with provisos such as 'least likely' and 'most likely'. Scenarios are also used to describe desirable future conditions, then goals can be set and a path to goal attainment mapped out in a logic model.

The starting point will most likely be a specific project: a proposed event, conference centre or arena for example. Then, identify the uncertainties. These might be inherent in the project itself, such as "how large should it be" or "where will it be built?" Uncertainties might also be part of the ultimate impact, such as "will a new facility/event significantly disrupt traffic patterns?" or "how is the project going to affect residents?" Now some brainstorming is needed, both by experts and through stakeholder/public consultation, to come up with two or more scenarios. For each one, the implications have to be carefully assessed, including exact impacts, costs, and mediation.

Some examples are needed. In Figure 3.5 a new indoor sport venue is proposed. The two scenarios are deliberately designed to be quite different in terms of the scale and location of the venue so that major impact differences can be clearly identified. Scenario 1 is for a new arena to replace the existing one, with twice the seating capacity and using the same site (meaning the old one is to be demolished). Scenario 2 provides for a new arena on a new greenfield site (i.e., no infrastructure in place) but at the same capacity as the old one. A possible complication is that several alternative sites might have to be evaluated. As well, there might be a question of how many seats are really needed to meet demand, and the financial feasibility of building a large arena.

Note that the list of impact objects and subjects can be quite long, or narrow in scope. This is a list of potential types of impact (social, economic, ecological etc.) on different groups (residents, businesses, tourists, etc.). Like the Leopold matrix a variety of information can be included, but in this example conclusions of analysis and forecasts are cited so that costs and benefits can be compared.

Some perennial issues stand out in this simplistic comparison of contrasting development scenarios. There seems to be a very good case for the doubling of the arena's size, as it pays off in economic terms – especially tourism. But there will be heavy costs for the city, even if they can offset some of them through levies on commercial development (which assumes they already own the land) and taxes are likely to be increased. The smaller, suburban development costs less for construction, but requires all new infrastructure and will present few opportunities for increased commercial development. In growth-oriented cities there is a tendency for building big, new facilities and this option is likely to be chosen. Indeed, the trend has been away from suburban venues to major downtown projects that revitalize areas and encourage mixed-use re-development. But look carefully: are there equity issues and externalities to consider? What are they and how would they be resolved?

Given the comparison of scenarios in the figure, what is the best choice? That is not an answer that can be deduced from the evidence, it has to be debated. Even when impacts can be projected and rational analysis employed, there is no right or wrong decision. Are all the comparison points valid and are the forecasts reliable? What has been the experience in other cities? Are residents going to make one option or both options a major political issue? What lobby groups will make a case and what will be their arguments? Should there be a plebiscite to let the voters decide?

Figure 3.5: Two simple impact scenarios for a new sport arena

SCENARIO 1:	SCENARIO 2:
Build a large indoor arena (20,000 seating capacity) to replace the existing small facility (10,000 seats), on the same site	Build a smaller venue (10,000 seat capacity) on a new, greenfield site in the far suburbs
BUILT ENVIRONMENT IMPACTS	BUILT ENVIRONMENT IMPACTS
Infrastructure: most or all services are available but underground services have to be enlarged to handle additional demands	Infrastructure: completely new services are needed: roads, water, sewerage, electricity
Traffic: potential doubling of auto traffic, leading to more noise, pollution, disruption to neighbours; doubling of parking is needed	No increase in volumes, and perhaps a decrease, but different areas will be affected; there are few nearby residents
Land Use: The venue's "footprint" will increase substantially, especially for parking	Land use altered permanently, from greenfield to urban uses
ECOLOGICAL; NATURE	ECOLOGICAL; NATURE
Water, Drainage: existing piped infrastructure will have to be enlarged to provide water and handle increased runoff; storm-water retention ponds are needed	An assessment of potential ecological impacts for this new site reveals that mitigation is needed to prevent erosion and damage to nearby wildlife habitat
Air: employing a carbon calculator to estimate increases in emissions, it was determined that the affected area will receive excessive air pollution unless mass transit is provided and private auto use discouraged	There is no existing public transit; a complete reliance on private autos would add considerably to carbon emissions and would diminish air quality in a rural area
Sustainability: the new, larger facility will incorporate all sustainability systems, but its doubling in size means there is a net increase in energy and water consumption	The new location will permit installation of systems to reduce waste and energy and water consumption, and to employ sustainable sources; but some external increases occur in carbon emissions and energy consumption due to increased distance from suppliers.

SOCIAL AND CULTURAL	SOCIAL AND CULTURAL
Social Impacts: already feeling inconveniences and amenity loss, nearby residents will undoubtedly object to this increase in scale; entertainment and event options for the city will be enhanced	Increases in commuting will occur, for workers living a distance from the new site; people without private autos might not be able to attend events in the new location; no net increase in entertainment or cultural opportunities, and there might actually be a loss if groups do not or cannot access the new site
Cultural: more opportunities will be created for cultural festivals and celebrations	
ECONOMIC	**ECONOMIC**
Employment: A doubling of permanent jobs is forecast for the expanded arena; construction jobs are substantial over a two-year period	No increase in permanent jobs, but substantial construction jobs are created over two years.
Tourism: projected increases in event numbers and attractiveness will lead to heightened competitiveness, reduced seasonality and less vulnerability to shifts in market conditions	Minor changes are expected in tourism attractiveness and yield; the new site will shift demand slightly
Business: Many new small business opportunities are created for the surrounding area and within the large venue; the surrounding district will become a magnet for residents and tourists, increasing overall business volumes	Some businesses and sales volume will be diverted to the new location
Cost: The higher cost requires a public-private partnership, but the public share can be offset by imposing a levy on new commercial developments such as hotels and shopping around the facility	There is no real opportunity for the city to offset costs; the construction costs are much lower, but land has to be purchased and all new infrastructure built.
Taxes: substantial increase in business taxes are expected for the city; an increase in resident and business property taxes throughout the city is required owing to the debt that has to be incurred	There are no net tax benefits for the city; debt will require some increase in resident property and business taxes throughout the city, unless other capital projects are foregone or delayed

With scenarios some degree of generalization is beneficial so that stakeholders and decision-makers can grasp the consequences of their actions. Basically, each scenario contains forecasts of a future state in which impacts are quite different, as the following example demonstrates in the context of strategy, rather than development options.

♦   *Scenario 1*: The city builds a major convention and exhibition centre that will attract many events and generate large economic impacts; primary direct beneficiaries are the tourism, hospitality and retail sectors, but many jobs will be created and potentially new business opportunities created. This is the economic development scenario pursued by many cities where venues and events are instruments of economic and place-marketing strategies.

♦   *Scenario 2*: The city invests in community festivals, leisure centres and amateur sport facilities, largely to meet social, health and cultural policy aims. Capital costs are much lower, and so is job creation. Residents and social groups get direct benefits from their taxes.

Are these scenarios mutually exclusive? Of course not, but they illustrate how strategic impact assessment can employ this method. Another scenario could be formed around a diverse portfolio strategy that pursues both economic and social aims.

3.4.8 Mapping

The traditional form of cartographic maps is often employed, aided by advances in computerized GIS (Geographic Information System) which can capture, store, manipulate, analyse, manage and present all types of data. Mapping can be both an analytical tool, especially to establish the baseline, and used to present results in forms readily comprehensible to stakeholders and decision makers. Here are some IA uses:

♦   Identify alternative sites or routes and their relationship to the other variables such as drainage, sensitive nature preserves, residential communities.

♦   Map areas that will be affected by development or event-related activity, such as:

  ❖ noise cones (e.g., varying decibel levels surrounding concert sites)

  ❖ traffic flows (e.g., zones with increased traffic/noise)

  ❖ visual impact assessment: what can be seen, from where; can be combined with an evaluation of aesthetics and design)

  ❖ hazard mapping related to possible changes (steep slopes, unstable soils, erosion or slippage, flooding, avalanche risk assessment)

  ❖ sensitive environments: parks, reserves, vegetation, wildlife movement corridors, wildlife habitat, drainage and water that might be impacted

- ❖ heritage: e.g., listed buildings, sites and monuments that should be preserved or might be impacted

- ❖ social/cultural: locations of events; sites of importance to groups; demographic and population zones; housing conditions; access to parks and leisure facilities

Overlaying maps can provide visual, and in some cases numeric quantification of general patterns. For example, where there are a number of negative impacts converging on one sensitive ecosystem or a neighbourhood, special attention has to be given to prevention and mitigation.

3.4.9 Decision trees

IA applications for decision trees include a comparison of options (i.e., what are the likely impacts of each?) and identifying decision points when planning a project (e.g., "if the project proposal costs over X amount, do we abandon or modify it?"). This can be combined with traditional cost-benefit analysis.

Figure 3.6: Sample decision tree

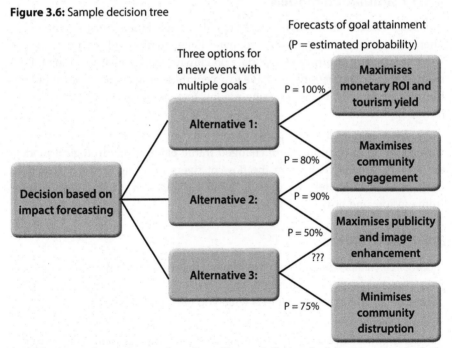

With three alternative projects (see Figure 3.6) the decision tree can include estimates of outcome probabilities, such as "for option 1 the probability of generating intolerable ecological damage is high, for option 2 it is medium, and for option 3 it is low". Or, "the probability of opposition from residents for option 1 is high". Any variable can be compared, and some (e.g., carbon emissions generated) can be quantified through simulation modelling. The best option might be the one that minimizes risks and costs or the one that maximises benefits, if costs and risks are tolerable. If monetary comparisons are desired, the expected net value of each option can become the main point of comparison.

An alternative is to design the decision tree as a series of yes/no branches. This is a way to consider all the main variables for a project, including its potential costs, benefits and negative impacts. Here is an example:

Decision point 1: Does the project cost exceed X amount?". If yes, then cancel or modify the proposal, but if no, then proceed to the next decision point.

DP 2: Will the project generate a positive ROI for the owners and the city? If yes, proceed.

DP 3: Will the project generate unacceptable social/cultural/economic/environmental impacts? If yes, cancel or modify the proposal.

There really is no limit to the branches permitted, especially if available software is employed, but it could get very complicated.

3.4.10 Simulation models

A range of simulation models exists to aid in impact forecasting and analysis. There are whole-planet models for climate change that provide future scenarios – with increasing accuracy as real data on climate change is incorporated. Like all modeling or simulations, we have to accept that complete certainty about the future is impossible, therefore using models to generate a range of scenarios is a wise approach.

Air dispersion models can predict emissions and pollution concentrations at various locations resulting from changed traffic patterns. Hydrological models are used to predict changes in the flow of rivers resulting from construction. Other ecological models are used to predict changes in water quality arising from erosion, and how that will affect fish.

3.4.11 Calculators

Carbon calculators are quite easy to find online, with applications ranging from your personal household emissions or to an event's. The tricky part is getting good data for these models. Here is what you need for an event:

♦ *Ecological footprint:* These models attempt to estimate the total environmental impact of an event, or of humans in general. But this method is currently restricted by a lack of accessible models, as they have to be constructed for particular countries, regions and cities. A short-form footprint analysis can be conducted using a number of indicators – see Chapter 7.

♦ *Direct Economic Contribution:* As discussed in Chapter 8, this is the preferred method of estimating the economic impact of events – not econometric models or multipliers. The site EventImpacts provides such a calculator, useful in making impact forecasts. They are only as good as the data put into them, and can be improved only through meta-analysis of standardized, post-event economic impact assessments.

3.4.12 Visualizations

A number of visualization techniques exist to help in the IA process, with matrices being the most common. Mind maps, concept mapping and storyboarding can also assist in the process of exploring complex situations, especially within public consultation exercises.

Concept Maps are a visualization technique for organizing and communicating knowledge, such as: "In this IA project we want to determine the existing and future potential impacts of event tourism on our destination." They can be done by experts, but are perhaps more useful for public consultations or focus groups wherein a lot of data might be counterproductive or implicit and tacit knowledge is being requested.

A starting point could be to ask respondents to describe their community and their environment, the good and the bad, then ask what they think will happen if a new event is created, a venue built, a resort developed, etc. Symbols, words or pictures are used to represent concepts like: sense of community/happy people, environmental quality/parks, economic benefits/jobs. To avoid bogging down in details, cover the major issues first (or only).

Lines or arrows link concepts, with text to relate them, such as: "a new arena will attract more event tourists and create jobs for residents, but it will also affect the community and environment in other ways – what are they?" A hierarchical arrangement is desirable for impact assessments (as in a logic model) but that might not emerge in initial mapping, it might require refinement through multiple sessions. An expert moderator might go through a series of refined maps, the first ones being messy and incomplete.

Link prior (implicit or tacit) knowledge to new knowledge, such as what participants think about the impact chain compared to what models are forecasting.

Emotional considerations

A concept map can include boxes and text for concepts like: fear or anxiety (e.g., "we worry about our children being able to remain in this community"); place attachment ("everyone here feels part of a strong community and we want to stay here"); optimism ("the future looks bright, assuming we make the right investments") or mistrust ("too many experts are saying this is good for us, but we do not believe them").

The end point, or conclusions of concept mapping (its main value is the process, not the diagram) is an understanding of impacts (real or forecast) and what they mean to the participants. This might take the form of a set of principles to guide development, propositions about what people think will happen if....., or a recommendation (e.g., proceed, modify, terminate). To those charged with doing an IA, the results can be incorporated into a summary document of all inputs and analyses, with consideration of the relative importance of the concept mapping and surrounding consultations.

3.4.13 Cost-Benefit Analysis

Forecasts of cost versus benefits are common for major projects and events. They are usually focused on economic quantifiables measured in monetary units, but can include intangibles – either by employing surrogate monetary measures (like 'consumer surplus' or putting a dollar value on amenity loss) or compiled separate from the economic metrics. The pioneering assessment of the costs and benefits of the Adelaide Grand Prix (Burns et al., 1986) opened new avenues of measurement for evaluators, including 'psychic benefits'.

Post-event CBA evaluations are rare, as are general tourism CBA evaluations. Complexity is one issue (discussed later), but a general unwillingness to be systematic, transparent and accountable is a larger problem and is political in nature. CBA is discussed in the concluding chapter where its limitations are highlighted and a short-form outlined.

3.5 Forecasting

Forecasting is an integral part of many IA projects, and especially critical is the prediction of mega event and venue-development impacts. It is beyond the scope of this book to cover forecasting methods in detail, however a number of important issues must be discussed, and several methods presented.

There are established methods of forecasting, but they all share one thing in common – uncertainty. A degree of risk therefore accompanies all predictions. Simulation models depend upon knowledge gained from past experiences and meta-analysis. Judgment depends upon the knowledge of experts and (sometimes) the reliability of their simulation models.

In this chapter, two useful non-forecasting methods have been discussed, trend analysis and scenarios. But both can be used in forecasting. When trends have been described, or quantified, 'trend extrapolation' can then be used to see where they will lead if the underlying forces remain constant. This assumption might hold true in the short term, but it is unreliable for the long term and in very complex and dynamic situations. Scenarios are also not forecasting tools, but more appropriately weigh alternatives by considering future conditions, or determining how to attain or avoid them. When a scenario has been selected as a preferred option, goals can then be set and a logic model or theory of change model developed, leading to an action plan, IA and evaluation. The logic and

TOC models are in fact forecasting impacts that will result from action pathways.

'Leading indicators' are often used by economists to forecast future economic conditions. They are considered to be the most important signs that the economy is moving in a certain direction. In IA we use key impact indicators that are believed to be most important in the context of the projects' aims and some of these can be important leading indicators as well. For example, public opinion surveys on perceptions of event-tourism impacts both reveal impacts and can be used to predict what will happen if conditions change – such as when a major new event venue is planned. The voices of the media and politicians representing communities can be leading indicators of protests to come.

The direct economic contribution (DEC) calculator discussed in Chapter 8 is not really a forecasting tool, but an algorithm that crunches numbers. It requires input data in the form of forecasts about the number of visitors expected and how much they will spend, so the actual forecasting is done before the calculator can be used. Users can consult previous studies of similar events and draw conclusions about theirs, but caution is required. Ramchandani & Coleman (2012) compared forecasts with post-event estimates of direct visitor expenditure and found that three were over and three were underestimated. They determined that a major source of error is visitor spending, which is more unpredictable than organisational spending, and especially for spectators at free-to-view events. To make a good forecast there has to be precise segmentation of the attendees, and/or participants, and especially important is a projection of the number of overnight, dedicated event tourists – those who travel because of the event.

A series of what-if scenarios is a good idea, to see what the forecasts would be under different assumptions. This is an example of 'sensitivity analysis' designed to reveal how much variation occurs in the output when one input is altered. If we predict fewer international tourists or shorter lengths of stay, the calculator will estimate the change in potential economic contribution. A high, medium and low forecast can assist in planning. The post-event assessment then has to determine how accurate the forecasts were, and why divergence occurred.

3.5.1 Qualitative Forecasting Methods

Harvard Business Review provides a summary and comparison of forecasting methods, both qualitative and quantitative (https://hbr.org/1971/07/how-to-choose-the-right-forecasting-technique).

Stakeholder input (voices)

Many of the consultation techniques employed in IA are intended to aid in the forecasting of potential impacts, often based on what stakeholders say has already happened, or derived from their knowledge of local conditions. That information goes into visualisations and matrices and enables impact assessors to make judgments about the probability and severity of certain impacts.

The reliability of *voices* is always a concern, as a number of biases can be at work, yet resident and other stakeholder opinions have to be given weight in predicting future impacts. If residents say they will lose amenity value in their neighbourhoods, this is important enough to warrant serious investigation. But it also has to be tempered by research, data analysis and discussion of possible mitigation.

Expert testimony and judgment

When experts are consulted in a formal manner, such as through a Delphi panel, with several rounds of prediction and discussion, forecasts can emerge about the probability and importance of future conditions. This, however, is seldom going to be practical for a specific IA project. More common will be a reliance on experts who provide input, and in some cases testify, that in their opinion (based on considerable experience and education, we hope) certain impacts are likely to occur. In other words, the predictions (such as we find in a Leopold matrix) are based on theory or propositions derived from accumulating knowledge.

Market research and polling

Analysis of market research can be an input to trend analysis and provide leading indicators that forecasters can use. Examples include the testing of new event ideas (e.g., to determine what proportion of the market might attend an expo, from where, and at what price) and estimation of the proportion of house-holds visiting certain events and venues, over time.

'Market penetration' studies are done for major events, with tracking start-ing years in advance and progressing right up to the event. For small festivals, sports and entertainment events most of the attendance might be local, whereas for international-class events (many conferences, sports, and fairs) it can be expected that there will be three or four market areas, from local to international. What forecasters want to know is how many will attend from each zone, and in what segments – with segmentation focussing on implications for event and within-scope expenditure. They test awareness (have you heard about it?), the event concept (is it appealing?), interest in attending (under what conditions and at what price) and most importantly the intention of people in various segments and market zones (from local to international) to attend given a fixed date and price. "Willingness to pay" questions are included to determine price sensitiv-ity and help in forecasting revenue. Accuracy of forecasts is likely to improve as the event nears. Further discussion can be found in *Event Tourism* (Getz, 2013, pp.184-6) and in an article by Xie and Smith (2000).

Polling is common before elections and can be used to predict outcomes, although the track record of pollsters is not all that laudable. The basic difficul-ties lie in getting a sample representative of all voting intentions, in the fact that many people do not know enough or care about outcomes, and the fact that minds get changed during campaigns. When it comes to 'selling' people on a proposed bid for a mega event, advice is readily available on what points to emphasize and what topics to avoid – all with the intent of changing people's minds or swaying the pattern of voting (i.e. who votes and who stays home) if there is a plebiscite.

Future studies

Futurists do not necessarily predict the future, but they study it and consider possibilities and the validity of forecasts. Scenarios are often used to explore how trends might change society or the economy, and alternative future states are compared.

From the Wikipedia article 'Future Studies' comes this quote about forecasting and trends:

> *'Futures studies' — sometimes referred to as futurology, futures research, and foresight — can be summarized as being concerned with 'three Ps and a W', i.e. 'possible, probable, and preferable' futures, plus 'wildcards', which are low-probability, high-impact events, should they occur. Even with high-profile, probable events, such as the fall of telecommunications costs, the growth of the internet, or the aging demographics of particular countries, there is often significant uncertainty in the rate or continuation of a trend. Thus, a key part of futures analysis is the managing of uncertainty and risk.*

The notion of 'wildcards' seems to be increasingly important. Some futurists believe we have entered an unstable period in which predictions are less reliable, that the time-frame for useful extrapolation of trends has shrunk, and major changes are impacting on society with alarming frequency. So be warned, trend analysis and forecasting is a very risky business.

3.5.2 Quantitative forecasting methods

Time-series

Trend analysis can lead to extrapolation, and with more sophisticated statistical methods such as moving averages that smooth the trend line. Again, without understanding of causal forces, extrapolation of trends into the future is only for the short term and even then must be used with caution. Economic conditions can change in a hurry, cities and regions can differ greatly in their growth rates, and past experience with events does not always suggest future resident reactions.

Trend spotting

Professional trend spotters are easy to find, with plenty of advice on what will be the 'next hot thing'. Common methods include monitoring online search trends (i.e., what are people looking for?), behavioural analysis indicated by participation in groups and discussions, highly-segmented focus groups and interviews, literature reviews (especially those pertaining to social and cultural trends, technology and business) and field experiments to test new ideas. Data mining of social media and online shopping does reveal trends, but also generates controversy about privacy and security. People use, but are also afraid of 'big data', the analysis of which has the power to spot trends early, correlate diverse and seemingly unrelated facts, and generate new insights to old problems.

Causal models

So-called 'causal models' attempt to link trends and forecasts to underlying forces, such as linking consumer demand for events in general to growth or decline in disposable incomes, which in turn is dependent in part on economic growth within cities, regions and nations. These forecasts can be more accurate through the medium term. Regression analysis and econometric models are examples.

Input-Output models

Much-cited in the literature on economic impacts, and criticised by many for its assumptions and exaggeration of purported benefits of events and tourism, I-O models are mostly used to calculate multipliers. These, in turn, can be forecasting tools, for example in predicting what an injection of new money by event tourism will generate in secondary and tertiary income for a region. See the discussion in Dwyer and Forsyth (2017).

CGE models

As noted by Dwyer and Forsyth (2017, p.108) Computable Equilibrium modelling (CGE models) is better at dealing with the complexities of impacts related to an economic shock on the demand side, such as a substantial increase in event tourism associated with a mega event. "In contrast to I–O analysis, which always produces a positive gain to the economy, however disastrous the event, CGE modelling recognizes that price rises due to resource constraints may limit the increase in economic activity occasioned by a special event, and may even lead to contractions in economic activity in some sectors or the whole economy."

Life-cycle considerations

In the marketing literature there is emphasis on product life cycles, examining their testing, introduction, growth, maturity and decline as measured by variables like sales, profits, market share or brand value. If you believe there is a natural evolution, then forecasts can be made on the assumption that growth will inevitably turn into maturity and then decline. But these stages do not necessarily apply to events and tourism. It would be unwise to predict the future of an event or tourism on this hypothetical evolutionary model, as we know that some events can endure potentially forever while others never get off the ground.

Life-cycle in the context of organisational ecology has been examined by Getz and Andersson (2016). In this theoretical context the viability and evolution of events is in part determined by external forces, despite strategy and marketing efforts. Competition for resources has to be considered a primary influence, and this is linked to stakeholder relationships, consumer demand and political decisions. The causes of event failure have received very little research, and while financial difficulties are probably the most common cause (Getz, 2002) you also have to consider mismanagement, event population dynamics, portfolio-related goals, general economic trends, demographic shifts, and consumer fads. More recent studies of event failure include Parent and Seguin (2007), Carlsen et al. (2010), Nordvall (2015), and Nordvall and Hedlt (2017).

Study questions

1   Compare the four IA planning-process models with regard to the steps to be taken and appropriate methods. Give examples of how and where each might be applied to events and tourism.

2   Discuss the critical role of indicators in impact assessment. How are they determined and used? What variables have to be considered?

3   Illustrate how to use a matrix in IA, with the example of a proposed major event venue.

4   Why are true experiments so difficult for impact assessment in events and tourism? What are the possible alternatives to provide convincing "evidence"?

5   Outline two future scenarios that can be useful in forecasting the impacts of alternative policies for developing an event portfolio. What visualizations would you use?

Recommended additional readings and sources

Chambers, J., Mullick, S. & Smith, D. (1971). How to Choose the Right Forecasting Technique. *Harvard Business Review*, July, (https://hbr.org/1971/07/how-to-choose-the-right-forecasting-technique)

Dwyer, L. & Forsyth, P. (2017). Event evaluation: Approaches and new challenges. In, Lundberg, E., Armbrecht, J., Andersson, T. & Getz, D. (Eds.). (2017). *The Value of Events*, pp. 105-123. London: Routledge.

EventImpacts (http://www.eventimpacts.com/)

Fox, D., Gouthro, M., Morakabati, Y. & and Brackstone, J. (2014). Doing Events Research: From theory to practice. London: Routledge.

Veal, A. & Burton, C. (2014). *Research Methods for Arts and Event Management*, Pearson Higher Ed.

4 Social Impact Assessment

Learning objectives

Know how to conduct a Social Impact Assessment (SIA) for events and tourism.

Understand how events and tourism generate social impacts on:

- ☐ Individuals and families
- ☐ Social groups and sub-cultures
- ☐ Communities (where people live)
- ☐ Events and event organisations
- ☐ Businesses
- ☐ Tourist destinations
- ☐ Politics and government
- ☐ Whole societies and nations

Learn SIA methods with relevance to events and tourism:

- ☐ Resident and stakeholder surveys
- ☐ Ethnography (participant observation)
- ☐ Socio-cultural data analysis
- ☐ Case studies
- ☐ Measuring social capital

4.1 Introduction

Social and cultural change can occur slowly, sometimes invisibly, and in many directions at once. It will usually be difficult to differentiate the changes caused or influenced by events and tourism from wider forces and trends in society. The approach taken in this chapter is to first define social impacts and social impact assessment, then examine the wide range of social impacts that could be the subjects of SIA.

A series of figures presents types of social impacts that should be considered for the major subjects of IA, starting with individuals and ending with whole societies. In each of these tables there are suggested goals, methods and indicators. Specific types of social impact are expressed as goal statements, mostly benefits to achieve. The SIA process is then discussed, including methods of particular relevance to SIA for events and tourism.

Special attention is given to the concept of *social capital* and how it can be assessed. Not only is social capital an important topic in the literature and apparently of interest to many policy makers, but exploring how to measure this concept is indicative of the challenges related to other social and cultural theories and concepts. Refer back to Chapter 3 for a parallel discussion of how to construct a theory of change model for social integration and inclusion.

For related history and topical overviews, readers are encouraged to consult books that give the big picture, including *Exploring the Social Impacts of Events*, edited by Richards et al. (2013), and *Event Studies* by Getz and Page (3d. ed., 2016).

4.2 Social impacts

There has been a tradition of blaming tourism and events for many negative social impacts, and the list of these is long: crime, prostitution, gambling, inflation, displacement of the poor from affordable housing, in-migration for jobs resulting in conflicts, and a general failure to ensure that all residents benefit from economic development. Most recently the conversion of housing to temporary rental accommodation has become a major issue in many cities, giving rise to protests by residents who feel displaced from affordable housing by an influx of tourists.

'*Over tourism*' no doubt means a lot of different things, but exceeding capacity is clearly implied, and the debate inevitably turns to regulation and imposing limits. Although Edinburgh is a world-renowned festival city and most residents are supportive, an article in the newspaper *The Scotsman* in 2018 illustrates some of the concerns people have when event tourism becomes dominant. Brian Ferguson authored this piece. The headline was "The future of Edinburgh's world-famous festivals is at risk by growing public anger over their impact, an official report has revealed", and specifically the article claimed that "dissatisfaction has been growing steadily over the last five years, according to the findings of new opinion polling carried out among people living and working in the city." Problems were attributed to the large influx of tourists into the historic heart of the city at peak periods, resulting in traffic and crowd congestion. In turn, this made it more difficult for residents to use public transit and "get on with normal life". (https://www.scotsman.com/lifestyle/public-fury-at-festival-impact-reaches-an-all-time-peak-1-4737466).

Edinburgh's festival impact studies measure social impact in a number of ways. In 2015 (BOP Consulting, 2016a) a set of social-impact questions were asked across all the events, finding that 75% of respondents agreed or strongly agreed that "attending the festival has given me the opportunity to spend some quality time together with family and friends", and 57% agreeing or strongly agreeing that "the festival is an event that brings your community together". Regarding civic pride, 89% of residents agreed or strongly agreed that "the festival increases my pride in Edinburgh as a city". For construction of a civic-pride scale, see Wood (2006).

Tourism and events are also frequently credited with positive consequences, including host-guest relations leading to peace and understanding. Add to this heritage preservation, including the valued cultural traditions performed at events, community development and urban renewal, and the broad notion of enhancing quality of life through events. Other potential benefits are provision of new leisure and entertainment facilities and more choice through events, community development, and economic prosperity.

Social capital has become a major area of interest for researchers, including questions of its definition, origins and uses. This connects to discussions of event goals and legacies. Individual, group, place and national identity have been attracting a lot of attention from event scholars. Engagement, involvement and transformational outcomes of event participation are a relatively new and challenging topic. Other important themes, many in need of theoretical development, include: events as places for socialization (linked to co-creation of experiences and social integration); social inclusion (linked to issues of power and equity in society); host-guest bridging and the fostering of understanding; elitism versus democratization; emancipation of women and groups without power; attracting attention and the legitimation of groups, nations and ideals; the capacity of communities to host events, the growing use of social media, and impacts on diverse stakeholder groups.

The discourse on social impacts continues to expand. Moscardo (2007) pointed to social capital formation, enhancing community capacity and support for non-tourism related products and services as three areas of social impact that support regional development, while Reid (2007) examined the social impacts of events in rural areas. Reid argued against a simplistic labelling of positives and negatives, and identified several little-discussed themes: trust and respect; breaking down social barriers; releasing stress and tension; forgetting hard times; being affiliated with success; a resistance to change; the affects of costs associated with attending; expectation of government assistance; and greed.

Sharpley and Stone (2012) identified three potential social impacts of events that benefit from multidimensional analysis. The first is place identity/meaning, which from the resident's perspective can include place attachment. There are socially constructed meanings for events and places, events provide one important experience of community, and events and tourism can alter the physical environment. However, events lacking in cultural authenticity are not likely to foster place meaning for residents and might convey the wrong impression to visitors. The second impact these authors discussed is social capital, referencing Arcodia and Whitford (2006), who proposed events can contribute to its formation in three ways: building community networks, resources, knowledge and skills; fostering social cohesiveness; and celebration. Authorised transgression is the third potential social impact, and this is an enduring theme in the social-anthropological literature – especially in the context of carnival.

Social impacts can be linked to specific types of events. With regard to sport, Hover et al. (2016) identified three themes: (1) sport and sport participation: the degree to which sport events stimulate the sport sector and especially stimulate participation in sport; (2) attitudes and beliefs: the degree to which sport events influence people's beliefs, attitudes, norms and values (e.g. pride, happiness, 'feeling good'), and (3) social cohesion, which is the process of developing a community of shared values, shared challenges and equal opportunities, based on a sense of trust, hope and reciprocity.

4.2.1 Definitions

According to the International Association for Impact Assessment (IAIA.org):

"Social impact assessment includes the processes of analyzing, monitoring and managing the intended and unintended social consequences, both positive and negative, of planned interventions (policies, programs, plans, projects) and any social change processes invoked by those interventions. Its primary purpose is to bring about a more sustainable and equitable biophysical and human environment."

SIA can be viewed both as an element in environmental impact assessments, the kind often mandated by law, and as a separate field of practice with its own theoretical and methodological foundations. If we view SIA in the context of evaluation theory, it is evident that many practitioners follow an 'interpretive' and/or 'participatory' paradigm in which the views of stakeholders are critical and in some cases the purpose is to 'emancipate' or 'empower' those affected by vents, projects, or phenomena such as tourism. The SIA process is detailed after the ensuing discussion of social impacts.

Delamere, et al (2001) and Delamere (2001) proposed that the socio-cultural impacts of events can be grouped into four broad categories:

1 *Community benefits:* e.g., celebration, identity, image, cohesion, well-being, community life, self pride through participation, shared ideas.

2 *Quality of life concerns:* crime, vandalism, traffic, overcrowding, litter, ecological damage, reduced privacy, noise, disruption of routines, overuse of community facilities.

3 *Cultural/educational benefits:* new experiences, learning, showcasing new ideas, developing new skills, exposure to new cultural experiences, strengthening friendships, lasting positive impacts, achievement of common goals.

4 *Community resource concerns:* increased disagreements, event as all work no play, excessive demand on human or financial resources, highlighting cultural stereotypes, unequal distribution of benefits, weakened identity, potential sense of failure.

Vanclay (2003, pp. 5-11) is widely cited in the SIA literature and he defined social impacts very broadly, incorporating economic, cultural and environmental categories that we consider in other chapters. The main categories of social are related to way of life, community, political systems, health and wellbeing, personal and property rights, fears and aspirations.

4.2.2 Mega event social impacts

Some of the typical social benefits associated with mega events are disputable, while many negatives are obvious. Do the biggest events foster civic and national pride, or are they propaganda tools for repressive or undemocratic regimes? Are there positive housing legacies, or are poor people displaced and the homeless rounded up because image is all? Is spectacle and world-class entertainment good for people, or a way to keep them passive?

Mega event planning is often the realm of boosterism and influence-peddling. Proponents often get their way, and indeed advice is readily available from 'experts' on how to 'sell' the purported benefits to an ill-informed population, including politicians. As determined by Matheson (2006) the asymmetry of mega-events' beneficial impacts means that community participation and collaborative planning are going to be minimal, while Pappas (2014; 2017) stressed that residents' decision-making engagement in mega-events is limited.

Some of the legacy goals of mega events are social in nature, and grandiose in scale, including the possibility of providing low-cost housing in refurbished athlete villages, engaging children and people with special needs in activities and causes, raising money for charities, or providing inspiration and hope for the downtrodden. How to attain these goals and prove their attainment is a difficult IA assignment. The article by Misener and Schulenkorf (2016: see the research note) refers to social leveraging for sport events, while Schulenkorf and Schlenker (2017) reported on research in Samoa that examined social and community leveraging of sport events, including participatory, educational, health-related, and reputational leverage.

4.3 The objects and subjects of SIA for events and tourism

Figure 4.1 (A to I), below, identifies possible social impacts (i.e., the 'objects' of IA) for a wide range of 'subjects', starting with individuals and families. The specific types of impacts are stated as goals, mostly things to achieve, but some to prevent. What is positive or negative, important or not, is open to interpretation and must be assessed through the IA process including stakeholder input.

Research note

Misener, L. & Schulenkorf, N. (2016). Rethinking the Social Value of Sport Events Through an Asset-Based Community Development (ABCD) Perspective. *Journal of Sport Management, 30,* 329-340.

Abstract: With an increasing emphasis on the social value of sport and events, there has been a shift in focus regarding the management and development process of event projects as well as their associated outcomes. This shift is about emphasizing a more strategic approach to developing social benefits by recognizing and utilizing leverageable resources related to sport events as a means of fostering lasting social and economic change (Chalip, 2006; O'Brien & Chalip, 2007; Schulenkorf & Edwards, 2012). In this paper, we adapt and apply the asset-based community development (ABCD) approach as a means of developing a more action-oriented, community-based approach to leveraging the social assets of sporting events. In applying the ABCD approach, we aim to shift the focus of event-led projects away from attempts to "solve" social problems (i.e., deficit perspective) to enhancing the existing strengths of communities (i.e., strengths perspective). We reflect on case study findings that highlight the challenges and opportunities in realizing an ABCD approach for disadvantaged communities through an examination of a healthy lifestyle community event initiative in the Pacific Islands.

Keywords: sport event, leverage, community development, sport for development

4.3.1 Personal and family impacts

A review by Deery and Jago (2010) concluded that 'social exchange theory' was employed to explain variations in perceptions of impacts, meaning that people who feel they gain from events and tourism should largely be supportive, and perceive fewer or lesser negative effects. But these researchers cautioned that communities are never homogeneous in their perceptions of impacts. Pearce et al. (1996) applied 'social representation theory' in arguing that people do not always rationally assess the costs and benefits of events or tourism as they hold attitudes based on personal experience and media coverage.

Most studies of residents and impacts have focused on assessing perceptions, employing various scales. We can draw upon a number of studies, including Delamere and Hinch (1994), Delamere (2001), Delamere et al. (2001), Fredline et al. (2003; 2013), Small et al. (2005), Schlenker et al. (2005), Wood (2006), Small, 2007, Woosnam et al. (2013), Misener and Schulenkorf (2016) to compile lists of possible outcomes, but in SIA we also need methods to elicit perceptions of impact direction (positive or negative), importance (severe or not, and to whom?) and other variables. It is also very useful to explore attitudes towards events and tourism, as well as use and non-use values both for planning purposes and to draw inferences about impacts and change processes.

There are direct and indirect impacts to consider. Event and travel experiences can have direct affects on those participating and attending, and there are be indirect and cumulative impacts of events and tourism on all residents. Both psychological (e.g., psychic benefits or harm) and physical impacts have to be considered. Small (2007) emphasized that people perceive personal-level and community-level impacts, not always in dichotomous terms like positive and negative, and these differences have to be taken into account. The size and location of events might also lead to important variations.

The personal impacts of experiences

In the age of the 'experience economy' and 'experiential marketing' there is often an expectation that travel and events will somehow change people. From a commercial or corporate perspective this means influencing their brand perceptions and consumer behaviour, whereas from a social-psychological point of view (which is important in leisure theory) experiences can help create and affirm personal and social identity. Indeed, the range of purported and desired life-altering benefits of events and travel are frequently discussed.

Benckendorff and Pearce (2012), writing on the Psychology of Events, provided a framework that examined pre-experience, on-site and post-event experiences for spectators and attendees, performers and participants, and elite participants. The post-experience impacts identified include satisfaction and loyalty, 'self-actualisation' and 'personal development quality', and for elite athletes 'superior performance'. In that context they discussed the relevance of personality traits, role theory and identity, motivation, the nature of experience (cognitive, affective and behavioural), emotional states and wellbeing – in other words, a vast array of social and psychology theory is applicable. If one understands the underlying motivations (e.g. Aicher et al., 2015) as well as specific motives for attending particular events, that goes a long way to crafting a theory of change model.

'Return on Experience' has entered the vocabulary of those engaged in business events, the idea being that a meeting, convention or exhibition should be designed as an engaging, memorable and transforming experience with benefits to the participants and the corporations organising the events. Just how this ROE is to be evaluated is a real challenge, and one that is discussed in the book *Event Evaluation*.

Leisure theory has been heavily influenced by social-psychology, and Patterson and Getz (2013) discussed how event and leisure studies both focus on the nature of experience and its effects on people and society. This relationship also applies to closely related fields like sports, arts, tourism and hospitality management. 'Serious leisure' theory (Stebbins, 1992, 2001; Green and Jones, 2005) has been very influential, with other important constructs being 'social worlds' (Unruh, 1980), 'involvement' (Kyle et al., 2007; Robinson & Getz, 2016) and 'commitment'. The 'event-tourist career trajectory', (Getz and Andersson, 2010; Getz and McConnell ,2011, 2014; Lamont et al., 2012; Buning and Gibson, 2015, 2016), arises from the above-mentioned theoretical perspectives and states propositions about why and how people change over time, in terms of motivation and behaviour, as they become more involved in leisure, sport or lifestyle pursuits.

When it comes to using any of these theoretical foundations in event design, the use of theory of change models is essential. The event that seeks transformational changes will have to give a great deal of thought to how programming, setting, inter-personal interactions and management systems all combine to make it happen.

The main point of this discussion of theory is that in IA we are going to be focused on obtaining evidence of impacts and how to interpret it, not necessarily on proving cause and effect. It usually boils down to deciding what evidence will suffice to demonstrate impacts, then developing the appropriate indicators and methods of data collection and analysis.

Impacts on the family

Exploring the impacts of events on families is a very recent line of inquiry. Jepson and Stadler (2017) and Stadler and Jepson (2017) have done research on how festivals and events affect families, children within families, and quality of life (QOL). They discussed how QOL research is carried out, with a focus on time & space, money/wealth, rest, health & happiness. Their work sheds light on the conditions events should provide to foster social bonding, belonging, and attachment to place.

Special cases of impacts on individuals

Figure 4.1 (B) provides some additional material on the impacts associated with a select number of categories of individuals, namely business-event attendees, exhibitors and suppliers, amateur athletes in participation events, elite athletes, volunteers, staff, event tourists, and special-need groups. Sample goals are suggested for each category, plus methods and indicators that can be used in SIA for these persons with somewhat unique motivations and special needs.

Figure 4.1 (A): Personal and family impacts, with sample methods and indicators

Sample goals for personal & family social impacts	Sample methods and indicators
Personal impacts (expressed as goals) Foster personal and social identity building and affirmation, a sense of well-being, spirituality, transformation, or inspiration. Increase personal leisure choices Facilitate health benefits from participation in events, and potential inspiration effects leading to increased activity & event-related activity Enhance learning & educational/skill attainment (applies both to business events and the role of events as conveyors of information) Ensure the safety and security of all residents, including at events Civil liberties and property rights to be respected at all times Prevent discrimination and exclusion on the basis of gender, race, ethnicity, social status etc. Provide equitable opportunities (this might require subsidies) Foster community engagement through volunteering Facilitate mutually beneficial host-guest interactions	**Interviews, surveys, & focus groups to measure:** Cognitive, affective and behavioural measures of the impacts of experiences (e.g., learning, expressions of happiness, mastery of skills, increased physical activity) Self identification (e.g., a sense of belonging to groups) Perceived impacts and their direction and importance (e.g., gains from new employment and leisure opportunities) Use and non-use values (see 4.5.2) Attitudes and attitude changes; (e.g., support for events and tourism; expression of use and non-use values ascribed to events) Satisfaction with access to events and leisure venues and quality of life Involvement scales and behavioural indicators **Participant Observation** is appropriate for a more subjective examination of benefits gained and the possibility of personal transformation
Impacts on Families Provide more family-oriented leisure and cultural opportunities Provide a more family-friendly environment at events Ensure equitable access to parks and nature Ensure safe, supportive cities and events for children	Special ethical issues apply, and clearance is often needed when researching children Use time diaries and/or experience sampling to evaluate family leisure and event experiences

Figure 4.1 (B): Special cases of impacts on individuals

Category	Personal impact goals	Methods & indicators
Meeting attendees & convention delegates	Group identity building and cohesion Strengthened networking and resultant collaboration or innovation; career enhancement	Surveys and interviews using personal development indicators such as: satisfaction; learning; motivation and commitment for the job; loyalty related to the organisation
Exhibitors and suppliers	Secure and develop business to business relationships; sales; marketing the brand	Measure networking (e.g., contacts made), marketing effectiveness (e.g., sales, qualified leads) and profit attributable to the event
Amateur athletes in participation sports	Advance their serious leisure careers Facilitate communitas (belong and sharing) Enable personal development (as defined by meeting challenges, improving health and skills, realizing lifestyle goals)	Surveys, interviews and participant observation to measure: -Health benefits: e.g., improved health and fitness; weight reduction; muscle tone; endurance; overcoming disability -Athletic benefits: e.g., improved performance (measured against personal aims) -Psychological benefits: e.g., self-development and actualisation (i.e., becoming the person we want to be); personal and social identity building and reinforcement ("this is who I am")
Elite athletes	Enable them to improve their skills and performance	Direct feedback to measure: skill and performance improvements; tangible rewards such as prize money
Staff	Ensure satisfying, safe and healthy work experiences; facilitate career advancement	Use self-reporting on goal attainment, satisfaction, critical incidents, and commitment
Volunteers	Foster altruism; enable learning and networking; provide career-oriented training; foster social identity and communitas	Self-reporting and participant observation to measure: self-development through altruism, hedonism, material rewards and learning
Event tourists	Provide quality social experiences for families and interest groups Facilitate nostalgia and social identity building /reinforcement	Netnography and surveys to measure: -memorable travel experiences -social and cultural capital formation
Special Needs -Provide for distinct requirements, e.g handicap access, sight and hearing aids, medical assistance, interpretation	Provide safe, healthy & enjoyable experiences in accordance with special needs and preferences Facilitate personal growth and development (psychological and physical) Enable the experience of belonging and sharing equal to all other attendees and participants	Employ consultations with organisations that enable special-needs groups Make individual contacts to assess needs and confirm self-perceived outcomes

The Inspiration (or Demonstration) Effect

Sometimes this is a justification for investing in sport events – the claim that they inspire people – both spectators and other viewers – to do more and better, such as take up physical activity and engage in healthier lifestyles. Proof of this social-marketing claim has not been forthcoming and the evidence is unconvincing (Hover et al., 2016). Ramchandani et al. (2017, p. 137) reviewed previous research on the subject and concluded: "Evidence that mega events such as the Olympic Games create a 'demonstration effect' or 'trickle-down effect', whereby people are inspired by elite sporting events and as a result increase their participation in physical and sporting activity is both mixed and limited."

Research by Ramchandani et al. (2017) led to the caution that, even if increased participation occurs, it is too simplistic to attribute causality to a single event. They recommended collaboration among stakeholders (i.e., organisers, funders, sport development agencies and national governing bodies) well in advance of hosting an event. That is a view shared by Taks et al. (2014) who studied the impacts of the 2005 Pan American Junior Athletics Championships and concluded (p.29): "Most outcomes were perceived to have occurred because of the facility legacy; no other intentional strategies were revealed that led to sport participation and development. There is some evidence to support the 'trickle down' or the 'demonstration effect' in that the event created opportunities for sport development, but not for new sport participation. The facility was instrumental to the overall success and likely any additional sport development opportunities."

Reis et al. (2017) concluded that "Overall, what the three case studies presented indicate is that there is limited evidence available to demonstrate that Organizing Committees and relevant government bodies have effectively attempted to strategically leverage the Games with the purpose of developing a sport participation legacy for the wider population, beyond the elite end of the spectrum, leaving this challenge for the next generation of Olympic host candidates". An even broader critique was made by McPherson et al. (2017) who said "There is ample research evidence available to suggest that major sporting events are limited in their ability to bring about and sustain social change. Although we recognize that host cities have a responsibility to pursue social goals when the events they host involve significant public investments, our findings also suggest that these goals need to be realistic if they are to be meaningful."

4.3.2 Social impacts on groups and sub-cultures

'Social groups' as a category includes clubs, teams, fans and other special-interest groups that participate in or travel to events, and ethnic groups or sub-cultures defined as being distinct from the cultural mainstream. Green and Chalip (1998) studied one such sub-culture with reference to how an event celebrated the sub culture.

Groups visit 'iconic events' (discussed alongside 'hallmark events' in Getz et al., 2012) that hold symbolic value, offer benefits that are oriented to their motivations, and facilitate *communitas* – the belonging and sharing that social and cultural groups relish.

Sharing with others is also hallmark of multicultural events, so inter-group collaborations and the building of trust and mutual respect is a goal. In some parts of the world the right to assemble, protest or express different values and lifestyles is restricted, whereas in most democracies these rights are protected.

Figure 4.1 (C): Social impacts on social groups and sub-cultures

Sample goals for social impacts on groups and sub-cultures	Sample methods and indicators
Facilitate development of iconic events for special-interest groups Meet special needs (defined by (dis)ability, gender, age, etc.) Enable and encourage collaboration among groups and organisations Ensure social and cultural inclusiveness at events Moderate conflicting views about the meanings and messages associated with events Ensure the freedom to assemble, celebrate and share Facilitate & legitimise social identity	Interviews, surveys, focus groups: obtain perceptions of costs and benefits and attitudes towards events and tourism Participant observation and self-reporting (systematic observation of what groups are participating in, and their experiences) Netnography (examine blogs, commercial and non-profit sites for information and opinions, meanings and priorities)

Figure 4.1 (D): Social impacts on events and event organisations

Sample social impact goals for events and event organisations	Sample methods and indicators
Increase opportunities to form interest-specific event organisations By solving important social problems, strive for institutional status Ensure safety and health at events; combat anti-social behaviour, hooliganism, crime Work for the legitimation of various types of events, serving all interests Practice social marketing and social leveraging in support of community and charitable causes Enhance opportunities for social entrepreneurship Facilitate social interaction at events Facilitate positive host-guest interactions Prevent exclusion, conflict and crime at events	Interviews with owners and managers: assess mission, strategy, goals, and evaluation / IA systems for comprehensiveness Document review: where possible, conduct meta-analysis of comparable impact studies and evaluation reports Stakeholder input: through interviews or surveys determine stakeholder congruence with event goals and satisfaction with goal attainment and reporting; look for consensus on what evidence of impacts is acceptable

4.3.3 Social impacts on events and event organisations

Events and their organisers have to respond to the needs and preferences of their clients and customers, to political pressures, and to PEST forces including changing societal values. This means they need to understand what impacts they have, regardless of their goals, and then respond or adapt. As well, new events are springing up all the time, many of which are aimed at specific groups and causes; they are part of social change processes.

4.2.4 Social impacts on communities and cities

The term 'community' has the connotation of shared interests of some kind, perhaps shared values (as in a religious community), or leisure or lifestyle interests (as in foodies or amateur distance runners). 'Communities' in this section are the places in which people live, from small neighbourhoods to entire cities, and at a minimum there is a shared interest in the various components that make places safe, healthy, liveable and attractive.

While many of these social impacts are also relevant at the scale of region or nation, what makes this 'subject' of impact assessment important is immediacy and scale, meaning that what happens at the neighbourhood, community or city level can impact on everyone who lives there, and they usually have political representation that must respond to community wishes. Accordingly, the proposal to bid on a mega event or build a venue, or the management of an event portfolio for multiple policy goals, is of importance to all residents – they must be consulted and their assessment of impacts must be given a lot of weight.

4.2.5 Social impacts on businesses

Businesses, both small ones and international corporations, are part of the event and tourism "industry". They sponsor and produce events, engage in "experience marketing" through the media of events, supply to events, and provide visitors with essential services that include travel, tour organisation, accommodation, food and beverages, retailing and advice. Many event producers are in the private sector. What they all have in common with regard to social impacts as that they are collectively and individually part of the process that generates impacts, and they must respond to social policies and community needs.

Figure 4.1 (E): Social impacts on communities and cities

Sample goals for social impacts on communities and cities	Sample methods and indicators
Advance social inclusion and integration through the media of events, venues and tourism Foster creative cities attracting investment, skilled workers Enhance city image and brand Prevent over-use, crowding, and displacement of residents from their normal activities and use of venues/resources Pursue culture-led urban regeneration including public art, festival places, events and other animated spaces for socialization Ensure provision of essential services and facilities for all residents Provide affordable housing and protect the integrity of residential communities Provide or support celebrations to bring all residents together in sharing and accepting diverse values and lifestyles Enhance civic pride, place identity and attachment through events and tourism Facilitate social capital formation through building trust, networking, collaboration through the media of events, tourism and venues Favour community ownership and development; foster capacity building Create a legacy program for long-term benefits Take action to integrate immigrants	Periodic resident surveys: to enable trend analysis and better forecasting, monitor satisfaction, attitudes, perceived impacts, use and non-use value Community-based open houses: determine issues and impacts specific to neighbourhoods and residential communities; consult on projects and events Stakeholder input (e.g., city agencies; business groups; event producers; service clubs and charities): obtain particular insights from both expert opinion and available data

Figure 4.1 (F): Social impacts on businesses

Sample goals for social impacts on businesses	Sample methods and indicators
Ensure workplace health and safety, for staff and volunteers Practice social responsibility through charitable acts, outreach to engage and meet community needs Support causes and events with positive social outcomes Work with community groups, cities and other organisations to realise the benefits of events, venues and tourism Combat negative impacts	Direct input from individual entrepreneurs and from business groups to measure: the extent of collaboration with other organisations in meeting social needs; specifics of CSR strategies and actions; funding through sponsorship and charitable donations

4.2.6 Social impacts on tourist destinations

The tourist destination in many ways cannot be separated from the community, city and nation, but there are some special impact considerations. These start with the overall image and attractiveness of destinations, and elements of competitiveness that can easily be damaged by internal problems such as poor living conditions, unhappy citizens, and very high costs. Although in many places the DMO (destination marketing organisation) is strictly in the business of marketing and development, there are also many places in which cities are in charge or are partners. Either way, tourism organisations will ignore social and other impacts at their peril.

Figure 4.1 (G): Social impacts on tourist destinations

Sample goals for social impacts on tourist destinations	Sample methods and indicators
Facilitate social and pro-poor event tourism Sustain a positive image and reputation related to social conditions in the destination and openness to all visitors Improve choice, affordability and the quality of visitor experiences Practice sustainable tourism Grow the destination's tourist attractiveness through social responsibility that gains resident and political support	Direct input from DMOs, Chambers of Commerce, hotel and restaurant associations, tour companies: document specifics of CSR actions; assess collaboration on identifying and solving social issues; measure effectiveness in developing social and cultural tourism Periodic visitor surveys to measure: image, reputation, brand recognition, satisfaction with experiences

4.2.7 Social impacts on politics and government

'Governance' in a broad sense refers both to control and the ways in which different stakeholders collaborate to share decision-making. In SIA this covers the necessity of consulting with residents and other stakeholders, and meaningfully engaging them in the IA process and corresponding decision making. In turn, politicians can never ignore the demands of voters, and those elected to office must never take it for granted that real or imagined impacts of events and tourism are inconsequential, acceptable or hidden. Full transparency and accountability are everywhere being demanded.

4.2.8 Social impacts on society as a whole; the nation

This category encompasses all of the above categories, but there are some distinct considerations. 'Society as a whole' is not always identical to the nation because some countries are divided and people are in conflict. In some countries there are policies for events and tourism, and in others these are of minor concern to national governments.

Figure 4.1 (H): Social impacts on politics and government

Sample goals for social impacts on politics and government	Sample methods and indicators
Encourage and enable full participation in decisions related to events and tourism Prevent the use of events as propaganda Adopt a comprehensive sustainability policy Practice bottom-up, community-based planning and governance for events, venues and tourism Ensure transparent decision making and accountability	Surveys: monitor trends in citizen opinions on accountability and transparency of government decisions and programmes Analyse media reports on politics, policies, and impacts Obtain direct input from politicians and political parties on priorities, goals, and responses to issues and complaints Undertake policy reviews (explicit policy statements and evidence from action or inaction) on how impacts are assessed and mitigated

Figure 4.1 (I): Social impacts on society as a whole or the nation

Sample goals for social impacts on society or the nation	Sample methods and indicators
Improve the health and welfare of all residents Foster a peaceful, integrated society Foster national identity and pride Prevent transmission of diseases through tourism and events Foster civil society (voluntarism, institutions, governance) Effectively manage in-migration and population growth	Develop public discourse and media coverage of events, venues and tourism-related issues Develop and monitor trends in national measures of economic, social and environmental progress; health trends; crime rates; population and demographic trends Identify and consult with national institutions that deal with social issues

4.4 The process of social impact assessment

Vanclay (2003, p. 6) discussed the evolution of SIA:

Originally SIA was a technique for predicting the social impacts of a project as part of an environmental impact assessment (EIA). Now, contemporary SIA researchers and practitioners are interested in the "processes of analysing, monitoring and managing the intended and unintended social consequences, both positive and negative, of planned interventions and any social changes processes invoked by those interventions so as to bring about a more sustainable and equitable biophysical and human environment."

Vanclay and Esteves (2011, pp. 12–17) proposed a number of principles for all impact assessments, and I have summarized and adapted them as follows:

♦ Conduct IA ethically: incorporate and respect human rights; meaningfully engage public and stakeholder input; consider gender impacts and the differential distribution of impacts; ensure free, prior and informed consent

(FPIC) (i.e., people have to be informed and want and want to give permission to be subjects or respondents

◆ For legitimacy, community-led processes will often be desirable, especially in Indigenous communities

◆ SIA should be more oriented towards how affected peoples can benefit from projects (not just identifying impacts and prescribing mitigation)

◆ SIA should take a holistic approach and be integrated with human health and wellbeing issues, and broader social, economic and ecological sustainability

◆ SIA must be anchored in ethically robust theoretical foundations related to social change. SIA requires a greater understanding of foundational concepts such as scale, power, justice and sustainability, as well as the theoretical frameworks around inclusive, pluralist and participatory approaches

Esteves, Franks, & Vanclay, (2012) have emphasised that SIA is a process of managing social issues, not just identifying them. It therefore has to be participatory, support affected peoples, and contribute to improved understanding of change and responses to change.

4.4.1 Generic SIA process

The SIA process is heavy on consultations and working with affected residents and communities (IAIA 2009; Vanclay and Esteves, 2011). Figure 4.3 is an adaptation of the typical SIA process, to illustrate two applications: (a) forecasting impacts on a city for a proposed major event, and (b) a retrospective assessment of the social impacts of a managed portfolio of events. Elements are not necessarily sequential, and while an 'initiation' is needed in all cases, the SIA process can be built into strategic planning and policy making, making it cyclical in nature.

Figure 4.3: Elements In the SIA process (forecasting and retrospective)

Elements	(A) Forecasting the social impacts of a proposed major event on a city	(B) Retrospective assessment of social impacts from a city-managed event portfolio
INITIATION Establish a participatory process, facilitate discourse, inform those potentially affected, and lay the groundwork for eventual agreement on evaluation, how decisions will be made and potential mitigation.	**Context:** a new event or venue is proposed, with SIA incorporated into the feasibility study; government regulations determine if IA is required Local governments should have citizen and stakeholder consultation processes in place There is a need for media management The SIA process has to be monitored/documented, as well as longer-term mitigation effectiveness Who watches the evaluators? Enforce transparency and accountability	**Context:** local government and the tourism agency agree to study the impacts of events (their portfolios) and tourism as inputs to strategic planning. Complaints or protests can motivate politicians to conduct IAs of existing events or venues and related developments Citizen advisory committees are one option
SCOPING Determine if it is a separate, comprehensive SIA, or part of a broader IA	A detailed project/event description and feasibility study is required How will the scope of the SIA be determined? through stakeholder consultations? How firm are the proposals and how far along in the approval process? this can affect the IA and its perceived legitimacy	Residents and community groups are generally focussed on their 'back yards' (i.e., issues that directly affect them), but a retrospective SIA will likely have to be broader The scope of the retrospective SIA can be open-ended, with issues arising during the study
BASELINE Establish the existing conditions against which changes will be measured In SIA it is necessary to involve and profile the affected populations and groups	What are the existing conditions (i.e., the baseline) against which changes and forecast impacts will be compared? Social and cultural conditions can be difficult to measure and open to wide interpretation, necessitating consultations with all stakeholders	Available data from the census, tax records, police, parks/recreation, conservation authorities etc. can be a first reference point for a baseline assessment Residents and groups will have to be asked to provide profiles of their communities and document what has changed
FORECASTS Use an IA matrix as a first step in identifying the need to forecast particular social impacts Make forecasts of the social changes that may result from the event, venue, policy or development Forecast the magnitude & importance of predicted changes, from different perspectives Determine how the various affected groups and communities will likely respond and the mitigation they might need	Is the SIA to be a technical process conducted by 'experts' or is it open to full stakeholder input? Theory of Change models can be used to designate desired and expected impacts Must be accompanied by a risk analysis (assign probabilities to forecasts and likely consequences) There are no 'calculators' to predict social change, but social impacts do link to ecological and economic forecasts	Rather than making forecasts, the retrospective SIA makes inferences about what has changed, and why The need is for evidence deemed appropriate to determine the impacts of past actions and trends Analysis can be used to formulate future scenarios and make forecasts, plus determination of appropriate policies, strategies and mitigation

Elements	(A) Forecasting the social impacts of a proposed major event on a city	(B) Retrospective assessment of social impacts from a city-managed event portfolio
ALTERNATIVES Examine and compare alternatives including forecasts and identification of potential benefits, costs and needed mitigation.	Opportunity costs are often ignored in impact assessments, as are externalities Politicians and lobby groups should be able to call any proposal or funding project into question with regard to how the same resources could alternatively achieve the same benefits	Scenarios can be used to examine what might have happened had alternatives been pursued Conclusions from the SIA will help in assessing future options
OPPORTUNITIES Forecast benefits that could be realised or maximised when considering social impacts	New venues present opportunities for new sports, leisure pursuits, and events If economic benefits are desired, then specify conditions to maximise local income	Retrospective SIA might identify missed opportunities, and should lead to conclusions about how to achieve benefits
MITIGATION	Problems or costs that might or will occur (risk assessment) Specification of mitigation strategies and actions, with costs and probability of success	One goal should be to examine the effectiveness and cost of any past mitigation efforts, drawing on resident and other stakeholder perceptions
REPORT, FINDINGS & RECOMMENDATIONS	Reports should be available to all stakeholders	Reports should be available to all stakeholders
FEEDBACK AND DECISION a choice from the alternatives might be made, or a decision to not proceed.	Ensure wide discussion with adequate time to respond It is reasonable to expect that not all stakeholders will agree with IA conclusions and recommendations	Stakeholders will want to discuss the thoroughness and validity of results and implications for the future
ACTION PLAN Develop and implement a social impact management plan (SIMP) with built- in monitoring	Collaboration among stakeholders; full involvement of affected people	A new, forward-looking plan might be the logical output of the retrospective IA, building on lessons learned
MONITORING; REVISIONS	Who does monitoring after the SIA project is over? Form a community monitoring group or place responsibility with an existing consortium of community groups	Permanent processes of accountability, transparency and monitoring are essential.

4.5 Methods

Discussed in this section are methods particularly important for social impact assessment, as a supplement to the generic methods presented in Chapter. 3.

4.5.1 Resident surveys

The principle method in SIA for events and tourism has been that of consulting and surveying residents (and specific stakeholder groups) regarding their perceptions of impacts, as well as attitudes towards events and tourism. After all, residents of affected areas should know best what is happening to them, and they will usually have opinions to share.

Articles pertaining to scale development and generating lists of positive and negative perceived impacts have been cited earlier in this chapter. Variations on resident samples include obtaining the opinions of event organisers (Mayfield and Crompton, 1995; Gursoy et al., 2004). Figure 4.4 provides a framework for a survey to obtain resident and stakeholder input on perceived impacts, their direction (positive or negative) and importance, to the individual responding and their family. There are numerous possible impacts, and the lists should be customized on the basis of consultations and/or available information about the people and community in question.

In sections A and B it might be wise to include a Do Not Know option. Crosstabulation with important variables like demographics, length of residence, employment, etc. is then analysed for significant differences. Several hypotheses derived from social exchange theory can be tested:

H1: those respondents living close to event venues will have different perceptions of impacts and their direction and importance (i.e., they should feel impacts more directly)

H2: respondents with employment in events, tourism, hospitality sectors will have significantly different perceptions (i.e., exchange theory suggests they will be more positive about impacts)

Figure 4.4: Suggested questions and format for examining perceived impacts of events and tourism by residents or other stakeholders

(A) Possible impacts on you and your family	For each possible impact, indicate on the scale of 1-5 if you believe it is a negative (cost or problem), or positive (a benefit)	For each possible impact indicate how important you think it is.
Possible impacts: -leisure opportunities for me and my family - jobs/income - daily routine - quality of life Please add others:	For each item: 1 means very negative 2 means somewhat negative 3 means neither a cost nor a benefit 4 means somewhat positive 5 means very positive	For each item: 1 means not very important (for me or my family) 2 means somewhat important 3 means very important
(B) Possible impacts on the community and your living environment		
Possible impacts: -effects on our economy -effects on young people and future generations -effects on entertainment options for everyone Please add others:	As an alternative to a scale, respondents can be asked to make written comments on what impacts they perceive to exist - this should reveal perceptions indicating positive or negative.	Another alternative is to ask respondents to rank a list of impacts as to their relative importance.
(C) What other issues related to events and tourism do you think are important? Please write them here.		

4.5.2 Use and non-use values

Do people value events and venues even if they do not use them? Research suggests that they do (see, for example: Andersson, Armbrecht and Lundberg, 2012, 2017; Gration et al, 2016). *'Use values'* relate to the value people place on their experiences, and this can be measured qualitatively (e.g., "I place high value on the events I attend") or quantitatively, using 'willingness to pay' (e.g., "I would pay X amount to attend (or more than I did to attend) that event"). Use values have to be assessed in the context of information about attending a particular event, or all events in the past year, and what was paid. This is related to economic impact assessment in the sense that monetary amounts can be given to resident spending on local events. That is not 'new money' for the within-scope area, but it is 'retained'. It is also a measure of the importance of events to a community or destination.

Non-use values are related to SIA in this way: if residents are unhappy about the impacts of events and tourism they can be expected to hold attitudes that are negative, and therefore assign low value to them. In Figure 4.4 section (B) there are three items that help measure non-use values. *'Existence value'* is a recognition that events, venues or tourism are good for the economy, community, culture or a particular social condition like employment and housing. *'Bequest value'* considers what should be passed on to the next generation (e.g., "more for youth") or the heritage value of events, buildings and places that should be preserved. *'Option value'* comes from having choices, with more venues and events giving people the option of attending in the future. A full discussion is included in two chapters in the book *The Value of Events* (2017).

4.5.3 Additional questions for residents and stakeholders about impacts

Below are more optional questions for SIA surveys. If they are incorporated into periodic omnibus resident surveys, trend analysis will be possible.

Q: What do you think are the most POSITIVE impacts of (*Event Name OR events in the city*)? The answers should be open-ended (written in) and precede the lists.

Q: What do you think are the most NEGATIVE impacts of (*Event Name OR events in the city*)? (write in)

Q: Is there any event held in the city that you think is particularly good or bad? Name(s); Your reasons?

Q: For (*name of event*) do you agree or disagree with the following statements? 1 means you totally disagree and 7 means you totally agree with the statement.

I have no involvement with this event and no opinion on it.

I love this event and hope it continues.

This event is a tradition that must be preserved.

This event is good for the economy.

I would like to see this event sustained through government support.

I would like to see this event terminated or moved out of the city.

This event is great for families (or youth).

I tolerate the inconveniences associated with it because overall I think it is good for the community.

I have to adjust my lifestyle to avoid the inconveniences associated with this event.

I stay away from the area during the event because I dislike the inconveniences associated with it.

I dislike this event and would be happier if it didn't continue in future years.

4.5.4 Ethnographic methods

Ethnographic methods, particularly participant observation, can be preferable when assessing the impacts of events and tourism in creating or reinforcing social and cultural capital, or other positive outcomes such as social integration and inclusion, community development, quality of life, or cultural preservation. Developing theory of change models in a social-intervention context can benefit from immersion in social groups and self-reflection. This methodology has been employed by leisure and event researchers seeking insights on social worlds, involvement and the nature of event and travel experiences. See the discussion and case study on participant observation by Richard Shipway in the companion book *Event Evaluation*.

4.5.5 Socio-cultural data analysis

Socio-cultural data analysis entails the systematic collection of appropriate data and secondary analysis based on key impact indicators, with time-series impact assessments as a possible product. Detailed analysis of housing, mobility, employment, voting patterns, media content, leisure opportunities or community life before, during and after a mega event or construction of a new venue is one application. Retrospective IAs will require a wide range of data and analysis from all levels of government, social agencies, not-for-profit groups and other sources. Full stakeholder input might reveal unexpected sources.

Local authorities and other government agencies collect a lot of data that can be useful in SIA, such as:

◆ *Census data*: trends in population growth and demographics (age, gender, family formation); of particular concern are the changing needs of families with young children, seniors, and disadvantaged groups – are they benefitting from convenient and affordable access to events, venues and tourism?

◆ *Leisure data*: What activities are popular and growing, or declining? Are certain sports holding more or fewer events? Are venues suitable for local, regional, national or international events? Do residents and tourists compete for use? Are they affordable to all residents?

◆ *Transportation data*: What is the level of private car use? Who uses public transport, and is it the best way to get to event venues? Is there traffic congestion around events?

- *Crime statistics*: Do police have specific challenges regarding events, venues or tourism? What are the crime trends?
- *Health*: What provisions are made for emergencies? Data on accidents and health issues from events should be available.

4.5.6 Case studies

Case studies can be useful in identifying possible social impacts and mitigation strategies. For example, Pentifallo and VanWynsberghe (2015) undertook an embedded case study of social housing impacts of the 2010 Vancouver Winter Olympics. The accumulating evidence from many case studies can be important in theory development, forming the basis for theory of change models. When standardized methods and measures are used, meta-analysis becomes possible, yielding much greater confidence in conclusions.

4.6 Measuring social capital

Bourdieu (1972, 1986) identified several types of capital, namely economic, social, symbolic and cultural. 'Capital' is usually defined as money to invest or assets constituting wealth. Acquiring 'financial capital' is obviously needed to produce events, but so too is 'social capital' in the form of inter-organisational trust, networking and collaboration, plus respect and reputation as reflected in consumer demand. Gaining institutional status, derived from long service to the community, ensures that social capital is available for investment. But can social capital be created or facilitated by events?

Arai and Pedlar (2003: 185) believed that public celebrations and other community gatherings engender social capital through enhanced social cohesion, trust, mutuality, cooperation and openness. Quinn (2013) believed there was rising interest in the relationship between social capital and planned events because of a general decline of social connections, trust, goodwill, cooperation, and reciprocity in society.

Putnam (1995, 2001, 2004) placed emphasis on the benefits of social capital to the community, while Bourdieu (1972, 1986) and Coleman (1988, 1990) conceptualized social capital at the level of individuals. Those theorists have given rise to several categories of social capital: '*bonding* capital' refers to identity ties between people, including families, communities of interest or ethnicity; '*bridging* capital' is needed to bring disparate people and groups together, for example across lines of race, social class, or religion, to share or collaborate or simply to get along, and '*linking* capital' occurs through social ties that enable people to access power or resources from institutions beyond one's own community.

Wilks (2011) tested these ideas at a music festival and found that it was not the kind of event that could be expected to generate social capital, nor meet policy aims such as combatting social exclusion. This has implications for theory of change models that incorporate social goals. More research will be needed on what actions, and what kinds of events can produce these desired outcomes – and how to measure them.

According to the Social Capital website (https://www.socialcapitalresearch.com/measure-social-capital/) the measurement of social capital has employed single indicators like trust, or complicated indices. They favour a multi-dimensional approach with a wide range of indicators, and provide a model that has potential application to SIA for events and tourism – not just for social capital, but also for examining other forms of desired social impacts. Their model embodies three dimensions of social capital (structural, cognitive and relational) and six sets of outcome indicators pertaining to trust, social networks, network structure, social cohesion, civic engagement, and norms and values. The *structural* dimension of social capital refers to creating opportunities for attaining goals. *Cognitive* elements in social capital include shared norms, values, attitudes and beliefs that predispose people to collaborate. *Relational* elements are social relationships between individuals, based in large part on trust.

Figure 4.5 is an adaptation to an event context in which the SIA must establish indicators for determining if social capital has been realised, although these should ideally have been established within a theory of change model to guide the design and production of the event.

Figure 4.5: Indicators for measuring the social-capital outcomes of events

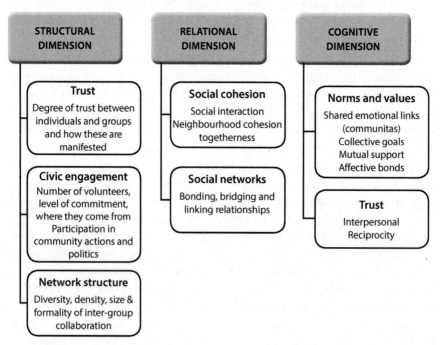

Many of the indicators in the figure are merely starting points for developing specific key impact indicators. 'Trust' has to be operationalized, and while it could mean a belief in the reliability, truth, ability, or strength of someone or something (that is a dictionary definition), what does it mean in the context of generating social capital through the medium of an event? Possible indicators for trust and the other elements of social capital are provided in Figure 4.6.

Figure 4.6: Elements of social capital and suggested indicators

Social capital elements	Suggested indicators
Trust -Interpersonal and inter-organisational -Reciprocity (mutual exchange; reacting to kindness or considerations in the same way)	Opinions: -Explicit survey or interview questions about trust, such as: "Do you trust your collaborators or partners in this event to always consult you and meaningfully consider your views?" Yes, No, Don't Know -On a scale of 1-7, with 7 meaning completely agree, what is your level of agreement with these statements? -The event has brought us closer working relations with other organisations -We trust the organisers more than we did before the event Observable conditions: -length of time groups have worked together -sharing of resources including personnel -cross-membership on boards of directors
Civic Engagement -Voluntarism -Participation in community actions and the political process	Opinions (perhaps best obtained through interviews and focus groups): -"Does your group's involvement with events result in having more legitimacy and influence on local government decisions?" -"Do organisations that collaborate on events gain wider inter-organisational benefits such as sharing resources or working on other community projects?" Observable Conditions: -numbers of volunteers and where they come from (i.e., which organisations?) -the roles of volunteers from different organisations or groups (e.g., do they have equal decision-making power?) -actions of lobby groups, their causes, and effectiveness of actions
Network Structure -inter-group collaboration	Opinions (possibly obtained in the context of constructing a network diagram, or a stakeholder map): "Please identify the links you have with other organisations, the nature of the relationship and how these links are managed; what issues or challenges exist? Do you think these links can be improved? How?" Observable conditions of the relevant network (i.e., the links between organisations collaborating or otherwise involved in planning and producing the event): density, or the numbers involved; formality of relationships; central and bridging organisations (with power or gatekeeping status), diversity or representativeness of the society/culture, gaps and clusters

Social Cohesion	Opinions:
-social interaction -neighbourhood cohesion -togetherness	"Do you believe that events are fostering social integration and togetherness in your neighbourhood? In the city? Why or why not?" Observable conditions: -measures of togetherness versus exclusion (which groups participate and who does not?) -participant observation to evaluate "communitas", or the belonging and sharing among equals -number of events or social occasions that link groups and neighbourhoods
Social Networks	Opinions:
-bonding, bridging and linking relationships	"In what ways do your events (or the city's events) bring individuals and groups together? Can you give examples of how social interaction is being fostered through your event (the city's events)?" Observable conditions: -data from surveys on how family and friends or social groups participate in events, their experiences and reflections on benefits -data on social programmes to overcome barriers and gaps (such as efforts to engage youth, recent immigrants, special-needs groups)
Norms and Values	Opinions:
-shared emotional links -collective goals -mutual support -affective bonds	-"Do you believe your event (or the city's events) reflect shared goals and aspirations? What kind?" -"when working with others to produce the event, have you developed emotional ties with the others?" Observable conditions: -data from surveys of residents and stakeholder groups on their goals, collaborations efforts, and the nature of their network links

When it comes to assessing collaboration around events and how different stakeholders deal with issues of power, negotiation, alliances, legitimacy, trust and identity-building, the notion of a "political market square" might help (Larson and Wikstrom, 2002; Larson, 2009). Larson observed that event networks fall into three categories, being tumultuous, dynamic and institutionalized, all of which can affect social capital investment and formation.

Study questions

1 Discuss methods and related challenges for obtaining resident perceptions of impacts and attitudes towards events and tourism. Why would you include use and non-use values?

2 Are individuals impacted or transformed in permanent ways by attendance and/or participation in events? Suggest methods and key impact indicators for transformational experiences associated with different types of events.

3 Compare the forecasting and retrospective SIA processes in terms of steps and issues.

4 Explain the particular challenges associated with assessing social-capital formation through events. What methods and measures can be used? Be sure to define what you mean by 'social capital'.

Recommended readings and additional sources

Becker, H. & Vanclay, F. (2003). *The International Handbook of Social Impact Assessment: Conceptual and Methodological Advances.* Cheltenham: Edward Elgar.

socialcapitalresearch (https://www.socialcapitalresearch.com/measure-social-capital/)

Schlenker, K., Foley, C. & Getz, D. (2005). *Encore: Event Evaluation Kit -Review and Redevelopment.* Sustainable Tourism Cooperative Research Centre, Griffith University, Gold Coast, Queensland.

Vanclay, F. (Ed.) (2014). *Developments in Social Impact Assessment.* Cheltenham: Edward Elgar.

Vanclay, F. & Esteves, A. (2011)(Eds.). *New Directions in Social Impact Assessment: Conceptual and Methodological Advances.* Cheltenham: Edward Elgar.

5 Cultural Impacts

5.1 Introduction

Cultural impact assessment (CIA) is often combined with social impacts, but there are often very good reasons for a separate approach. CIA is especially relevant for festivals and cultural celebrations, and any event featuring ethnic, indigenous and multicultural themes, or events and tourism located in sensitive cultural communities.

This chapter starts with definitions of culture and its elements, leading to an overview of the main related themes found in the tourism and event literature. A set of goals, related methods and key impact indicators is presented as a way to begin thinking about cultural impact assessment. The process and methods of CIA is then detailed, incorporating concepts and methods from earlier chapters.

5.2 Definition, and elements of culture

The United Nations Educational, Scientific and Cultural Organization (UNESCO, 2002) defined culture as

"the set of distinctive spiritual, material, intellectual and emotional features of society or a social group, and that it encompasses, in addition to art and literature, lifestyles, ways of living together, value systems, traditions and beliefs".

As to the elements of culture to be considered in impact assessment, with many related specifically to native/aboriginal groups or well-defined ethnicities, the UNESCO list of 'intangible heritage' is useful.

"The term 'cultural heritage' has changed content considerably in recent decades, partially owing to the instruments developed by UNESCO. Cultural heritage does not end at monuments and collections of objects. It also includes traditions or living expressions inherited from our ancestors and passed on to our descendants, such as oral traditions, performing arts, social practices, rituals, festive events, knowledge and practices concerning nature and the universe or the knowledge and skills to produce traditional crafts."

(Source: https://ich.unesco.org/en/what-is-intangible-heritage-00003)

5.2.1 Events, tourism and cultural impacts

Anthropologists have traditionally studied the nature and important roles of rituals, festivals and events in human cultures (e.g. van Gennep, 1909; Turner, 1969; Falassi, 1987), and also with regard to negative impacts on culture. Enduring themes include 'acculturation' through host-guest interactions (e.g., see Nunez in the classic book *Hosts and Guests,* edited by Valene Smith, 1989), where interacting cultures begin to share elements and a weaker culture might lose its identity. It is often heard that tourism can 'commodify' events and rituals for commercial gain, thereby damaging cultural 'authenticity' (e.g., Greenwood, 1972; Shaw and Williams, 2004).

Events can be viewed either as agents of change or manifestations of important cultural components, or both. And following the logic of Greenwood (1989) who re-thought his critique by noting the importance of cultural evolution, and of Cohen (1988) who described 'emergent authenticity' in the context of how new events can evolve into authentic traditions, we have to conclude that a static view of impacts should never be taken. Planned events, tourism and culture evolve together.

It is generally believed that searching for 'authentic' experiences is a hallmark of the experience economy (see Gilmore and Pine, 2007) but the search for authenticity is a theme made popular by earlier theorists like Goffman (1959) and MacCannell (1973, 1976), and it has been the subject of much debate. Are people disappointed when they do not find authentic cultural experiences? Do they even know what they are? Without interpretation, many event experiences that have local meaning will only be entertainment to outsiders. Accordingly, when IA searches for impacts on authenticity, definition and measurement become critical.

Scholars have noted the importance of authenticity to special-interest groups such as 'foodies' (Getz et al., 2014). Quinn (2013) described authenticity as a key concept in event management, although it should be remembered that many planned events do not attempt to provide cultural experiences or meanings. Being authentic means different things to people. To a museum curator it often means 'original' or 'unchanged'. But according to Richards (2007), residents are more likely to emphasize familiar cultural norms like traditions and language, and visitors might emphasize their own enjoyment and socializing when it comes to defining what is an authentic experience.

Both positives and negatives can be identified, with lots of grey areas, and there will almost always be different value perspectives – both on the perception of impacts and their importance. Those stressing economic development often appear to downplay the negative cultural impacts of events and tourism, while festival producers are usually engaged in fostering one or more cultural benefits – from arts development to multi-cultural inclusiveness. Cultural impacts will certainly come to the fore when ethnic, native and minority groups are involved as participants, organisers or host communities. By way of example, Whitford and Ruhanen (2013) conducted a sociocultural analysis of an Australian indigenous event.

In *Eventful Cities* (Richards and Palmer, 2010, pp. 359-364) the European Cities of Culture programme is discussed, for which a number of indicators have been developed for assessing cultural impacts:

♦   Participation (e.g., audience and tourist data; increased access for all residents)

♦   Collaboration between cultural organisations (i.e., synergistic effects)

♦   Levels of cultural production (e.g., number of cultural enterprises)

♦   Changes in cultural funding (both public and sponsorship)

♦   Number of new creations (plays, music, books, etc.).

The arts community is diverse, and each form of art (e.g., visual, performing, written) will have a different set of goals and indicators to be assessed. Artists want opportunities to innovate, perform and earn money. Fostering arts appreciation is a general goal, and many arts agencies are interested in making international links. Keep in mind that outputs (e.g., attendance and ticket revenues, numbers of performances, amounts of grants received) are easier to measure and are not long-term impacts.

Meyrick (2015, p. 102) argued for a 'total cultural value' approach, saying:

"The aim of the Total Cultural Value assessment exercise is to capture as many proofs of worth as possible and turn these into descriptions – numerical or verbal – that best represent the value of a cultural activity to its communities (not just the present community, but also past and future communities). The aim is not to make assessment of culture easier for either organisations or government agencies. In fact, it may make it harder." The evidence is to be reported by cultural organisations, including events, as their best expression of worth, being its value to various communities or stakeholders. This would consist of: (a) historical data, including its mission and evolution as well as attendance and financial figures; (b) peer reviews (as evidence of esteem, authenticity, and impact; (c) responses by patrons and the community (tourism figures, sales, endorsements, satisfaction, experiences); (d)

current strategic planning; (e) future mapping and (f) self accounting for total value, both in qualitative and quantitative terms.

The Edinburgh Festivals Impact Study (BOP Consulting, 2016a) identified a number of cultural goals that have been measured through visitor and stakeholder surveys: provide enriching, world-class cultural experiences; widen access, and develop audiences for the future; enrich cultural learning for students. Two questions in their surveys pertained to audience development: "Attending the festival has made me more likely to attend another similar cultural event than before my visit" (68% agreed or strongly agreed); "The festival has given me the opportunity to discover new talent, styles or genres (76% agreeing or strongly agreeing)". Note that these data can be indicators for impact studies, but without follow-up research or corroborating audience data it remains uncertain that merely attending festivals has the desired effect.

5.2.2 Mega event cultural impacts

Garcia (2012), in the book *The Olympic Games and Cultural Policy*, explored the relationships between culture, communication and mega events. The IOC requires cultural programming, and usually an arts festival is a major component. Garcia claims the Olympic cultural programme has become a laboratory for policy development and legacy building.

As media events, major sports competitions like the Olympics and World Cup have to show sensitivity to the host culture(s), balanced with the presentation of spectacle to a global audience. Hosts attempt to outdo each other to make their event the best ever, which can mean real economic impact through improved image and more tourism or trade.

European Capitals of Culture (ECOC) can be considered a cultural mega event. As discussed in Kania (2013) they promote social inclusion, cultural diversity and creativity, support social development of cities, and use culture as a catalyst for change. ECOC reflects a desire for European identity and unity, and is therefore political in nature. Cities compete to be a culture capital, and create and package events within the year-long celebration. Culture, in this context, is at once the production and consumption of arts and other cultural manifestations, and a medium for change. Cities want culture-led revitalization or repositioning, and events always figure prominently. New venues might result, improved networking among institutions, audience development and civic pride can all be part of the desired legacy.

5.3 The subjects and objects of cultural IA for events and tourism

Colombo (2016) provided a list of possible cultural benefits and costs associated with events, and an impact assessment approach that is similar to the SIA process discussed previously. These and other potential impacts identifiable in the literature have been incorporated into Figure 5.1 (A-I), following the approach taken for social impacts. Possible impacts are expressed as goals for each of the subjects of IA (from individuals and families to entire societies or countries), and sample methods and indicators are listed.

5.3.1 Individuals and families

Adoption of goals for positive cultural impacts, and related policies and actions to achieve them, is no guarantee that negative impacts will not occur. The range of goals indicated in Figure 5.1 (A) suggest the potential benefits to attain and some negatives to avoid, but to achieve these will require policies and actions from all levels of government, with support from businesses and the events sector.

There are always arts and cultural lobby groups that can be consulted, but they do not necessarily reflect the full diversity of interests, opinions and attitudes in a community. Local governments that regularly survey their citizens on a range of topics have the advantage of being able to monitor trends and make more reliable forecasts.

5.3.2 Groups and sub-cultures

Cultural groups may be defined by ethnicity or race, religion or language, or devotion to particular art forms and expressions of culture including music, visual and performing arts. These are the groups with vested interests in cultural impact assessment and they must be consulted during the CIA process. Also important are sub-cultures, being those groups possessing norms and values that distinguish them from the parent or encompassing culture. They are often associated with a deliberate break from the mainstream in some obvious manner like appearance, fashion, leisure pursuits or language. Social groups also have cultural elements, as identified by Unruh (1980) in his Social-World theory. There are indicators to consider, including ways of organising and making decisions, the values of founders and leaders, special symbols, iconic events that hold special meaning, and methods of communicating that are usually made through social media. Groups and social worlds can be local or global in their orientation and networks.

Figure 5.1 (A): Cultural impacts on individual and families (residents)

Sample cultural impact goals for individuals and families (residents)	Sample methods and indicators
Minimise potentially harmful demonstration effects on language, the arts, values, traditions	Exposure, awareness, and attitudes towards culture measured through surveys & focus groups
Foster personal enrichment and family bonding through engagement with cultural/multicultural events and the arts	Consult cultural organisations and lobby groups on participation rates and trends, among segments of the resident population
Help create and affirm cultural identity	Measure personal use of culture and event information (e.g. through local mass and popular social media)
Foster celebration and sharing of traditions and identity	
Knowledge and traditions to be preserved or passed along (through formal education, performances, or orally)	Participant observation/ethnography to assess potential impacts on quality of family life
Facilitate mutually beneficial interactions between hosts and guests	Monitor trends in participation rates in the arts and culture (attendance at events, sites; membership in clubs, groups)
Preserve access to resources (e.g., traditional hunting and fishing; transhumance; wildlife migration) and land ownership/use patterns.	Evaluate inspiration effects (increased participation, interest or support attributable to events)
Foster the formation of cultural capital at the level of individuals and families	Monitor trends in use of language, religion, symbols

Figure 5.1 (B): Impacts on groups and sub-cultures

Sample goals for cultural impacts on groups and sub-cultures	Sample methods and indicators
Foster cultural diversity (multiculturalism), collaboration and tolerance	Consultations to evaluate shared cultural experiences, collaborations, networks, identity, pride, issues
Facilitate expressions of identity, ethnicity, group values	
Respect gender roles and relationships	Assess the sustainability of cultural organisations (financial, organisational, operations)
Sustain traditional relations to the land and environment	Document and monitor trends in cultural celebrations (quantity, quality, durability)
Increase opportunities for participation and artistic performances by cultural groups	Media analysis to reveal issues, the perceived legitimacy of groups, public perceptions
Foster a sense of common identity in values, beliefs, ancestry, religion, spirituality, kinship	
Enhance the capacity of groups to deal with threats or participate in projects	
Protect vulnerable groups (owing to their size, history, conditions like disease, crime, substance abuse, housing, basic services) from acculturation; foster cultural renewal	

5.3.3 Events and event organisations

Although many planned events do not have specific cultural aims or components, they can be interpreted as expressions of culture. Festivals and commemorations in particular are explicit manifestations of some elements of culture or sub-culture.

A special category to consider in CIA consists of arts and cultural institutions, often associated with the term 'high culture', such as opera and theatre companies, philharmonic orchestras and the ballet, all of which produce events, as well as the museums and galleries, art centres, and heritage assets that also get involved with events. They might all be considered to be part of a 'cultural industry', at least when it comes to lobbying for pubic recognition and government support. Many planned events, however, are associated with 'popular culture' and their development is left to private enterprise or not-for-profits.

Figure 5.1 (C): Events and event organisations

Sample goals for cultural impacts on events and event organisations	Sample methods and indicators
Celebrate valued traditions & multiculturalism Collaborate with cultural institutions and sub-cultures	Within event portfolio analysis monitor the number and types of events, their programming and specific attention to cultural content
Protect the values associated with an event, tradition, or place (e.g., are certain rituals valued for their own sake or can they be exploited commercially?) Combat prejudice and misunderstandings	Assess the cultural programming, symbols and meanings of event programmes from multiple stakeholder perspectives Obtain visitor feedback on the effectiveness of cultural information, interpretation, and story-telling
Work with stakeholders for a shared interpretation of authenticity and interpret this to residents and visitors	Quantify money raised for arts and cultural programmes or venues, and assess its uses
Showcase local cuisine, beverages, chefs, & farmers as expressions of culture	Resident input is important with regard to assessing impacts on cultural identity, values, attitudes, and behaviour (such as prejudice versus understanding and tolerance of cultural differences)

5.3.4 Businesses

Corporations and private businesses are expected to be profitable, but also to practice social responsibility and adhere to principles of sustainability. These guiding principles often lead to engagement with the arts and cultural groups that includes sponsorship, co-branding and sometimes the production of cultural events. Business organisations in each community should provide leadership, in particular for ensuring social cohesion and cultural development.

Figure 5.1 (D): Cultural impacts on businesses

Sample goals for cultural impacts on businesses	Sample methods and indicators
Encourage business support for the arts & cultural programming, e.g. through sponsoring events Help businesses to present valued cultural symbols, entertainment, stories Facilitate the creation and sustainability of cultural tourism services and experiences involving events	Consultations with sponsors and local business organisations to determine their level of support and the nature of their engagement with events Analysis of local sponsorship of the arts and cultural groups (i.e., amounts invested, perceived ROI for events and sponsors, trend analysis)

5.3.5 Communities and cities

The cultural impacts being discussed are of interest to most residents, as many impacts are felt in residential areas, and city-level organisations have important roles to play. Cultural policy at the city and community level can include support for events directly, or indirectly through support of cultural institutions and venues. Many cities manage a portfolio of cultural events.

Community development is generally a major concern, but it has many meanings. Essential elements include empowerment to make decisions locally, collaboration of the people and organisations within a given city or community for the purposes of solving problems, improving their environment, achieving self-sufficiency and becoming more resilient in the face of external forces. The International Association for Community Development (www.iacdglobal. org) defines it as "a practice-based profession and an academic discipline that promotes participative democracy, sustainable development, rights, economic opportunity, equality and social justice, through the organisation, education and empowerment of people within their communities, whether these be of locality, identity or interest, in urban and rural settings".

Planning and producing events can be an instrument of community development, although positive outcomes cannot always be assured because of the possibility that such collaboration generates or exasperates cultural and social divisions, or that event failure damages capacity to move forward.

Figure 5.1 (E): Communities and cities

Sample goals for cultural impacts on communities & cities	Sample methods and indicators
Support local arts organisations, artists, and cultural events Foster community development through events Foster cultural capital formation by making opportunities for residents, community groups & visitors to engage with local traditions & cultural events Preserve authentic cultural elements through events; interpret them to residents & visitors	Periodic omnibus surveys of residents to obtain data on perceived cultural impacts and the authenticity of events, attitudes towards cultural policies and events, & valued traditions Community-group engagement in policy, strategy and events programming; encourage groups to conduct culture inventories and identify issues Measure institutional networking and collaboration within the arts and cultural groups

5.3.6 Tourist destinations

DMOs and the tourism and hospitality industry have recognized the high value derived from all forms of cultural tourism, and there are several books on the subject (e.g., Richards, 2007; Timothy, 2011; du Cros and McKercher, 2014). It can be very broadly defined to include special-purpose travel for events, immersion in a different culture or lifestyle, cultural experiences such as food and beverages, as well as visits to heritage sites, attending concerts and visiting galleries or museums. There has also been a recognition that damage to heritage and cultural assets accompanies over-tourism or inadequate management, and the literature also warns that acculturation and demonstration effects of tourism can be very damaging to authenticity. Sustainable destinations need to consider limits on use, at least at peak season, and how to extract sufficient financial resources from tourism to pay for upkeep and preservation.

Figure 5.1 (F): Tourist destinations

Sample goals for cultural impacts on tourism destinations	Sample methods and indicators
Attract cultural tourists, including diverse interests such as food, visual and performing arts, ethnic festivals and music concerts	Visitor surveys to obtain data on: perceptions of image, cultural opportunities, authenticity, interpretation, information available, their satisfaction and preferences
Ensure that every visitor enjoys a cultural experience (beginning with food, but also including entertainment, host-guest interaction and the arts)	Monitoring attendance at events and venues, linked to capacity
Work with stakeholders to preserve and enhance authentic cultural experiences	Assessments of capacity and over-use at sites and venues, with multi-stakeholder input
Protect tangible and intangible heritage from over-use or misuse; tourists should help pay for upkeep & preservation	

5.3.7 Politics and government

Most cities have cultural departments, or at least explicit cultural policies and programmes. These might overlap or be integrated with the programmes of senior levels of government and tourism organisations. Typical examples of cultural action include investment in museums, galleries, public art, employment of artists and performers, and supporting a portfolio of cultural events.

Political ideology is often manifested in events and cultural policy in the form of symbolism (e.g., display of flags, singing of national anthems, speeches), propaganda (meaning overt political messages) and performances that reflect dominant values. Particularly surrounding heritage commemorations there can be serious disagreements about expressed values and the meanings of programming (see the book *Commemorative Events* by Frost and Laing, 2013).

Figure 5.1 (G): Politics and government

Sample goals for cultural impacts on politics and government	Sample methods and indicators
Create and manage a portfolio of cultural events Support cultural institutions and groups Commemorate important historical events and persons Secure broad agreement on cultural values and meanings, and tolerate dissent when it arises	Stakeholder input will reveal the degree of support or dissent on cultural expressions and interpretation Assessment of government policies should reveal values and priorities, although actions (events produced, their programming, and support for institutions) might be a better indicator

5.3.8 Whole cultures or the nation

At the national level events are often used as symbols of identity and unity, although these can be disputed and politicized. There are cultural landscapes, national identity, valued customs and heritage sites, even cuisine that are recognisable as national culture.

Mega events tend to be showcases of culture, embodying elements considered to be distinctive, and perhaps cynically, to be 'marketable'. Support for events can be a reflection of a country's policies towards cultural hegemony or multiculturalism, and in the past have frequently been viewed as useful propaganda tools. Preserving valued traditions through support to events is a legitimate goal for nations.

Figure 5.1 (H): Whole cultures or nations

Sample goals for cultural impacts on whole cultures or nations	Sample methods and indicators
Showcase distinctive elements of culture Protect cultural landscapes (their meanings, aesthetics, and uses) Enhance national identity and unity Preserve and enhance national traditions (intangible heritage)	Surveys to determine awareness, national image and reputation outside the country Resident surveys within the country to assess identity Input from agencies and groups devoted to heritage preservation

5.4 Cultural impact assessment: the process

CIA can follow the generic IA process, with some adaptations. This is particularly true where aboriginal, ethnic or multicultural events and communities are the focus of attention. Similar to SIA, the conduct of CIA is often part of planning or feasibility studies, aimed at forecasting impacts and including mitigation strategies. The International Network for Cultural Diversity's Working Group on CIA defined it this way (from Sagnia 2004, p. 9):

"a process of evaluating the likely impacts of a proposed development on the way of life of a particular group or community of people, with full involvement of this group or community of people and possibly undertaken by this group or community of people. A CIA will generally address the impacts, both beneficial and adverse, of a proposed development that may affect, for example, the values, belief systems, customary laws, language(s), customs, economy, relationships with the local environment and particular species, social organization and traditions of the affected community."

Note that full involvement by the affected people is inherent in CIA, reflecting the fact that outsiders cannot possibly identify all cultural elements, processes and impacts, or correctly interpret the possible affects of an event or tourism on cultural groups.

5.4.1 Scoping and consultations

The scoping stage of CIA should consider the following:

♦ Cultural context (the environment, history, documentation of baseline conditions and trends, local knowledge).

♦ Meaningful consultation among stakeholders; local control asserted where appropriate and feasible.

♦ Understanding what elements of culture are important to whom, and why.

♦ Determining which elements of culture might be impacted (use the matrix).

♦ Comparisons and case studies (what has been learned in the past or elsewhere).

♦ Appropriateness: the scope of study must match the nature of the threat; are there specific impacts to be given priority? what do stakeholders emphasize?

Colombo's (2016) model is specifically designed for assessing the cultural impacts of events, and is based on the perceptions of residents; identified impacts are subjective and personal in nature. Colombo listed potential benefits and negatives that should be examined, provided indicators for each, and advocated a method for obtaining resident input on the following:

♦ *Perceived or not:* yes it is a likely/existing impact, no it is not

♦ *Considered positive or negative*: this can be from the individual's or community's perspective

♦ *The intensity of the impact on individuals and on the community is evaluated:* (on an intensity scale, say from 1-10)

♦ *Considered intentional or not.* The evaluator could ask respondents if they think an impact was intentional or not, or draw this conclusion from the event organisers or observation and document review.

The point of determining if an impact is intentional or not (either through objective analysis and/or resident perceptions) is related the need to avoid the tunnel vision that occurs when assessors only look at intended outcomes.

The variables age, gender, place of birth, educational attainment, native language, nationality, participation in the event or events, and place of residence were considered by Colombo to be important to cross-tabulate with the above responses.

Issues identification is one aim of early consultations. What are people talking about, on social media or in focus groups and community meetings? Asking what worries them is partly a threat assessment related to the event(s) in question and partly a means to induce open discussion of concerns. What evidence of impacts is already visible or suspected?

There might be many issues that seem to have little or nothing to do with the event or project in question, but links might be revealed through further analysis of results. And it should be cautioned that any issue, however trivial or irrelevant it might initially appear, could come back to be important in the light of actual development. Here are some possible issues that will be identified:

♦   A general worry that change will disrupt the community or have negative cultural impact (sometimes this will be alleviated by more information).

♦   Specific concerns about an event or project's potential impacts on the community, its way of life or its values (be aware of the 'not in my backyard' syndrome, where people are mostly concerned about impacts on their own property or lifestyle).

♦   Acceptance or not of the CIA process (is it legitimate, and are the assessors trustworthy?

♦   Concerns that that community or resident input is not valued and will have no impact on the project (do they have control over the process?)

♦   Debates over what is claimed to be knowledge (either by the assessors or by residents; what is credible and acceptable evidence of impacts or potential impacts will be a matter for debate and possibly compromise).

Traditional use and knowledge studies

Professionals tend to think they know a lot, and can learn everything that is needed through observation and research, but local people often know more than outsiders can ever discover. It is important to ask residents, particularly in societies close to the land, what resources they use and how, and to obtain as much information they can provide about how an event or project might affect traditional uses.

A pertinent question is "what do you know about your environment that can help identify potential and existing impacts?" Sometimes this involves place-name geography, meaning "what do you call this place?" or, "does that place have special meaning?" In fact, residents of any community will be able to identify and possibly map their patterns of life, objects and places of importance, such as meeting places, and intangibles that have particular importance such as green spaces or access to the countryside.

Consultations have to be accompanied by research and analysis, and there are a number of methods especially important to cultural impacts that can be added to the SIA methods.

5.5 Methods

Mapping the cultural landscape is a valuable tool, with cognitive and mind mapping being discussed first. Next the potential applicability of LAC is discussed, focussing on the issues of whether there are limits that can be expressed in cultural terms. Then we examine cultural capital, what it means and how it can be assessed. The final topic concerns how to address the impacts of cultural engagement, for individuals and communities.

5.5.1 Mapping

How land and water resources have been influenced by human activity can be of importance. This can be called 'cultural landscape mapping' and can include landscape aesthetics, although different cultures have quite different ideas about what is beautiful or worth preserving. Events held at, or near important archaeological or heritage sites and buildings could impinge on their meaning or preservation, with over-use a major issue. IA will ask: "what is the capacity of the landscape and of sites and buildings to sustainably accommodate events in both physical and cultural terms?"

'Cognitive mapping' (or mental maps) is a tool for SIA and CIA and specifically can be used for defining cultural landscape, spaces and places. Respondents can be asked to identify and map buildings, areas, places and routes of importance to them, and questioned about how they make sense of their physical environment. This will not always correspond to actual maps, but will reveal much about how residents perceive and interact with their environment.

Lask (see the research note) used this technique to assess potential impacts of an event on 'cultural habitus', a term used by Bourdieu that refers to the deeply ingrained habits and dispositions of people that come from life experiences. Habitus is related to cultural capital and how we acquire it, as our backgrounds shape relationships with the outside world. Habitus also helps explain one's taste for art and other cultural objects, being linked to social class in Bourdieu's theory.

Research Note

Lask, T. (2011). Cognitive maps: A sustainable tool for impact evaluation. *Journal of Policy Research in Tourism, Leisure and Events, 3* (1), 44-62.

Abstract: The objective of the research on which this paper is based is to find out what impact Liverpool 08 will have on local cultural habitus, and how the sustainability of this impact can be measured and monitored. Too often, evaluation became a box-ticking exercise for decision makers to demonstrate transparency and to objectively prove results. However, evaluations are usually ephemeral, and do not systematically integrate inputs from the end-receivers/consumers of public policies. Decision makers prefer quantitative indicators, that are well known, easily applied and comprehensible to a broad audience, but leave out emotional and participatory aspects. Introducing a hermeneutical approach to understand the impacts of cultural policy allows access to the emotional and qualitative experience of policy impacts on everyday cultural life. This paper suggests that cognitive mapping turned into an evaluation method promotes residents as local experts on everyday construction of cultural space, and gives them an opportunity to participate in the evaluation process. The geography of the local population's interaction with urban space as a creative force conveys emotional attachment to particular parts of the city, determines the essential elements for cultural life and space and its comparison to the city's legitimised cultural space shows how far the bottom-up and the top-down approaches match: the smaller the gap between them, the higher the sustainability of cultural policy.

5.5.2 Mind mapping

One of several visualization techniques that can be used in consultations and reporting, mind mapping aims to elicit a flow of thoughts about perceived impacts, their direction (positive of negative) and their importance. Figure 5.2 illustrates a kind of mind map, but there are many sources of software available for more elaborate graphics. The approach taken in this diagram is to start with a discussion of all the major types of potential impacts, then proceed to greater detail. Impacts thought to be immediate are likely to arise first, but longer-term implications should then be addressed. This can be done with individuals, but probably will get better results in focus groups.

Interrelationships can be more clearly revealed in some graphic software programmes, such as lines showing how economic impacts might directly produce higher incomes and in the longer-term increased prosperity and in-migration, or how land use changes might directly affect access to nature and subsequently have a negative impact on ecological processes and wildlife. The caution, as with all forms of input, is that perceptions might be influenced by inadequate or mis-information. Also consider that this kind of input from stakeholders can be informed by theory of change models, simulations and other forecasting analysis.

Figure 5.2: Mind mapping for consultations in CIA

CULTURAL IMPACTS
Are there potential benefits or negative impacts to your distinctive culture & heritage?

BUILT ENVIRONMENT IMPACTS

More traffic in neighbourhood
New commercial cluster formed with permanent land-use changes that will impact of daily life

PROPOSED MAJOR EVENT VENUE

ECONOMIC IMPACTS

Perceived immediate social/culture impacts
Daily routines altered
Increased incomes
Population growth
Less contact with nature
More leisure opportunities
Noise & safety concerns

Temporary and permanent jobs created
Many future events and an increase in tourism

SOCIAL IMPACTS
Are there potential benefits or negative impacts on your quality of life?

ECOLOGICAL IMPACTS

Perceived longer term effects
Demographic shifts owing to in-migration
Threats to traditions & language
Possible diminished quality of life
Hopeful of improvement in services for health, education & leisure

Increase in carbon emissions/ pollution
Permanent land-use changes with effects on parkland & wildlife

5.5.3 Limits of Acceptable Change

Can residents sense what is a threat, or when a tipping point or limit has been reached? The problem is that events, tourism, venues, and in fact most developments are part of a much larger change process and disentangling specific causes and effects is quite difficult. Within an SIA or CIA the assessors might very well hear "enough is enough!" or "it's too much, its happening too fast, it's not acceptable to us!" Do these expressions of fear or dissatisfaction mean that limits have been reached and nothing else should be allowed to change? Or do they mean there is fear based on inadequate or misinformation, that residents sense they have no control over the process, or perhaps that not all voices in the community are being heard?

It is almost certain than some people and interest groups will be opposed to major development proposals, including mega events or portfolio strategies, sometimes merely on the principle that people do not like change. Therefore SIA and CIA cannot rest entirely on perceptions and opinions. Objective analysis of the facts, reasoned forecasts and justifiable proposals for mitigation must accompany consultations. In the end, most major decisions will be political in nature and out of the hands of impact assessors. The strength of evidence and arguments will be important.

In retrospective IAs the scenarios are quite different. In these processes the consultations and visualizations will be focussed on what has happened, so that perceptions of impacts can be matched by analysis of what has actually changed. It will be the attribution of impacts to causes that matters the most. Are residents correct in believing that venue development and event tourism, cumulatively, altered the demographics of their community? Or were observable changes in social and cultural life simply reflective of broader societal changes?

5.5.4 Assessing cultural capital

Similar to measuring social capital, it is a challenge to demonstrate the creation of cultural capital and particularly how to deal with it in a cultural IA. First we have to define it. Attributed to Bourdieu and Passeron from their book *Cultural Reproduction and Social Reproduction* (1977), 'cultural capital' is in fact a sociological concept.

Bourdieu's theory deals with the symbolism attached to skills, tastes, mannerisms, belongings or credentials that are acquired within social classes. Collective identity arises from sharing these elements of culture, but it also fosters social inequality. Three forms of cultural capital were identified by Bourdieu. '*Embodied*' cultural capital refers to the person's accent or mannerisms, while '*objectified*' cultural capital refers to possessions and material things. '*Institutionalized*' cultural capital includes titles and qualifications, such as those bestowed by a university degree.

If we have financial capital we have money to invest (or assets that can be converted to money), whereas cultural capital consists of all the assets needed for social success and mobility, even for power, including our education, skills, intellect, mannerisms and style. What is valued and influential will vary from culture to culture. For example, in some societies attending the 'right schools' is more important than having a degree. Social relations are often crucial, as in "who you know".

What has this got to do with events and impact assessment? One of the goals of some events or organisations supporting them is to foster or increase cultural capital, especially among disadvantaged or marginalised groups, so that they can improve their position in society, or at least get a good job and thereby improve their quality of life. How is that possible? The base has to be exposure to cultural expressions like art and performances, and increased knowledge of culture, keeping in mind that often 'high culture' is valued more by the elite. When individuals and groups are exposed, and preferably engaged in cultural productions, there should be some transfer of knowledge, hopefully increased appreciation of cultural elements, and ultimately participation.

5.5.5 The personal impacts of cultural engagement

The underlying theory is that exposure, and especially higher levels of engagement in arts and cultural pursuits will lead to greater understanding and appreciation, and possibly to more profound changes that can be termed personal development or self actualization.

A schema for assessing the outcomes of cultural engagement has been provided by the Cultural Development Network in Australia.

Five domains of outcomes are detailed: cultural, social, economic, environmental and governance. In Figure 5.3, adapted from the original, measures and methods are suggested including questions for interviewers or surveys. The table considers individuals on the left side and communities, or possibly entire societies and cultures on the right.

Figure 5.3: Assessing cultural impacts of events on individuals and communities or society (Adapted from: http://www.culturaldevelopment.net.au/outcome)

Sample Q & indicators for individuals	Sample Q & indicators for communities/society
Creativity stimulated Q: Through your participation in (name of this event or activity) was your creativity stimulated? In what ways? -experienced emotional highs? -inspired by what I saw/did?	**Arts & cultural development** Q: How have the arts been fostered in your community? -more public art? -increased participation? -more positive attitudes? -increased funding?
Aesthetic enrichment experienced Q: Did your experiences of art, beauty or cultural productions move you or inspire you? -I gained new insights -It expanded my appreciation	**Enhanced quality of cultural life** Q: How has the community/city benefitted or changed as a result of…(event or project) -more access for all residents? -a broader portfolio of art and events? -better cooperation through networking? -a more animated, dynamic cultural community? -civic design enhanced?
New knowledge, insights and ideas gained Q: What have you learned from your engagement with the event(s)? -more critical reflection? -increased knowledge of art /other cultures?	**Cultural richness fostered** Q: Has cultural and artistic diversity been improved / increased? -more sustainable institutions? -more programming or productions? -broader participation by groups? -increased attendance?

Cultural diversity appreciated	Cultural diversity manifested in the community
Q: As a result of your participation are you more aware and tolerant of cultural differences? In what ways? -knowledge gained of others? -working together /collaborations/links forged? -attitude changes? -behavioural changes?	Q: are events in this community more or less inclusive? Accessible to all? Responsive to community needs? -measures: involvement by different segments and groups; (multi)cultural events fostered; formal networks and collaborations established
Sense of belonging to shared heritage experienced Q: Are you more attached to your city? More proud of your community? More appreciative and protective of your collective heritage? -measure: knowledge gained and shared; financial or volunteer contributions to heritage preservation and interpretation	Heritage and cultural identity Q: Does your community now understand and value its heritage more? In what ways? -manage a portfolio of community commemorations? -more residents and visitors have access to and use local heritage resources?

Study questions

1   Discuss the differences between social and cultural impacts, giving examples pertinent to events and tourism.

2   What goals do the arts community and artists have for events and tourism?

3   Outline a consultation process for a retrospective CIA pertaining to a city's event portfolio. What visualization techniques will you recommend?

4   Will engagement with culture transform individuals and communities? How can you assess these potential impacts? Is this the same as cultural capital?

Recommended additional readings and sources

duCros, H. & McKercher   (2014) *Cultural Tourism* (2d.ed.), London: Routledge

Cultural Development Network (http://www.culturaldevelopment.net.au/)

UNESCO (https://ich.unesco.org/en/what-is-intangible-heritage-00003)

Built Environment

Learning objectives

☐ Learn the range of impacts that events and tourism can have on the built environment.

☐ Learn why and how events and tourism contribute to urban development, renewal and re-positioning.

☐ Understand the issues associated with events as animators of public spaces.

☐ Be able to take into account life-cycle issues when conducting IA

☐ Be able to recommend strategies and actions for image, reputation, brand and place marketing to attain desired outcomes from events and tourism.

☐ Know how media management can influence the impacts of events and tourism.

6.1 Introduction

Built environment refers to the places in which we live and work, the services that meet our needs, and everything humans do by way of physical planning, design, development and controls to ensure our basic needs are met and quality of life maximised. This broad definition encompasses residential neighbourhoods, transport systems, farmland and industrial zones. It is also worth distinguishing between 'spaces' where things can be built and activities occur, and 'places' which have meaning – such as play and work spaces, living and meeting places, all within social and cultural value systems.

Impacts of tourism and events on the built environment are of increasing importance, particularly because so many cities have pursued tourism and culture-based development or re-positioning strategies. There are many examples of using events, venues, iconic architecture, tourism and culture synergistically, with profound effects on the urban landscape, its image and liveability. In small towns the impacts of development can be more noticeable and have more profound impacts on residents.

In the literature on events and the built environment the focus has often been on the effects of mega events that require enormous investment in infrastructure and venues. However, construction and operation of sport arenas and stadia, major arts and culture facilities, as well as convention and exhibition centres all have profound implications for cities.

In this chapter the starting point is a discussion of the roles of events and venues in urban development and renewal, a theme that incorporates the concepts of liveability (or quality of life), community development, healthy and creative cities. A second theme is the use of public spaces by events, looking at both the positives and negatives. The influence of the environment upon events and tourism has to be mentioned, although it is not part of the objects of impact assessment considered in this book. Within 'environmental psychology' there is the principle of 'setting affordances', meaning what the environment allows (or lends itself to) by way of events and tourism. For example, many urban spaces with heritage status and unique design are popular venues for festivals and other events, but with possible negative impacts owing to crowd activities and, over time, the accompanying change in the character of the place. Parks and streets lend themselves to parades and open-air events, but at a potential cost.

Attention is then directed at place making and place marketing and the interdependent elements of image, reputation, positioning and brand. In recent years the communicative properties of events have come to the fore, and in many cases even replacing the emphasis on events as attractions. We live in a networked world, with mass and social media presenting global opportunities to both market events (especially to special interest segments) and to exploit events and related images for broader political, economic and social purposes.

Completing this chapter is a case study from Rudi Hartmann about events and the evolution of the resort town of Vail, Colorado. A number of themes are reinforced, and new theoretical perspectives introduced.

6.2 Events, tourism and urban development or renewal

Several themes are discerned in the literature, starting with the roles of events and tourism in urban development and renewal. This is a multi-dimensional process of change, involving the creation of event places, image management, repositioning, animation of new development and existing spaces or facilities, and employing event venues as catalysts for economic transformation.

This is not a completely new theme. Mules (1993) examined how a special event was designed to draw people to a redevelopment area in Adelaide, South Australia, as an integral part of urban renewal, and to change the image so that the area would become associated with leisure and tourism with a maritime flavour. More recently, Xie and Gu (2015) also examined events at the waterfront, in Auckland New Zealand, observing that the America's Cup and the Rugby World Cup aided in its redevelopment.

Research Note

Xie, P. & Gu, K. (2015). The changing urban morphology: Waterfront redevelopment and event tourism in New Zealand. *Tourism Management Perspectives 15*, 105–114.

Abstract: This study addresses the changing morphology of the commercial waterfront in Auckland, New Zealand. It seeks to examine the wider impacts and implications of hosting special events such as that provide an impetus for the redevelopment of an underutilized waterfront area. By using an evolutionary analysis of the spatial structure of the waterfront landscape, it demonstrates that government development agencies and event tourism have been the key agents of change in influencing its redevelopment at different phases. The findings illustrate the role of government in the context of economic restructuring and the embrace of tourism as a significant element in the waterfront planning. This study proposes to establish a systematic understanding of morphological change in order to create a sound base for waterfront landscape management and tourism planning.

Van Aalst and van Melik (2012) wrote a case study of a festival that was moved from one city to another, focusing on the question of place identity and dependency. Although the festival is a showcase for Rotterdam, findings suggested that the event and not the city was the destination; its audience cared most about the festival programme and site. The implication is that a lot of thought has to go into embedding an event in a particular place in the hope that it will somehow transform its environment.

6.2.1 Mega event impacts on the built environment

There is a long tradition of examining mega event impacts on host cities. Mendell et al. (1983) observed that the Knoxville World's Fair was conceived as an urban-renewal project and created a legacy of improved infrastructure, a new convention centre and private investments that improved the city's tax base. Dungan (1984) reported on a variety of mega event legacies including airports, subways, freeways, fairground renovations, parks, and the landmark structures that have become iconic in a number of cities (e.g., the Eiffel Tower and Seattle's space needle). Mihalik (1994) said the Atlanta Summer Olympics of 1996 generated two billion dollars worth of construction projects and were a catalyst in obtaining federal money for low-income housing.

Essex and Chalkey (1998) reviewed how the Olympic Games emerged as a catalyst of urban change and a key instrument of urban policy for host cities.

Sadd (2012) discussed the London Olympics and event-led urban regeneration, pointing out the difference between helping those who need it most and 'gentrification', in which housing moves upmarket and poor people are displaced.

Urban regeneration and the role of events have been examined by Pacione (2012) who observed that urban and cultural geographers are particularly interested in how events influence both form and function in communities. Pacione examined the case of Glasgow's efforts to use culture and events in re-positioning and regeneration, noting the discourse this has engendered within the city on such matters as whose culture, and what cultural should be displayed and celebrated in the 2008 European Capital of Culture. Rogerson (2016) also examined Glasgow, specifically in the context of hosting the Commonwealth Games and two aspects of its planned legacy: increasing participation in sport and physical activity, and community regeneration.

Andrew Smith's book *Events and Urban Regeneration: The Strategic Use of Events to Revitalise Cities* (2012) examined the different ways that events can assist regeneration, as well as related problems. McGillivray & Turner, (2018: *Event Bidding: Politics, Persuasion and Resistance*) critically examined bidding and the benefits and costs of hosting mega events. They stressed growing ethical and governance issues, and documented increasing opposition. *Circus Maximus*, the book by sport-economist Andrew Zimbalist (2015a), makes it clear that bidding on mega events is an 'economic gamble', and points specifically to the numerous 'white elephants' that were no-doubt trumpeted as 'benefits' when bids were made. There is more on Zimbalist's analysis in Chapter 8.

It is true that a lot of infrastructure gets built because of mega events, but it always has to be asked if the event was a catalyst in getting a necessary improvement done, or were the improvements a cost of hosting the event? Sometimes the costs of unnecessary developments are claimed to be benefits, which is obfuscation. Another obvious legacy on the landscape of cities has been a myriad of 'white elephant' facilities that are too large or single-purpose for viable after-use, and too expensive to keep operational.

6.3 Events and the use of public spaces

As animators, planned events have the potential to turn busy streets and passive parks into public celebration spaces, albeit temporarily. The animation of spaces through events is also a feature of housing and commercial projects, many of which incorporate design features to ensure that event-led animation can be permanent. Use of public space for events is often a matter of public policy, but there is also pressure from many groups in society to gain access for their own celebrations, demonstrations, exhibitions or games.

In reviewing this phenomenon, Andrew Smith (2016; 2017) examined the pros and cons, and pointed to a relatively new issue – making money from public spaces. The book is entitled *Events in the City: Using Public Spaces as Event Venues* (2016) in which Smith talks about 'the urbanization of events'. Public space is both 'performed and consumed' by this trend, and it can be witnessed especially in historical cities and precincts where the backdrop of public squares, heritage buildings and monuments are a large part of the attraction. A related trend is to use sport events, such as marathons and bicycle races, as media for showcasing cities and countryside, with the Tour de France as a prime example, and this reflects modern practices in place marketing and branding.

While there are likely to be a number of stakeholder groups to consult in such examples, the views of residents must be paramount in assessing related impacts. It is one thing to find out that they are opposed and angry, and another to demonstrate that serious harm has been done to the environment. Exclusion from using public spaces at specific event times can be controversial, with one group of users lining up against another, but are they really harmed by the occasional event or is the community enriched?

6.3.1 Life cycle considerations

Change is constant. That means impacts have to be measured and evaluated in a way that reflects stages of development, or the ways in which change is being managed. When an event plays a role in urban renewal, its impacts will be different – some intentionally and some not – ten years later. Goals for a start-up event have to be different from those for a well-established event, and so do impact methods and measures. If an event can last ten or twenty years or more it might become a permanent institution, and therefor it is expected to play important roles in various aspects of community life.

As mentioned earlier, the legacy of mega events has often been that of sport and other facilities that have no practical after-use and consume a lot of money to maintain them, pay off debt, and eventually de-commission them. This kind of all-too-common life cycle represents a failure of governance. In such cases comprehensive IA and evaluation is not produced, nor is it wanted by those responsible. (See also the discussion of life cycles in 3.5.2 and the case study ending this chapter).

6.4 Subjects and objects

Events, venues and tourism require development, and that alters the built environment (being the 'object' of IA). The first consideration should be how these changes affect residents, and in this chapter we start by looking at individuals and families (the 'subject' of IA). Because many of the impacts of changes to our built environment will be social, ecological cultural and economic, and are covered in the other chapters, the approach taken in Figure 6.1 (A-H) is to suggest goals pertaining to what benefits should be pursued from changes in the built environment, and what should be prevented or mitigated when the built environment is altered by development and events. Sample methods for IA, with some key indicators, are suggested.

6.4.1 Individuals and families (residents)

Residents feel the impacts of events and tourism on their living environment, sometimes in direct ways when venues are built and events held nearby, and sometimes indirectly through changes to traffic, land use or amenities.

Figure 6.1 (A): Individuals and Families

Sample goals for built environment impacts on individuals & families (residents)	Sample methods and indicators
Venues are to provide needed leisure opportunities to residents; in a tourism context, hosts and guests are to equitably share spaces	Resident and stakeholder consultations & surveys: assess issues, satisfaction levels, complaints, needs
Infrastructure is to improve essential services to residents	Focus on family use of events and venues, and interactions with tourists
Prevent displacement of the poor; add to the affordable housing supply	Measure venue use trends (residents and tourists)
Animate public spaces & facilities with events	Analyse attendance & segmentation data from event organisers (host and guest interactions; conflicts)
Help prevent social/cultural exclusion in spaces and venues through design and access standards	Conduct expert review of spaces and venues (design, use, contribution to liveability)
Enhance residential and work-related amenities (e.g., parks, leisure facilities, art, design)	Measure new and improved housing, recreation facilities & infrastructure for residents, and housing deficiencies
Use design and events to help create safer communities	Monitor crime rates, types, locations
Minimise disturbances to residential and work places (e.g., noise, pollution, congestion)	Conduct business surveys: are they catering to residents or tourists?
	Analyse local government data and professional opinions on the adequacy of essential services for residents (police, fire, building inspection, design, planning, infrastructure)

6.4.2 Groups and sub-cultures

Places and venues of importance to groups and sub-cultures can be altered by events and tourism, or they can be removed from public use altogether. Community associations, representing residents in particular areas, will undoubtedly want to be involved in planning and evaluation.

Figure 6.1 (B): Groups and sub-groups

Sample goals for built environment impacts on groups and sub-cultures	Sample methods and indicators
Venues and events should be required to host diverse interest groups and sub-cultures: both their organization and activities/events Provide safe places for groups to meet and celebrate Prevent or minimize displacement of group activities from public spaces Manage event portfolios to include a variety of iconic events targeted at special-interest groups (both residents and tourists)	Stakeholder consultations and surveys: determine who uses venues and spaces, and for what purposes Engage special-interest, community and cultural groups in planning, design and operation of important spaces and venues and in event production

6.4.3: Events and event organisations

Every event needs a venue, whether indoors or outside, and this ensures a direct link with various aspects of the event environment. As users of built venues, whether arenas, stadia, theatres or convention centres, some of their main impacts (after construction) will stem from changes to land use and traffic patterns surrounding the venue. There will be differences between special-purpose venues, like sport fields, and multi-use facilities, but all facilities should be subject to regulations and various health, safety and sustainability standards. The bigger the venue, the larger the external impacts are likely to be, including traffic, noise, light, litter and even crime. As users of outdoor sites, such as parks and streets, urban plazas and natural areas, events can cause damage to ecological processes as well as to the atmosphere and aesthetics of communities.

Figure 6.1 (C): Goals for events and event organisations

Sample goals for built-environment impacts on events and event organisations	Sample methods and indicators
Events and venues will adopt design and sustainability standards to enhance aesthetics and liveability in their communities and in the natural environment Events within managed portfolios are to be positive forces in achieving goals for sustainable, creative and smart cities	Conduct periodic surveys of event organisations to obtain data on: venues used; issues that have been raised with stakeholders, and steps taken to improve the living environment.

6.4.4 Businesses

Business investment tends to concentrate in tourism districts and around major destinations like arenas and other event venues. This type of clustering can be planned, but it also happens naturally and can lead to displacement of resident-oriented retailing. Venues and event tourism should lead to more opportunities for small and local businesses, but that kind of development has to be facilitated through leveraging strategies. The business community should be collaborators in improvements to the physical environment, and individual business owners should be asked to partner with design improvements, public art and heritage conservation.

Figure 6.1 (D): Goals for impacts on businesses

Sample goals for built environment impacts on businesses	Sample methods and indicators
Minimise displacement of local businesses when new venues are built	Monitor trends in business start-ups & failures (focusing on preservation of resident-oriented retailing and services)
Prevent over-concentration of business development in congested areas	
Tourist Business Districts to be planned and designed with events as animators, and to facilitate equitable host-guest interactions	Assess business involvement in events (as organisers, sponsors, or suppliers)
Ensure that residential neighbourhoods retain adequate retailing and services	Conduct visitor surveys: compare attendance by residents and tourists - is there a balance?
Involve local businesses in planning and design around venues and tourism development	Ask stakeholders to map and evaluate the physical appearance of their communities & business districts, how they function, and needed improvements
Facilitate the restoration and re-use of old buildings and sites for commercial purposes (especially in tourism business districts)	

6.4.5 Communities and cities

At this level we are interested in what local governments can do with events and tourism to improve the built environment. The 'community' in this context are the places in which people live and work. Many of the negative impacts are felt at the neighbourhood level, but tourism and large-scale events can have major impacts on downtown areas and the districts surrounding major venues.

Events, culture, sport and business venues are frequently instruments of urban renewal, development and re-positioning strategies so they have to be integrated with a variety of other policy fields. For the goal of achieving a sustainable city, events must play a positive role in diverse strategies ranging from food-in-the-city to reduction of carbon emissions.

Some of the goals in 6.1 (E) are similar to those for individuals and families, as it is often the local authority that has jurisdiction and the means to set and achieve the goals.

6.4.6 Tourist destinations

Tourism organisations, and the industry, have a vested interest in maintaining the image and reality of safe, convenient, attractive and liveable environments. It is worth remembering that most of the world's tourism takes place between cities, and many resort areas are urban in nature. Cities are destinations for all forms of tourism that link with events: cultural, business, sport and entertainment.

Figure 6.1 (E): Goals for impacts on communities and cities

Sample goals for built environment impacts on communities and cities	Sample methods and indicators
Venues and infrastructure to assist in community renewal/ development by helping to attract & hold families, workers, businesses	Monitor business & land use change & activity patterns
Prevent traffic congestion, noise and loss of amenity in residential areas	Consult community groups regularly to identify local issues and needs
Minimise traffic volumes and avoid congestion associated with events	Enforce maximum decibel readings at the event and various distances from the event/tourist zone
Maximise use of public transit and shuttle services for events	Prevent excessive traffic in residential areas
Provide all communities with access to nature, recreation space	Obtain resident and police input on crime and safety
Enhance urban design and aesthetics	Measure resident and other stake-holder perceptions and attitudes toward redevelopment
Use events to rejuvenate or redevelop areas	Conduct expert reviews of policies, strategies and trends
Form public-private partnerships for development	
Improve the tax base	
Require sustainable event practices and certification	
Conserve heritage buildings, archaeological sites and symbolic places	
Integrate monuments, galleries and museums into the community (many of which host events and are tourist attractions)	

Figure 6.1 (F): Goals for impacts on tourist destinations

Sample goals for built environment impacts on tourist destinations	Sample methods and indicators
Enhance potential for event tourism through urban planning and design	Visitor surveys to measure perceptions and satisfaction
Facilitate mutually beneficial host-guest interactions	Market area surveys to assess image, reputation and positioning vis a vis other destinations
Make more efficient use of public facilities and spaces to the benefit of residents	
Improve destination competitiveness linked to design, liveability, and overall attractiveness	Resident surveys to monitor facility use and satisfaction trends

6.4.7 Politics and government

Political interest in events, venues and tourism has never been higher. Many politicians want to be associated with big events and projects, and are pro-development – but they cannot ignore the costs and risks. Over-tourism, high costs for bidding and building, debt financing and negative impacts on the environment generate opposition. When it comes to the built environment there is a common belief that all communities must have a range of events and venues, and that major cities must have the biggest and best – this reflects both the legitimation of events in popular culture and civic boosterism. Cities are competing for publicity, investment, attracting and retaining skilled and creative people, and in general satisfying consumer demands.

How decisions are made becomes critical, especially if a plebiscite is part of the process. In the early stages of a bid or development proposal impacts will be discussed, but probably without supporting data and analysis. This is the time to get IA integrated in the planning process, throughout implementation, and part of post-event or post-construction evaluation.

The rationality of political decision-making always has to be questioned. If the ideological foundation is clear, as in a bias towards free enterprise versus socialism, or perhaps a belief in private investment as opposed to government funding, then at least people know what their government is inclined to do. In all cases, stakeholders should be insisting on a rational planning and development process with full benefit and cost forecasts, a monitoring system, and key impact indicators in place.

Figure 6.1 (G): Goals for impacts on politics and government

Built environment: goals for impacts on politics and government	Sample methods and indicators
Governments at all levels should adopt clear, standard policies on how decisions are to be made regarding mega events and major venues, including the integration of impact assessment and evaluation processes	Review public documents, political speeches and the media for the ideological basis of tourism and event-related policies
Stakeholders, the media and lobby groups must hold politicians to public accountability; IA reports have to be freely available	Assess the political decision-making process for events, venues and tourism as to its comprehensiveness and transparency

6.4.8 The nation

Most of the political and legal considerations of built-environment impacts occur at the local and regional levels, but national governments often have urban policies, funding programmes and regulations that affect events, venues and tourism. When it comes to mega events, the support of the host nation is usually a prerequisite to making a bid. That provides the opportunity for setting conditions, such as the requirement for consultations, impact assessment and evaluation criteria.

Nations use events and their modern venues to showcase 'progress', reflect their ideology (i.e., events as propaganda), and support trade and investment strategies. This has resulted in the world's biggest events going to countries that can get away with making major financial commitments without having to subject the process to transparent public accounting – in other words, democratic principles are ignored or not even part of the equation.

Figure 6.1 (H): Goals for the nation

Sample goals for built environment impacts on the nation	Sample methods and indicators
Ensure there is full, transparent, public accountability for all major venue and event investments Require IA to be integrated in all decisions	Senior-government policies on event bidding, and on support for venues and tourism should be accessible to all citizens & reviewed regularly

6.5 Place making and place marketing

'*Place making*' has a number of connotations, starting in urban design and planning. The website Rethinkurban.com defines it this way:

> "*Placemaking is the process through which we work together to shape our public spaces. Rooted in community-based participation, Placemaking involves the planning, design, management and programming of shared use spaces. More than just designing spaces, Placemaking brings together diverse people (including professionals, elected officials, residents, and businesses) to improve a community's cultural, economic, social and ecological situation.*"

Richards (2017, p. 10) took a broader perspective specific to the eventful city, saying:

> "*In summary, therefore, the more holistic approaches to placemaking that have emerged and which events have now become a part of, consist of three important elements: the physical city itself, the lived experience of place that is shared among the stakeholders or users of the city and the symbolic imaginings of the city that are projected through city images and brands.*"

Derrett (2003; 2016) discussed the roles of festivals in creating a 'sense of place', referring to the various meanings held by people regarding their communities and natural environments. People form emotional and tangible attachments to places because of these meanings, and attachments can led to a sense of stewardship that embodies sustainability principles and a sense of community that generates celebrations and other collaborative action that can be called community development. 'Place identity' can refer to the meanings held by residents, including social representations that emerge from promotions, media coverage and communal events, and embodying ideas about social justice and inclusion or exclusion. Events take at least part of their identity from the unique combinations of setting and meanings attached to them, and this is paramount in the case of permanent Hallmark Events.

'*Place marketing*' is what tourism organisations do to attract visitors and events, but in a wider context it is everything cities, destinations and countries do to create an attractive brand and compete in various international marketplaces – including bidding on events. The roles of events in place marketing have become more and more important, going well beyond a tourism orientation to encompass (re)positioning, combatting negative publicity, and building or reinforcing a destination or city brand (Richards, 20217). The interests of event and venue sponsors, corporate partners and the media are substantial.

A number of key terms are defined in Figure 6.2, both for place making and place marketing, together with suggested methods and indicators for impact assessment. Positioning, Image, Reputation and Branding are all inter-related, and each presents challenges for evaluators.

Figure 6.2: Place making, place marketing, positioning, image, reputation and branding

Key terms	Suggested IA methods and indicators
Place making: originally referred to the collaborative design and use of city spaces; events can contribute to place meaning through experiences and symbolism by providing collective experiences of value that foster a positive image and place attachment.	The effectiveness of place making efforts should be assessed longitudinally or retrospectively. This is critical in evaluating event portfolio management. Residents' feelings of pride and attachment are the primary consideration and will have to be measured subjectively. Identity requires more in-depth evaluation of the meanings attached to places and events by all stakeholders.
Place marketing: Cities, regions, countries, and destinations engage in image communication and messages about brand values to specific target-market segments. Events often figure prominently in these strategies, particularly to convey a positive image of a place in which to visit, invest or live.	The effectiveness of place marketing has to be evaluated longitudinally, through various targeted surveys that measure awareness and respect for the brand and brand values, reputation vis a vis competitors, images held, and intent to visit or invest. Expert panels can be used to evaluate relative success in overall place marketing. Rankings in various media can be an indicator (such as top 100 food tourism destinations, or world's best sport destinations) but knowing their criteria is important and therefore rankings can potentially be manipulated.
Positioning: Conveying unique selling and/or value propositions in order to create a distinctive and attractive image in the minds of people, relative to competitors. Cities with many popular events, for example, can claim to be festival or sport 'capitals'. 'World Cities' tend to have the biggest and best venues and events. 'Iconic' events are positioned to hold symbolic value for special-interest groups. 'Hallmark' events are positioned as permanent traditions with institutional status.	Consumers, event owners, investors and other targeted groups can be asked to complete a positioning grid relative to competitors. Various attributes are ranked, such as "a great place to attend festivals". For events, thought has to be given to Unique Selling Propositions or the specific reasons for choosing the event over others, such as price, convenience, and quality. Authenticity and uniqueness are key USPs for both places and events.

Image: In marketing, image is a controlled viewpoint set by the marketers. In place marketing it is necessary to convey a desired image (one that is positive and attractive, but customized to particular segments). But this might not correspond with the image people have of a place or an event, and this requires research and corrective action.	Images and messages must be received, understood and be influential; respondents should discuss the impressions, emotions or messages they perceive from communications Image studies can use methods similar to positioning grids, comparing perceived images against competitors Longer-term changes in images and positioning have to be monitored through repeated surveys or focus groups.
Reputation: A social evaluation, using specific criteria related to the quality, or characteristics of a place or event as perceived by others. Reputation can be enhanced through holding successful events, or events can be used to combat a negative reputation. Major threats to the reputation of a place or event are crime, poor quality products and services, high prices, unattractive environments, disease, terrorism, and pollution, all of which can be exasperated by hostile media reports.	Content analysis of media reports, & monitoring trends in social media can reveal damage or threats to reputation Measuring the monetary value of media coverage (advertising equivalence value) is not as important as 'reach' (i.e., how many readers or viewers there are in key segments) and influence (are people's image, attitudes and intentions altered) Analysis of social media can be done quantitatively (using, for example Google Analytics) or qualitatively through netnography Expert panels can compare image and reputation with competitors for an impartial evaluation; report on changes over time
Branding: Branding starts with vision, incorporates the desired identity and brand values of a place or event, then develops a uniform approach to communicating those values. Branding mechanisms include logos and design standards for all communications, specific slogans and images that communicate brand values, and co-branding with sponsors and corporate partners, or between events and destinations. Consumers often chose products and services from known and trusted brands, so maintaining a positive reputation is crucial.	Brand values have to be communicated and correctly interpreted by the targets, so specific input is needed from target segments on awareness of the brand, what it stands for, and how it compares to others

6.5.1 Image change

Image enhancements can be short lived, even when mega-events provide a major boost in publicity. As recommended by Boo and Busser (2006), longitudinal research is needed when evaluating image and the effects of events on destination image. Longitudinal studies by Ritchie and Smith (1991) and Mihalik

(2000) demonstrate the necessity for periodic reinforcement of image, and point out the need for longitudinal research on all related matters including positioning, reputation and branding.

Richards and Palmer (2010, p. 378) reported on results of periodic assessments of city images conducted by the ATLAS surveys. An important observation made by those researchers was that new destinations and smaller, less-known places stand to gain the most, and this observation has also been made about the effects of mega events in general. Placing events in world cities will do little to increase awareness, and related images are likely to be already well formed.

6.5.2 Media management and impact assessment

Media management is a vital tool in all forms of place and event marketing, and it refers to how all the modes of communications are used in marketing, and how media people are treated. The general aim is to receive fair, and ideally positive coverage (we can call that the *output*) which changes image, reputation, and positioning in desired ways and strengthens the brand (these are the *outcomes* or *impacts*).

Media management should involve being proactive with the media (as they also want a rewarding event experience) as well as monitoring all media coverage and reacting to issues or reputation damage. The target segments include media employees, residents, known and potential customers, and other stakeholders such as event owners, sponsors and advertisers. It is now essential to develop specific strategies for social media, and this requires an online presence that reinforces brand values.

There have to be media-management goals pertaining to residents as well (see Figure 6.3), including fostering civic pride, positive attitudes and sustaining demand for events. Politicians can be influenced by the media, and political support can be translated into more effective event portfolios and venue development. The business sector advertises in all the media, therefore they want to see positive coverage of events and tourism, and perhaps they can be induced to undertake more sponsorship and collaborative marketing.

Potential tourists are a major consideration in media management. Events and place-marketing organisations, including DMOs, want to have a positive image translated into demand and loyalty (repeat visits). Therefore the impacts they want to see demonstrated pertain to sustainable competitiveness and/or growth. Positioning and branding strategies have the same long-term goal.

Figure 6.3: Media goals, methods and indicators

Sample media goals	Sample methods	Sample indicators
Maximize positive image effects for the local area and the country (while combatting negative news and images)	Commissioned evaluations of social and mass media coverage Feedback from event attendees, residents and other stakeholders Reports from expert panels in target market areas or by reference to social media interest groups	Reach (what coverage is accessible by target segments?) Coverage in all media types that cover the event (TV, radio, press, social) Evaluate content and tone (positive or negative? what is featured?) Trend analysis; measure changes in awareness, image & reputation within target markets Surveys to measure images held and attitudes among attendees, residents and other stakeholders - towards events and the destination or host city Measure awareness and positive perception of specific images, brand values and messages conveyed through the event and related media coverage Assess changes in intention to travel, demand and loyalty; changes relative to competitors
Effectively manage the media	Direct feedback from media Reports from the event's or destination's media management team Monitoring of social media	Measure the number and types of accredited national and international media attending the event Surveys and focus groups to reveal perceptions and satisfaction of media personnel, bloggers Quantify the numbers and types of reports, broadcasts, and other communications that convey desired images and messages (e.g., logos, stories, images); have expert panels review the data for impartial evaluations
Produce broadcast and social-media content to enhance the event experience and generate favourable publicity	Feedback from target audiences Expert opinion	Attendee satisfaction ratings Positive effects reported by experts
Monitor and evaluate social media content and effects	Commissioned studies by media monitors	Positive coverage and image formation

6.5.3 Methods for assessing media impacts

The most common evaluation method is a poor surrogate measure. 'Advertising Equivalence Value' (AEV) assumes that all media reports have been purchased and the overall value can therefore be measured in monetary terms. But this reveals nothing about the tone of coverage (good, bad, indifferent), its reach (specific to high-value target segments) nor its long-term impacts on loyalty or repeat visits.

An alternative is to rely on experts or expert panels to provide feedback on media coverage and its effects from specific areas or for specific target market segments. For example, experts in travel industry packaging or airlines can be asked to comment on how events are received in specific cities, and whether or not there is an observable impact on trips offered and taken. Trends need to be established, and changes linked to marketing efforts.

Increasingly events and destinations produce their own media for which special evaluation methods are required. Three broad types have to be considered:

1   Productions for broadcast through normal media outlets (such as background stories, travelogues, and photo opportunities)

2   Those for on-site consumption, to augment the experience (e.g. fan zones)

3   Those for social media to foster positive interaction before, during and after the event (e.g., between organisers and potential customers; among attendees; among communities of interest)

Some of the major effects of social media can be measured through visitor surveys that include questions to obtain respondents' awareness and evaluation of marketing and communications and of course how it influenced their decisions. Real-time website and social-media monitoring, including dealing with questions and complaints, is gaining acceptance by event organisers.

Social media coverage that is beyond the control of organisers needs to be evaluated in different ways, and the assistance of media or marketing companies can be obtained (at a cost) to monitor key e-zines, blogs, and person-to-person sites for the volume and tone of discussions. Expert panels can be formed to provide subjective evaluations of media coverage and effects in key target markets defined by demographics or special interests.

6.6 Case study

The following case study discusses the theoretical perspectives of resilience, evolutionary paths, life-cycles, and events as path-shaping moments in the context of the development of a ski resort. When reading the case, consider how these ideas link to the Forces-Pressure-State-Impact-Response and Theory of Change models. Note specific references to innovation, image (or 'self representation'), sustainability, economic and built-environment impacts.

Explaining growth dynamics of resort areas: human agency, pro-active and reactive responses to trends in ski resort development in Vail, Colorado

By: Rudi Hartmann, Department of Geography and Environmental Sciences, University of Colorado Denver (rudi.hartmann@ucdenver.edu)

Resort areas, including ski resorts, are dynamic entities in the present-day tourism landscape. They represent tourist destinations which have undergone or undergo change. Frequently, the size and extent of the resort areas as well as the populations residing there have increased with distinct economic, social and environmental implications for the area in question. The purpose of this case study is to examine the growth dynamics of resort areas and to assess the impact these changes have had over time.

How have scholars in the interdisciplinary tourism study field tried to explain growth and change in/of tourist destination areas? What are viable models and approaches in the explanation of the growth dynamics? It is argued here that three models and explanatory approaches have been widely used in the examination of resort areas and tourist destinations. The most common model and framework in the study of the evolution of resort areas and destinations is the *Tourism Area Life Cycle (TALC)* introduced by Richard Butler in his seminal article 'The Concept of a Tourist Area Cycle of Evolution' (1980). Butler's TALC model, with parallels to the 'product life cycle' in market research, has been applied and modified in many case studies as well as critically appraised (see, for instance, Butler, 2006a and 2006b, and Brouder et al., 2017).

A second more recently applied theoretical framework is based on the notion of *resilience* of resort and tourist destination areas. Resilience thinking has been introduced across many disciplines studying the capacity of natural and social systems to absorb disturbances while maintaining its functions. Resilience has been described "as a theory of change, a new development paradigm, a defining metaphor for our era, and a buzzword" (Brown, 2016, p. 5). Recently, the discussed adaptive capacity cycles in resilience have also been examined in the tourism study field (see, for instance, Lew & Cheer, 2017; Cheer and Lew, 2017).

A third approach to the study of growth and change of tourism places comes from evolutionary economic geography (EEG). In the analysis of the evolution of tourist destinations the EEG approach employs the path metaphor. Here, the concepts of *path creation* (with important *moments* that shape and shift the path), *path plasticity* and *path dependence* are distinguished (see, for instance, Sanza-Ibanez, Wilson and Clave, 2017). This case study applies the EEG approach to explaining the evolution of Vail and Vail Valley in the High Country of Colorado.

Vail, Colorado: A leading ski area and highly frequented tourist destination area

In 1962, Vail started as a new ski area and ski town, as a recreational environment used mainly during the winter season. The appeal of this new destination area in the High Country of Colorado was closely tied to the increasing popularity of skiing and ski racing in the 1960s/70s/80s. By the mid-1970s Vail ranked as the leading ski area in North America (by size and visitation numbers). In 1989, 1999 and in 2015 Vail and Beaver Creek, Vail Resorts' second ski area along Vail Valley, hosted the FIS World Alpine Ski Championships. Vail's transformation from a small attractive ski area with an alpine inspired village to an upscale four season resort environment with an extended down valley stretching now over fifty miles (70 km) is discussed in greater detail elsewhere (Hartmann, 2006; Hartmann, 2017a; and Hartmann, 2017b).

Application of the path metaphor to the evolution of Vail Valley

It is argued here that the World Alpine Ski Championships 1989, 1989 and 2015 were important *moments* in the evolution of Vail and Vail Valley, as they represented path-shaping evolutionary inflection points. The two-week high-powered, state-of-the-art events brought fundamental changes and challenges for the host community each time. The 1989 championships gave Vail broad international recognition for the first time in its history. The 1999 championships with the creation of the innovative 'Birds of Prey' race course helped to establish a new annual world cup event for Vail Valley. Whereas Beaver Creek could only provide a temporary basis for the 1989 events, a carefully crafted, posh village center was put in place in 1999. The 2015 championships saw crucial changes in mountain operations and the hospitality sector as well as revolutionized media relations. In a wider sense, the 2015 championships reformulated Vail Valley's self-representation (Hartmann, 2017a).

While preparing for a new ski season and forthcoming world cup races are part of a competitive routine to be performed each year (conceptually speaking, an expression of a *path dependence*), world alpine ski championships represent events with the potential of *path creation*. They left an innovative mark on the path Vail took, versus merely following established common practices industry wide.

The financial impacts of the three mega sports events in 1989, 1999 and 2015 held in the mountain environment of Colorado are hard to pin down in pecuniary terms, though. The reality is quite complex. While the majority of the Vail service enterprises and institutions gained from the two week events with more than a dozen race competitions and a large number of athletes staying in town, other Vail Valley businesses may have experienced financial losses since a part of the general public avoided the region which would otherwise be visited in high numbers during the ski season. The economic impact of the 1989 Championships was assessed at $55 million, with additional tax revenues of $1.45 million for Eagle County (Rosall Remmen and Cares, 1989). It can be argued that the investments made on and off the mountain in the preparation of the championships have had even a greater and lasting impact as they helped to 'put' Vail and Beaver Creek, Colorado 'on the map'. Regarding the 2015 events, $2 billion in renovation were invested, for instance, during the years leading up to the Championships. It has been estimated by the organizers that the 2015 Championships would cause "the flow of $120 million to the region". Internally, hosting mega events telecasted worldwide has resulted in waves of modernization in town like local initiatives of staying on the cutting edge in communication (Hartmann, 2017a).

Photo 6.1: Ski race at Vail

Vail, Colorado hosted the world alpine ski championship mega events three times. Only one other ski resort town, St. Moritz, Switzerland, was given the same honor within the last fifty years. While Vail & Beaver Creek's resort development accelerated each time markedly and had a lasting impact, Vail Valley missed out on hosting Olympic races. In a special election 1972, the Colorado voter rejected Denver's successful bid for the Winter Olympics 1976, a first in Olympic history (see Childers 2012). In the U.S., Winter Olympics were held in upstate New York (Lake Placid 1932 and 1980), in California (Squaw Valley 1960) and in Utah (2002). A later second Denver bid also fell short. Thus, Vail never had an 'Olympic moment'.

Root causes for change: pro-active decisions and reactive responses

Far-reaching changes in tourist destinations including *moments* as important inflection points in their evolution do not happen by chance. Frequently, they are the result of deliberate action. It is argued here that human agency in a given social setting (such as in a resort community) has to be examined for the explanation of change.

Human agency entails purposeful, goal-directed activities in the form of intentional actions of individuals, members of a group or groups within the context or limits of a given social structure (such as entrepreneurs in a resort town). Intentional actions made by individuals or a group can be distinguished as pro-active decisions or reactive responses.

A pro-active approach to change is often trying to capitalize on a potential future opportunity or to avoid a potential future threat. By contrast, reactive change occurs when an organization makes changes in its practices after some threat has already occurred and materialized or a given chance or opportunity for future development has passed.

It is argued here that the evolution of Vail/Vail Valley is marked by important pro-active decisions as well as reactive responses. From its very beginnings to more recent phases in the evolution of Vail and of the Valley as a whole a number of decisions stand out. In the following, the selected decisions are shown in chronological order in a scheme; they are grouped into a) pro-active decisions and b) reactive responses (see Figure 6.4).

In the following paragraphs several phases will be discussed including the establishment of Vail as a ski area and as a ski and resort town as well as more recent initiatives by Vail Associates/Vail Resorts, the owner and operator of the Vail and Beaver Creek ski areas in Vail Valley.

The initial situation for a new ski area venture in the High Country of Colorado was very much limited as preference was given to already existing towns and population centers (mostly from the mining area) by the National Forest Service, a federal agency with control over the lands used for new developments. Thus, the Vail venture was forced to respond to a challenging set-up. Despite the disadvantages, individual actions proceeded, with the discovery and eventual claim of the then unnamed mountain from 1957 until December 1962 when the new Vail Ski Area was opened to the public.

A similar pro-active decision was made with the planning and establishment of the Town of Vail 1966, of a second base of the ski area in 1968 and further expansions of the skiable terrain on the mountain which would become the leading ski area in the U.S. within a dozen years.

Photo 6.2: Summer attractions – farmer's market at Vail

Reactive responses were made in 1976 when a gondola accident with four fatalities occurred (with the closure of the ski area and an overhaul of the safety rules for uphill transportation on Vail Mountain) as well as after two snow-parched ski seasons in 1976/77 and 1980/81, with the introduction and implementation of a mountain wide snow-making system.

Pro-Active and Reactive Decisions in the Making of Vail Valley

Pro-Active	Reactive
	1950s/60s: Many Applications for New Ski Area Ventures in Colorado Restrictive Permit Policies by the National Forest Service
In March 1957: Unnamed (Vail) Mountain Discovered/Claimed by Pete Seibert & Earl Eaton A First 'Moment' in the Evolution of 'Vail' Seibert and Eaton Form Investor Group (Eventually Named "Vail Associates")/Buy up Land 1958/59 After First Rejection of Permit Application 1959 Political Intervention/Permit Granted Development of Ski Area/Installation Lifts & Gondola Opening of Vail Ski Area in December 1962	
Vail Village Base Area/Town of Vail Established 1963 – 1966	
Enlargement of Vail Ski Area, with Second Base Area 'Lionshead' Established in 1968/69 Vail Becomes the Largest/Most Visited Ski Area in the U.S. by the early/mid-1970s	
	Winter Olympics 1976 given to Denver/Vail, but Colorado Voters Reject Bid in Election 1972/Beaver Creek, Vail's Second Ski Area, Delayed
	March 1976 Gondola Accident with Four Fatalities/Ski Area Closed
	Snow Parched Winter Season 1976/77: Grappling with not enough Snow on the Mountain & Decision for Snow Making Equipment
	Late-1970s: Response to Carrying Capacity Problems in Town
Application for 1989 World Alpine Ski Championships: Vail Hosts the Two Week Mega Sports Event, a 'Moment' in the Evolution of Vail Valley	
Mid-90s: Restructuring of Vail Associates as Vail Resorts Inc (Public Company Owned by Wall Street Firm) Decision for Continued Growth Policies Including Category III Expansion of Skiable Terrain	
	Defensive Response to Public Criticism of the Resort Company's Expansion on the Mountain & Intrusion into Wildlife Habitats
	Earth Liberation Front's Arson Attack in October 1998
Formulation of 'Bigger Vail is a Better Vail' Goal Wins the Support of the Vail Valley Resort Community after the Arson Attack Another 'Moment' for Vail & Beaver Creek: the 1999 World Alpine Ski Championships	
	Slow Response to New Trends in Environmentally Friendly Mountain Management Delayed Implementation of Programs
2006 - 2014: New Leadership and Transition to Changed Goals Introduction of Vail Resorts' 'Epic' Brand and Embrace of a New Sustainability Philosophy	
Town of Vail Implementation of Sustainable Programs	
2015 World Alpine Ski Championships: A 'Mini'-Olympic Event for Vail & Beaver Creek	
Vail Resorts Becomes a Global Resort Company, with the Acquisition of Many More Ski Areas Collaboration with other Corporate Companies and Non-Profit-Organizations Formulation of New Environmental Goals for All Resorts under the Management of Vail Resorts	
	Slow Response to Global Warming/Climate Change

Figure 6.4: Pro-active and reactive decisions in the evolution of Vail 1957 - 2018

It is also maintained that Vail's run for hosting the World Alpine Ski Championships was a pro-active decision resulting in three important moments in the evolution of Vail and Vail Valley. Recently, Vail Resorts have made several pro-active decisions with the introduction of the new Epic brand, the decision to embrace a sustainable development philosophy and to assume a leading role for the corporation in the further globalization of the ski resort industry. On the other hand, decisions were very slow and tentative in response to climate change.

Conclusions

Vail/Vail Valley has seen distinct periods in its evolution; some were steered or guided by pro-active decisions while others marked reactive responses to existing problems in the ski area. The resort community and Vail Associates/Vail Resorts, the operator of the Vail and Beaver Creek ski areas, responded frequently with delay to new and innovative trends in ski area management initiated somewhere else. On the other hand, there were several *moments* in the evolution of Vail/Vail Valley where the local decision makers opted to pioneer new management approaches and went ahead with applications for mega ski events that would spur change and secured Vail's leading role among mountain resorts nationwide and globally. While Vail's strategic position in the further globalization of the resort industry has been recently strengthened, there is a lack in decision making regarding global warming and changing conditions for winter sports recreation in the High Country of Colorado.

Study questions

1 Use the FPSIR model to explain how events and tourism affect the built environment and in turn residents.

2 Give specific examples of how events, venue development and tourism have been used in urban development, renewal and (re)positioning; what are the equity issues?

3 Animation of public spaces is a frequent goal of cities, but it has costs and benefits. What are the issues and the potential solutions?

4 Compare place making and place marketing from the point of view of event producers.

5 How are image, reputation, and branding incorporated into place marketing? What are the roles played by events?

6 Compare social and mass media in terms of how they can influence the image of an event and a destination, from the perspectives of residents and potential tourists.

Recommended additional readings and sources

McGillivray, D. & Turner, D. (2018). *Event Bidding: Politics, Persuasion and Resistance.* London: Routledge.

Smith, A. (2012). *Events and Urban Regeneration: The strategic use of events to revitalise cities.* London: Routledge.

Smith, A. (2016). *Events in the City: Using public spaces as event venues.* London: Routlege.

7 Ecological Impacts

Learning objectives

- ☐ Distinguish between nature, ecology, and ecological processes
- ☐ Know how to assess the 'greening' of events and 'event sustainability'
- ☐ Learn how events impact upon, and are affected by the natural environment and ecological processes
- ☐ Understand the subjects and objects of EIA for events and tourism
- ☐ Know how to plan and conduct and EIA

7.1 Introduction

In this chapter we examine nature, ecology and ecological impacts, as distinct from the impacts of events and tourism on the built or human environment. This brings sustainability to the fore, and that is a term that has to be examined carefully with reference to the 'greening' of events, different interpretations of the meaning of sustainability, and how this influences evaluation and impact assessment.

It is also very useful to examine environmental impacts ON events, as opposed to the impacts OF events. This involves an illustration of the event settings spectrum that identifies important variables related to the differences between indoor events and those situated in natural environments.

The subjects and objects of ecological impact assessment for events and tourism are examined in detail, presenting goals, methods and indicators that can be applied to the full range of 'subjects' – individuals and families or the entire nation.

The process of EIA follows the generic IA process model, with a number of special considerations. Methods include the Leopold Matrix, Forces-Pressures-State-Impact-Response model, and carbon and ecological footprint analysis.

7.2 Nature and ecology

People understand 'nature' as being in opposition to environments where human influences are obviously dominant. 'Nature' covers the entire physical world, including plants, animals, geomorphology and geology, but we can also speak of 'natural forces' such as climate and weather that influence everything humans do. Within the study of nature there is the science of 'ecology' which covers interactions between organisms and their environment, including species-to-species and human-environment interactions. Two specific terms have to be defined:

♦ *Ecosystem:* A community of species within a supporting environment. Ecosystems are open systems, dependent upon flows of energy and materials to sustain them; they are subject to external forces and are seldom static.

♦ *Ecological processes:* Underlying forces or 'drivers' affect ecological processes and result in changes or impacts. The processes we are interested in depend upon the situation. For major events or new arena construction we will want to examine drainage, soil erosion, ground water retention, wildlife movement and habitat, carbon and other emissions from machinery, construction waste and its disposal, etc., all with a view to the accumulating impact on the natural (and built) environments.

Research on the ecological impacts of events has lagged behind the other 'objects' of IA. Jones et al. (2008) in the report *Assessing the Environmental Impact of Special Events* (conducted for the Cooperative Research Centre on Sustainable Tourism, Australia) noted the following potential impacts and the reasons why so few events were doing EIAs or adhering to sustainability standards:

"The environmental impacts identified by organisers and/or hosts as the most important were transport (parking and traffic), waste management (general rubbish collection, litter, recycling and the provision of toilets) and noise. For six of the events, mention was also made of putting measures in place to promote environmental awareness. Environmental impacts/issues perceived as less significant included the provision of power, (for outdoor events), air pollution (smoke haze and vehicle emissions), management of environmental risk and the minimisation of environmental harm. However, the calculation of environmental impacts is more problematic, due to the limited availability of data for most of the perceived environmental impacts and the limited enthusiasm of both organisers and hosts to collect such data."

There has been a limited amount of research published on the potential effects of climate change on events (Jones et al., 2006) and the influence of environmental values on events (Kim et al., 2006). However, a number of books on greening and the sustainability of events are available (e.g., Jones, 2018).

7.2.1 Sustainability and the greening of events

The sustainable events movement is a very positive development, although there is little evidence to demonstrate the extent of compliance, the cost implications, or the results for cities or regions. Certainly there is enough advice available, and examples to learn from, to enable every event organiser, regulator and facilitator to insist that available standards be met, yet that is not widely the case. One can easily get cynical by pointing to the rather obvious attempts by some events, corporations and governments to paint tourism and events as green, or carbon neutral by touting 'offsets' such as planting trees somewhere, or by easy efforts like recycling. Clearly more must be done to ensure compliance, assuming that we want the sustainability paradigm (Getz, 2009) to be universally accepted.

A review of the literature suggests there are two sets of applicable sustainability goals:

1) *The greening of events* as an important path to make events and tourism more sustainable. Standards of practice are available (e.g., ISO 20121) and books such as *Sustainable Event Management* (Jones, 2018) provide the foundation. This quote is from Meegan Jones (2018):

> *"ISO 20121 … includes requirements for an event to establish a statement of purpose and values as it relates to the principles of sustainable development. This standard prescribes, as a minimum, the sustainable development principles of inclusivity, transparency, integrity and stewardship."*

2) *A positive force for sustainability:* In this theme events are encouraged to not just 'go green' but to become a positive force for sustainable development, especially within the policy framework of communities seeking to be green and sustainable (Getz, 2017). Events are viewed as important media for social marketing and as agents for change, a view that is in accord with Theory of Change approach to impact assessment. This set of goals covers both the natural and built environments and embodies the inter-related concepts of sustainable development and social responsibility.

The term 'sustainable', however, is often used to describe *sustainable development or growth* which reflects a very narrow bias on the part of those operating a business or marketing a destination. Some business people do understand the triple bottom line and support ecological-sustainability initiatives, but others only understand money and growth.

Steady-state sustainability

An economic interpretation of sustainability starts with capital and equates natural resources with monetary capital – that is, things to invest for growth and a return on investment. Conservation and social programmes might detract from this goal. But the 'steady state' approach to sustainability requires that resources are not depleted – all must be renewable.

Short-term thinking is the anathema of the sustainability paradigm, no matter what perspective or model one takes. If we can develop appropriate concepts and methods for cumulative, long-term impact assessment, dealing with port-folios and populations of events and closely-related matters of tourism and venues, then perhaps we will be able to deal with the really big questions. In the meantime we can start to apply sustainability criteria through evaluation and impact assessment.

It is my contention that sustainability, whether viewed as sustainable develop-ment or steady-state resource management, is a process, not an end point. Along the path we pursue *continuous improvement,* not being satisfied with achieving standards or being able to boast of 'greenness'. The essence of the Event Com-pass as an evaluation system, explained in the companion book, is that progress has to be demonstrated within a TBL format for impacts and within all the man-agement functions, and when goals are met new and higher ones are set. In this way evaluation, impact assessment and strategic planning are integrated.

7.3 Environmental impacts *of* and *on* events

Robert Case, in the book *Events and The Environment* (2013), distinguished between events in terms of their relationship to the environment, noting that environmental factors influence the event and events have impacts on the envi-ronment. Events can be classified in terms of their relationship with, and location relative to nature, with wilderness events at one end of the spectrum and indoor urban events at the other. There are also events held in natural environments that require built facilities, and outdoor events held in the middle of cities in parks and on streets. These relationships have to be considered when construct-ing an EIA.

In Figure 7.1 a spectrum of event settings is illustrated, together with key impact indicators. Indoor settings are at one end, and these should have perma-nent environmental management systems that cover events. At the other end are outdoor settings in natural areas that can pose a threat to ecological processes and therefor require the imposition of strict environmental management sys-tems. The impact variables shown in the diagram apply to all events across the spectrum as questions to be asked by impact assessors: do the events require construction? is the necessary infrastructure (services) available? how do users access the site? is the venue protected or sensitive in any way? what is the capac-ity of the site? are there activity restrictions? management systems in place? do people live there, or nearby? Other variables can be added, but the main point is this: the relationship between events and nature (or ecosystems) is not fixed, it is highly variable, and therefore environmental impact assessments must be adapted to the context.

Figure 7.1: Event settings spectrum and key impact variables

Event settings spectrum

Impact variables
Construction needed/allowed
Permanent infrastructure available
Accessibility; public transit
Sensitivity; protected status

Indoor venues
Management systems
in place for events

Attendance limits; capacity
Use/activity restrictions
Management systems in place
Residential context (high density or none)

Outdoors
Nothing built
Temporary
infrastructure only

Increasingly urban ← → **Increasingly natural**

Convention & exhibition centres	City parks & streets used occasionally for events	Rural event sites with some permanent infrastructure	Natural areas with some event infrastructure; limited development	Wilderness areas hosting occasional events; no permanent development or changes allowed
Theatres; concert halls				
Galleries ; museums				
Schools; community centres				

7.3.1 Mega event ecological impacts

Reflecting on the event settings spectrum, most mega events are urban and venue dependent, with substantial impacts on the built environment. However, given the view that mega is a relative term, it can be argued that in some rural and wild settings almost any event could raise capacity issues.

Agencies bidding on mega events generally must provide social and environmental impact statements and mitigation plans, but the greening of mega events is a controversial subject. How can events that are heavily dependent on major insfrastructure development and mass tourism be considered in any way green or sustainable? C.M. Hall (2012) discussed mega-events in this context, including the Olympic's requirements on environmental sustainability and concluded (p. 128) "The small and slow is a beautiful approach embedded in steady-state sustainability does not apply to mega events. By definition they are grand statements of belief in the discourse of place competitiveness. A steady-state approach would not regard most, if any, mega events as sustainable in their current form…". Hall also argued (p. 129), "Instead, sustainable events are more likely to be found in the smaller localized community based events that run over the longer- term or at least help maximize the use of existing infrastructure."

7.4 Subjects and objects of ecological impact assessment

Tourism, venues and events have direct and indirect impacts on nature and ecological processes, and these in turn affect people and organisations, businesses and government. In this section the 'objects' of IA are expressed as goals pertaining to environmental impacts and how they relate to our 'subjects' – starting with individuals and families (residents). Sample methods and indicators are also listed in Figure 7.2 (A-H).

7.4.1 Ecological impacts on individuals and families (residents)

If the environment changes, for better or worse, people are affected. Bad air or water can kill, while loss of access to nature is a quality-of-life detractor. Residents want a healthy, sustainable environment and often insist that politicians implement related tourism policies, that events go green, and that ecological processes and nature are respected in all decisions.

Figure 7.2 (A): Goals for individuals and families (residents)

Sample goals for ecological impacts on individuals and families (residents)	Sample methods and indicators
Provide opportunities to learn about environmental issues and practices Encourage attitude and behavioural changes (e.g., in consumption, recycling, voting) through event experiences Ensure that all residents have access to nature and nature interpretation	Consultations and surveys to reveal knowledge, perceptions of impacts, attitudes towards sustainability, and changes in eco-friendly behaviours Observe behaviour at events to evaluate conformity with policies and practices such as reducing waste and water/energy consumption Measure access to parks and nature reserves Evaluate the reach and effectiveness of information and educational efforts

7.4.2 Groups and sub cultures

Some groups will pay more attention than others to the ecological impacts of events and tourism, notably environmental lobby groups, those living close to nature, and recreational groups using outdoor sites. They can be mobilized as allies for green practices and sustainability. Many events incorporate outreach programmes, especially through schools to reach children that can incorporate environmental messages.

Figure 7.2 (B): Goals for groups and sub cultures

Sample goals for ecological impacts on groups and sub cultures	Sample methods and indicators
Mobilize community and special-interest groups for environmental lobbying and action Provide educational and demonstration opportunities for environmental groups at events Conduct outreach programmes through schools to engage children	Consultations can include visualisation techniques, e.g. mind mapping, to identify perceived impacts (future or existing). Lobby groups should have data of value in assessing forces, trends, and impacts. School programmes can be evaluated in the short term by reference to numbers reached, but permanent changes in attitudes and behaviour will require the cooperation of educational institutions in longitudinal research

Figure 7.2 (C): Goals for events and event organisations

Sample goals for ecological impacts on events and event organisations	Sample methods and indicators
Implement sustainability standards for events Increase the development and use of sustainable energy sources Reduce consumption of energy, water, food/beverages, land and materials Reduce or eliminate waste (re-use material and recycle) Eliminate pollution of land, water, air (including by litter, chemical contamination, silt, etc.) Reduce or eliminate greenhouse gas emissions (e.g., water vapour, exhausts, smoke) contributing to climate change) Use supply chain management (i.e., green procurement) to implement standards Advance the discourse on ecological issues and sustainability practices Reduce reliance on private vehicles by providing shuttle busses If appropriate, employ carbon offsetting Contribute to nature conservation Contribute to land and water rehabilitation	ISO20121 certification is demonstration of commitment Use carbon calculators and measure reduction of emissions over time "Greening checklists" (results of actions measured against greening or sustainability standards) employ experts to assess effects on wildlife and habitat (e.g., disruption of movements, breeding, deforestation) Employ experts to assess effects on ecological processes (drainage, land-use changes, trampling of vegetation, introduction of new species, wildlife consumption) Stakeholder input to confirm procurement standards are implemented Visitor surveys can measure responses to social marketing and educational campaigns (awareness, changes in attitude and behaviour) Police data to confirm reductions in private auto use; also refer to parking counts Conservation agencies to provide feedback on effectiveness of environmental prevention and amelioration Monetary value of carbon offsets Amount of money spent on conservation and/or ecological restoration work Increased environmental awareness Increased public participation in environmental programmes attached to, or sponsored by the event More sustainable consumption linked to the initiatives of events

7.4.3 Events and event organisations

The onus is on venues and events to implement relevant sustainability standards, but they cannot act alone. There must also be green standards imposed on the supply chain (i.e., procurement). Methods like carbon and ecological footprint calculators are tools for event IA, but are just as pertinent for government agencies and tourism organisations.

Here are a number of key impact indicators recommended by EventImpacts: (http://www.eventimpacts.com/impact-types/environmental)

♦ Waste footprint of event-related visitors

♦ Proportion of waste classified as inert/hazardous

♦ Changed composition of event related waste streams

♦ Changes in amount of waste produced per event-related visitor/participant

♦ Changes in proportion of waste diverted from landfill (i.e. increase recycling and composting)

♦ Reduction in waste produced at event site

♦ Reduction in waste produced per event-related visitor

♦ Carbon footprint (CO_2 equivalent) associated with event-related visitation

♦ Carbon footprint per event-related visitor (CO_2 equivalent)

♦ Total event carbon footprint (CO_2 equivalent)

♦ Reductions in personal carbon footprint following events

♦ Quantity of water used (litres public water supply) at event site

♦ Changes in the proportion of visitors using public transport to travel to/from event

♦ Changes in the proportion of visitors driving to/from event by car

♦ Total distance (miles/km) travelled by visitors to /from the event

♦ Proportion of visitors using car-sharing schemes

♦ Quantity of food and drink consumed

♦ Quantity of food and drink consumed which is organic

♦ Quantity of food and drink sourced locally (i.e. produced within 100 miles or 160km of the event)

♦ Quantity of food and drink certified as Fairtrade or other eco-certification

7.4.4 Businesses

The business sector has to buy into green and sustainability programmes, especially when it comes to supplying events and servicing tourists. The voluntary adoption of green certification programmes gives businesses guidance and support for going green and using that fact in their branding.

Figure 7.2 (D): Goals for businesses

Sample goals for ecological impacts on businesses	Sample methods and indicators
Support events in their sustainability efforts (e.g., through adopting their own green practices, sponsorship, and co-marketing) Foster business partnerships with events and venues as sponsors and suppliers	DMOs and business organisations can obtain data from members on green certification Measure reductions (use trend analysis) in waste, energy and water consumption and carbon emissions throughout the supply chain

7.4.5 Communities and cities

In the eventful city we need both a supportive environment for sustainable events, and programmes to help the event sector become a positive force for sustainability. Communities have to manage ever-larger and more complex portfolios of events, serving different policy domains, and this could lead to setting limits on numbers, location, or the size of events.

Figure 7.2 (E): Goals for communities and cities

Sample goals for ecological impacts on communities and cities	Sample methods and indicators
Manage land use to protect sensitive areas and preserve essential ecological processes Manage portfolios of events to be a positive force for sustainability Set limits on event numbers, size, locations, where appropriate	Review public documentation to assess compliance with environmental regulations Employ experts to evaluate sustainability progress among events and venues; detect weaknesses and failures Work with stakeholders in assessing limits beyond which development, attendance or activities should not be permitted

7.4.6 Tourist destinations

DMOs should collaborate with government agencies, businesses, events and venues to ensure the implementation of environmental sustainability policies. Destinations with opportunities to host nature-tourists or develop ecotourism have a special interest in setting high standards. Capacity to absorb tourism development, activities and numbers will be a major concern in protected and sensitive areas. There is often an overlap between environmental and social/cultural impact assessment when native people are involved and traditional land-uses are an issue.

Figure 7.2 (F): Goals for tourist destinations

Sample goals for ecological impacts on tourist destinations	Sample methods and indicators
Employ 'green' branding in partnership with events Foster sustainable practices by events and all industry partners Implement ecotourism at a manageable scale through special events	Tourist surveys can reveal perceptions of environmental quality and threats Iconic events for eco-tourists provide the opportunity to test the effectiveness of educational campaigns, acceptance of standards and regulations, and perceptions of capacity limits

7.4.7 Politics and government

There is an opportunity for events and tourism to lobby, and exert pressure on politicians to enact firm sustainability policies and regulations covering these sectors. When faced with political resistance, which often accompanies pro-growth ideology, visitors, suppliers, sponsors and collaborators can employ social marketing campaigns to change attitudes.

Figure 7.2 (G): Goals for politics and government

Sample goals for ecological impacts on politics and government	Sample methods and indicators
Lobby to get governments to enact and enforce firm sustainability policies and regulations for events, venues and tourism Establish demonstration programmes at events and venues to convince political parties of their effectiveness	Review public documentation of sustainability policies and regulations Monitor progress across cities, regions and nations

7.4.8 Society as a whole; the nation

A number of environmental issues are of vital national concern, from meeting carbon-reduction commitments to ensuring safe, healthy, liveable cities. Biosecurity has become an issue that, alongside disease prevention and treatment, translates into extra attention on events and tourism as possible sources of contamination.

The resources of senior levels of government might be needed to develop and implement the tools needed for impact assessment, including ecological footprint calculators customized for the nation and its regions. When standards are set for sustainable events and impact assessment methods at the national level (usually pertaining to major events supported by the government) they can become models for all others.

Figure 7.2 (H): Goals for society as a whole; the nation

Goals for ecological impacts on whole societies or the nation	Sample methods and indicators
Maintain biosecurity (prevent contamination & invasive species) Protect biodiversity through conservation laws and funding programmes Ensure that sustainability is integral to all mega-event decisions	Ecological footprint analysis can be conducted for events, venues and all jurisdictions; customized calculators are needed.

7.5 The process of ecological impact assessment

The International Association for Impact Assessment (IAIA) defines an environmental impact assessment as "the process of identifying, predicting, evaluating and mitigating the biophysical, social, and other relevant effects of development proposals prior to major decisions being taken and commitments made." However, we have separate chapters on the social and built environment impacts.

Most EIAs are conducted prior to a project getting approval, and in the events and tourism contexts the EIA could be part of a feasibility study for a new event or venue. Typically they are done when there is reason to believe that nature and/or ecological processes will be compromised in some way, and this belief is usually based on experience with similar projects and direct stakeholder consultations.

Another application of EIA could be to determine the environmental effects of a condition like tourism, or events that have already taken place, but retrospective IAs are rare. Unless a comprehensive evaluation system is implemented it is unlikely that all outcomes will be considered. Furthermore, the assessment and evaluation of long-term, cumulative changes attributable to portfolios of events and tourism is virtually unexplored territory.

7.5.1 Steps in EIA

Under European Union directives, an EIA must provide information in seven key areas. The headings are listed below, with some contextual comments added, but the full document should be consulted (http://ec.europa.eu/environment/eia/pdf/EIA_Directive_informal.pdf).

1   Description of the project or event:

- breakdown into key components through construction, operations, and decommissioning
- for each component list all of the sources of environmental disturbance
- for each component all the inputs and outputs must be listed, (e.g., air pollution, noise, hydrology)
- a matrix is often used in the systematic examination of potential interactions

2 Alternatives considered:
- ♦ are there other possible locations? for energy, can wind or solar power be used?
- ♦ opportunity costs: what are the alternatives to the event or venue?

3 Description of the environment:
- ♦ list all aspects of the environment that may be affected by the development, corresponding with elements of the project, in a matrix
- ♦ what are the most likely impacts of construction? of events? of related traffic and visitor activities? what are likely cumulative impacts?
- ♦ consultations should reveal existing issues, fears, and potential impacts

4 Description of the significant effects on the environment:
- ♦ 'significant' must be defined by experts, stakeholders, and through consultations; scales can be used to indicate severity, perceived importance, duration, etc.

5 Mitigation:
- ♦ analyse potential ways to avoid or otherwise mitigate negative impacts
- ♦ consider how events can be moved in space and time, adopt green standards, limit attendance or types of activity, incorporate educational and social marketing campaigns, raise money for conservation, etc.

6 Non-technical summary:
- ♦ the EIA is in the public domain and to be used in the decision making process

7 Lack of know-how/technical difficulties:
- ♦ this section is to advise any areas of weakness in knowledge; it can be used to focus areas of future research

The primary difference between ecological impact assessments and others lies in the need for scientific and engineering theories, models and simulations of ecological processes, and therefore a range of expertise has to be on the IA team. Consultations alone will not suffice, and original research is usually needed for projects and events with potential to cause serious damage.

On the other hand, consultations with a range of experts and stakeholders, especially residents, will raise some issues that might escape the experts. Consider, for example, how residents use local parks and natural areas. Do they merely walk their dogs there (in which case alternative locations can likely be found), or do they assign spiritual meaning to the outdoor experience because of the smells, the pleasing landscape, sightings of animals and the spring flowers? Some aspects of nature cannot easily be quantified or explored with ecological process simulations.

7.6 EIA methods

Environmental Impact Assessment (EIA) is where IA professionalism began, and it came to encompass broader impacts (social and cultural) that are dealt with separately in this book. We still call it EIA, but remember that built environment impacts are not the same. The Leopold Matrix was invented for EIA, and the FPSIR model as well. More recently carbon and ecological footprint calculators have become important.

7.6.1 Forces-Pressure-State-Impact-Response model

This model is useful in specific ways for ecological impact assessment. Taking the example of a proposal for a new arena and an indoor event, these being the 'forces', IA will first consider the known and potential environmental 'pressures' generated by events and tourism, such as travel, consumption, visitor activities and related infrastructure development. There is constant interaction between human activity and the environment, so for impact assessment we need to know the 'state' of the affected environment (is it local or regional in scope?) and its dynamics, particularly through benchmarking and monitoring in those ecological systems impacted by the pressures. If there are sensitive natural areas or protected resources nearby or downstream (including parks, wildlife habitats and corridors, water reservoirs, and difficult terrain subject to erosion) then extra care is obviously required.

The list of potential 'impacts' has to be matched against elements of the project (see Figure 7.3). First comes investment and construction, then operations, with events held in the venue, and likely traffic and land-use changes in the foreseeable future. 'Responses' will include prevention and mitigation actions, monitoring, and perhaps more research, all constituting a learning system that hopefully leads to enhanced sustainability.

There is no doubt that new developments have major impacts, whereas the ongoing use of venues is a totally different picture. The exact 'stressors' or 'causal forces' for each project will depend upon what is already known and what is feared. Often various stakeholders suggest their concerns up front, while expert evaluators have experience to draw upon. In Figure 7.4 we can anticipate that the main stressors consist of investment, physical development, event tourism (although in most cases of new venues, local travel will be dominant), activities (what users do), land use changes, individual and community involvement, and media coverage. Each stressor can have single impacts, but for major projects we have to consider synergies and cumulative impacts.

Figure 7.3: Forecasting environmental impacts for a new arena and an indoor event

Stressors or causal forces	Potential ecological impacts	Possible responses (systems to be put in place)
Physical Development (A) New Arena: large cost; possible public-private partnership; large site with huge footprint (arena, parking, bus/rail access); multi-year project with considerable risks; temporary construction jobs and permanent operational jobs (B) Indoor Event: existing venue; rental costs only; venue management systems in place; no new venue jobs created, but possible event jobs	(A) Construction Stage: traffic, noise, emissions, earth moving, energy and resources consumed (e.g., steel, concrete, wood, water); possible drainage alterations, tree removal, habitat loss or impacts on movement Operational Life: altered land use, economic and traffic patterns; energy consumption and generation of wastes from arena activities; urbanization process accelerated; urban design and community life altered (B) Each event in the venue will have predictable environmental impacts; evidence accumulates	(A) Policies and regulations are needed for development and land use changes: avoid sensitive areas; enforce green venue and sustainable development standards -impose full life cycle accounting -use development to clean up damaged areas -impose design standards Mitigation: Construction almost always causes negative impacts that have to be monitored and mitigated (e.g., redesign of drainage system; restoration of ponds; tree protection and planting) (B) Ideally, the green certification of venues assures that each event is in compliance
Event Tourism (A) New Arena: tourism occurs after completion; might be synergistic effects with other developments (e.g., a new entertainment or sport district, added retail and offices) (B) Indoor Event: event traffic will be a mix of locals and tourists; capacity is known in advance	(A) Forecasts (with wide margins of error) can be made of the number of events and potential travel generated over the arena's hypothetical life cycle or a specified period of time; this permits estimation of the project's ecological footprint (B) A good estimate of induced tourist-traffic can be made, linked to venue capacity and target marketing, but high confidence in forecasts will depend upon past experience; accurate post-event calculations can be made of carbon emissions	(A) Requiring mass-transit links to the new arena will reduce emissions and congestion; favouring redevelopment over green-field sites limits ecological impact (B) Concentrating events spatially and favouring small-scale events minimises some environmental impacts and makes their management and mitigation more efficient
Activities of Users (A) New Arena: a multi-use arena can introduce new sports, entertainment events and associated retailing (B) Indoor Event: have known activity/experiential characteristics, mostly confined to the venue but sometimes spilling out (e.g. fan zones, parties)	(A) As a result of increased tourism and resident demand, visitor activities and crowding can be harmful to the environment directly (e.g., trampling and erosion) or indirectly (through resource consumption and waste generated) (B) The cumulative impact of many events can become a problem	(A) Require ISO certification and sustainable practices from the outset -link development of venues to supply-chain management -educate visitors (social marketing for attitude & behaviour change) (B) Require a permanent impact assessment system and monitor cumulative impacts -each event has known characteristics, based on experience, leading to more effective management and mitigation

Figure 7.3 (cont.): Forecasting environmental impacts for a new arena and an indoor

Land use changes (A) New Arena: likely to generate additional and new retailing on site and nearby; may be combined with urban re-development at a large scale (B) Indoor Event: no land use changes	(A) An environmental legacy of positive change, or damaged ecosystems (B) No likely impact on land use	(A) Community-based planning will be needed to accommodate and regulate use of the new venue -land use and environmental planners have to ensure that mitigation is fully implemented, as specified by IA (B) not applicable
Individual and community involvement (A) New Arena: a major development might be met with opposition and/or support; it is unlikely that a major facility will be community oriented (B) Indoor Event: each event can be linked to particular place or interest communities	(A) Residents will identify potential impacts on parks, protected areas, wildlife and ecological processes (B) Not usually applicable	(A) Development might lead to enhanced pressure or support for environmental management and integrated planning -lobbying by special interest groups can accompany major land-use changes -multi-stakeholder inputs needed to ensure identification and mitigation of all ecological impacts
Media coverage (A) New Arena: likely to generate considerable media coverage and possible controversy over costs and impacts (B) Indoor Event: a major facility can host events that attract publicity on impacts	(A) Media attention could help identify ecological impacts and possible mitigation (B) Assuming the enforcement of sustainability standards, each event should strive for reduction of carbon emissions and ecological footprint leading to image enhancement	(A) (B) Media coverage has a role in shaping public opinion and policy, with major events and venues attracting the most attention

7.6.2 Carbon calculators

To the extent that events and venues generate travel, these sectors must account for their carbon emissions and continuously do more to reduce them. Direct emissions are those generated by the use of fossil fuels at events and in venues, such as for heating/cooling, cooking, equipment and vehicles, and by event attendees who fly or drive to the event. Indirect emissions include those produced by the use of electricity, the problem being that so much of it is generated by burning fossil fuels. Consumption of all supplies and production of services for venues and events also leads, indirectly, to carbon emissions, making it important to apply sustainability standards throughout the supply chain. The tourism and hospitality sectors also make a big contribution to carbon emissions, with tourists demanding plenty of hot water, air conditioning, imported food and high levels of service.

Carbon calculators are available online, some of which appear to be 'black boxes' with unknown assumptions. Exactly what should be included, and how the data are to be collected, is still an open question. The website *greeneventbook* (www.greeneventbook.com/event-carbon-footprint-possible/) discusses these issues as well as the meaning of carbon offsetting and neutrality.

7.6.3 Ecological footprint analysis

The total impact of an event or tourism on the environment should have the smallest possible footprint. The ecological footprint is not a single measure, but an attempt to quantify the total demand an event makes (or for tourism, or your own household) on the earth's resources, thereby demonstrating how 'natural capital' is being depleted. Wackernagel et al. (2002, p. 1) defined the concept as:

"...the area of biologically productive land and water required to produce the resources consumed and to assimilate the wastes generated by humanity, under the predominant management and production practices in any given year"

Global Footprint Network's calculator (https://www.footprintnetwork.org/) estimates the amount of land and sea area needed to provide the resources a person needs (food, shelter, etc.), and absorb their carbon dioxide emissions. The ecological footprint is expressed in global hectares or acres.

According to Wikipedia:

"The Global Footprint Network, for instance, is an ecological organization that calculates a global ecological footprint from UN and other data, and publishes the result. They estimate that as of 2007, the planet uses up major ecological resources 1.5 times as fast as they are being renewed. . . This resource accounting is similar to life cycle analysis wherein the consumption of energy, biomass (food, fiber), building material, water and other resources are converted into a normalized measure of land area called global hectares (gha)."

It is not easy to do a full ecological footprint analysis for events because the data required have to be relevant to the area in question. The footprint of Europeans or North Americans, for example, is quite different from that of people in poorer parts of the world. As you would expect, in countries where consumption is high, the footprint of individuals, households, events and tourism is also very high.

In the events-specific research literature we have a few examples of applications (Collins et al., 2005; Collins and Flynn, 2008). Collins et al., 2005 employed this method in a study of the 2004 FA Cup final in Cardiff, Wales. Their analysis estimated that the event had a footprint equal to 3051 hectares. More than half of this footprint was generated by the travel of 73,000 attendees (totalling 2 million kilometres), and consumption of food was the second-largest contributor. Andersson & Lundberg (2013) and Andersson, Jutbring & Lundberg (2016) have used footprint analysis in Sweden as part of their triple-impact-assessment approach.

Food consumption and waste can be better managed to reduce the ecological footprint, such as by using less energy in its preparation and eliminating unnecessary packaging. In one atypical and controversial case, a music festival in Sweden banned meat sales on site, thereby substantially reducing its footprint (Andersson, Jutbring and Lundberg, 2013).

Knowing what generates the largest contributions to carbon emissions and the ecological footprint of events is much more important than being able to estimate the footprints in quantitative terms. The most important indicators, each being subject to standards and firm management action, are related to travel (i.e., minimise private auto travel), energy, food and water consumption, and waste reduction.

Because event tourism by definition involves travel, what can be done other than offering shuttle buses? I have always maintained that low volumes of high-yield tourists are more important and more sustainable than mass tourism. As a portfolio strategy for cities and destinations, avoid the largest events and concentrate on permanent, 'owned' events including small to medium-sized iconic events for special-interest tourists. Mega events not only maximise travel and consumption, they actively promote it through corporate sponsorship and media coverage.

Study questions

1   Use the FPSIR model to assess how a mega event could impact on nature and ecological processes. Discuss appropriate mitigation methods.

2   Events are held indoors in urban venues, outdoors and even in the wilderness. How does the setting affect the event, and in turn what kinds of IA methods are needed for events in different environments?

3   Explain the concepts of carbon calculators and ecological footprint, and the main problem areas for events and tourism. What are the best solutions?

Recommended additional readings and sources

Case, R. (2013). *Events and The Environment.* London: Routledge

Green Event Book (www.greeneventbook.com/event-carbon-footprint-possible/)

Global Footprint Network (https://www.footprintnetwork.org/)

Jones, M. (2018). *Sustainable Event Management A Practical Guide*, 3d. ed. London: Earthscan.

8 Economic Impact Assessment

Learning objectives

- ☐ Learn important principles for conducting economic IA
- ☐ Know the main potential costs and economic impacts (both positives and negatives) of events and tourism, and how to maximise local benefits
- ☐ Be able to plan and implement economic IA, including appropriate methods
- ☐ Learn how to forecast and estimate the direct economic contribution of events

8.1 Introduction

Concepts for understanding economic impacts, and valid methods of assessment are well developed. In fact, there is so much information available that this is the largest chapter in the book – not the most important. A thorough and accessible reference on the subject is the book *Tourism Economics and Policy* by Dwyer, Forsyth and Dwyer (2010) as it contains a full chapter on events. *Event Tourism* (Getz, 2013) also covers economic impact assessment in detail.

There have been well-documented problems with economic impact assessments for tourism and events (Matheson, 2002; Matheson and Baade, 2003; Crompton and McKay, 2004; Tyrell & Ismail, 2005; Crompton, 2006; Davies et al., 2013), pertaining to both how they are done and the purposes they serve. Dwyer and Jago (2014, p.130) identified three main types of criticisms associated with the assessment of the economic impacts of events, commencing with the exaggeration of benefits owing to either deliberate manipulation or faulty methods. Attention has often focused on the use of Input-Output tables to formulate 'multipliers', a practice which leads to exaggerated benefits, with a number of scholars preferring Computable General Equilibrium (CGE) modelling.

Most fundamental is the frequent failure to consider all costs and benefits, leading to calls for more comprehensive cost-benefit analysis (CBA). Most economic IAs have utilized only a narrow range of metrics, but even more unfortunate is the continued reliance on multipliers and econometric models, as these 'black-box' approaches tend to exaggerate imputed benefits while ignoring costs and equity issues. This is certainly not in keeping with principles of social responsibility and sustainability.

Dwyer et al (2010, p. 421), based on Blake (2005), developed a list of neglected issues pertaining to IA of large events, summarized below – to which I have added some additional comments:

♦ Commercial success has been declared even when huge debts have accumulated; taxation might increase to cover debt.

♦ Infrastructure is often viewed as a benefit, but at what (opportunity) cost?

♦ Full costs are seldom considered in IA: typically omitted are security costs and the costs associated with co-opted civil servants.

♦ Many claims of employment gains are exaggerated because of assumptions made about underemployment in economies; most events are too short to generate new jobs; construction does generate work, temporarily, but it might also 'steal' labour and resources from other parts of the economy and lead to shortages or to wage inflation.

♦ Distributional effects are seldom considered: who gains and who pays?

♦ Tax and lottery funds devoted to venues and events could be used elsewhere (again, opportunity costs).

♦ Displacement of tourists and residents is generally ignored.

♦ There is often deliberate exaggeration of imputed benefits or of projected revenues.

♦ Environmental costs are often ignored or under-estimated, especially congestion, local pollution, and greenhouse gas emissions contributing to climate change.

Another major misuse of feasibility studies, impact assessments and economic impact forecasts in particular is to exploit them to 'sell' an idea like bidding on a mega event, or to convince politicians to support a particular event or venue, or events and tourism in general. In this approach claims of benefits can be made and exaggerated, costs minimised, and potential negative impacts ignored completely. Post-event and retrospective impact assessments might then be avoided completely, or narrowly defined in order to avoid a direct comparison of prior claims with post-event reality.

8.1.1 Basic principles of economic IA

Several assertions are made below about what evaluators and researchers need to know and do, and these should be considered to be guiding principles.

1 As emphasized by Dwyer et al. (2010), the economic impacts of events and tourism are not necessarily benefits; impacts can positive, negative, neutral or disputed. This means that economic impact assessment should NEVER stand on its own when evaluating events and tourism.

2 It is essential to consider all tangible and intangible costs and benefits; the distribution of those impacts (who gains and who pays or loses?), and the

different stakeholder perceptions of the impacts and their importance. This is essential for the implementation of sustainability and social responsibility.

3   There is no point in examining economic impacts if nothing is to be done about them! All impact assessments are to be used as inputs to evaluations and planning, including the formulation of mitigation for costs and negatives and advancement of strategies for continuous improvement.

4   Only the forecasting and post-event estimation of the direct economic contribution of events and event tourism is necessary; the use of econometric models and multipliers is an unnecessary complication and is prone to abuse, but no doubt there will remain political interest in seeing them used.

5   Standardized methods and measures of economic impacts are needed for comparative purposes, and for meta-analysis that can shape theory and planning. Standardization is becoming essential for legitimacy in the minds of politicians and the public.

8.2 Potential economic impacts of events and tourism

As summarised in Figure 8.1, economic growth and development is the dominant theme.

This is a very big category, encompassing events as tourist attractions, animators, image makers and catalysts for change and development. Events in this context can be conceptualized as a 'business' sector contributing to economic growth and prosperity for all. Or it can be viewed as an 'export industry' generating foreign revenue by attracting tourists and generating new income for a city, region or country. At the national level, event tourism should be 'export ready', meaning events that play an economic development role should be attractive to international tourists, and ready to purchase from anywhere on the planet – in other words, a product to sell.

If events and tourism are to be sustainable, a lot of change is necessary, starting with comprehensive and valid impact assessment. O'Sullivan and Jackson (2002) called for greater comprehensiveness in economic impact assessment, specifically to examine the roles of events in capacity building, training, community enterprise, responsible business practices, equitable access to jobs, and local procurement. To these goals can be added a fuller set of aims arising from principles of sustainable development and social responsibility.

8.2.1 Costs and negative impacts

Investments are expected to have a return that exceeds costs – but what if the costs are social, cultural or environmental? Externalities occur beyond the usual accounting framework of events, but they can be real costs, including the negative effects of pollution, crime or noise. Another question pertains to opportunity costs, because if governments invest in events and tourism they should be obliged to consider what alternatives exist for achieving the same public good. Then there is the matter of who pays and who gains, or how costs and benefits are distributed – it is not always an equitable arrangement.

Opportunity costs occur when one investment precludes another, or alternatives are not even considered. For small events it is not usually an issue, as the public funding is typically small and there are many reasons for support, but for major venues and mega events there are always questions to ask about the wisdom of the investment and whether or not the same benefits could be achieved in other ways. It often appears that the taxpayer is left with a huge bill to pay, while some interest groups walk away with big profits and fancy new venues to play in.

On the other hand, real alternatives might not exist. In many areas tourism is the only feasible economic driver. And what communities do not want leisure and sport facilities to serve the residents? Some level of public provision is expected. Senior levels of government typically allocate funds to culture, business development and sport, so it becomes mostly a matter of where and when to invest. Supposing alternatives do exist, and the question of opportunity costs is raised, can they be quantified? Many intangibles might have to be considered, such as how many people are affected, their economic and social standing, and whether or not they have preferences?

Holger Preuss, writing on opportunity costs in the book *Event Tourism* (Getz, 2013; pp. 374-376), sought to clarify the issues associated with efficiency of event investments and opportunity costs. Several key points were raised:

◆ Projects can be valued only with regard to political goals

◆ The efficiency of an event differs with each stakeholder due to different inputs and outputs

◆ The spatial distribution of costs and benefits has to be factored into the evaluation of efficiency and opportunity costs

◆ For mega events, multiple projects usually have to be considered together

◆ Alternative uses of money are limited to the input each stakeholder gives (each one has its own calculations to make)

◆ Investment in one event can lead to other events, so there are future costs and benefits to consider

◆ Externalities must be considered.

Externalities are the costs and impacts that are not accounted for in event and tourism budgets or impact statements. When the organisation responsible for a major event declares it to be 'carbon neutral' we should ask for the proof, and when the same organisation declares that it balanced its budget we must ask what exactly was included and excluded from their accounts. One of the biggest costs for mega events is security, and this is generally the responsibility of senior governments – not the event organisers.

'Distributional' impacts are often ignored in economic IA, and this might be the most important issue to assess. Does economic gain for business (i.e., profits) or government (e.g., tax revenue, jobs created) justify incurring debt to be paid off over many years by the average taxpayer? This is clearly a political issue, but discussion of who gains and who pays is seldom included in feasibility studies, economic forecasts or post-event accounts. Some of these equity issues do generate public opposition and political debate from time to time, such as increased inflation, loss of affordable housing, land-use changes that affect residents' lives, and of course social and cultural losses for marginalised groups.

In Figure 8.1 the typical major goals related to economic growth and development are identified, these being major objects of economic IA. In Figure 8.2 major potential costs and negative impacts are listed, and these provide instruction to impact assessors on what to measure. Subsequently, in Figure 8.3 (A-H) each of the subjects is considered in turn, starting with the perspective of individuals and families (the residents).

Figure 8.1: Major economic development and growth goals and specific objectives

Develop event tourism as an export industry
Attract international, high-yield tourists to improve the nation's balance of payments through foreign earnings
Assist events to be 'export ready' for easy purchase from anywhere
Use events and venues as catalysts for development and change
Assist in modernization (e.g., Through new modes of business and employment)
Stimulate community economic development
Foster entrepreneurship and innovation through events and tourism
Enhance destination marketing
Maximise potential to attract future events through venue development & infrastructure improvements
Spread development geographically by stimulating growth through events and tourism
Assist events in rural areas and small towns to become tourist attractions and image makers
Bid on events that can be located elsewhere than major cities
Reduce or eliminate seasonality of demand with events
Situate more events in low-demand periods to create greater economic impact by stimulating demand for travel and hospitality services
Foster the image of an all-season destination
Create income and jobs in events and related businesses
Develop local supply chains (i.e., backward linkages)
Train volunteers for future employment
Increase tourist length of stay and spending
Use events in branding and positioning
Create positive images in target markets
Combat negative publicity

Figure 8.2: Major economic costs and negative impacts

Debt
Public-sector borrowing for mega-event construction, related infrastructure and operating costs can lead to long-term debt, and might result in higher taxes
Debt incurred by not-for-profit organisations might not be sustainable, resulting in failure
Disruption of normal activities
Increased travel time owing to congestion
Loss of amenity might depress property values
Investment
Private capital invested in bidding on events, venues and event organisations is expected to generate public good
Private investment is expected to earn a positive ROI
Operating costs
Producing events
Operating venues
Marketing events and tourism
Risk management including insurance
Life-cycle costs including de-commissioning venues, and mitigation efforts
Externalities
Pollution and ecological damage not covered by event and tourism budgets
Social and cultural costs not covered
Security costs borne by senior levels of government
Seconded staff
Inflation
Rising prices for residents because of tourism demand and investments
Displacement
Of residents, during events
Of residents from affordable housing owing to tourism demand and conversion of housing to commercial accommodation
Of businesses from one area to another; of demand during events
Of tourists from one city/region to another because of mega-event attractiveness
Of regular visitors by event-tourists during peak demand periods
Opportunity costs
Investment in events and tourism can result in less money for social or environmental programmes or other projects with the same economic benefits

8.2.2 Return on Investment (ROI) and the economic worth of events

ROI is not in itself a usual measure of economic impact, but one of financial performance – alongside ROA (return on assets) and ROE (return on equity or return on experience). It could be a desired impact of a change in strategy or tactics within an organisation or destination, however, as expressed this way: "our new strategy will produce a higher return on our investment in research and marketing", in which case the impact assessors have to demonstrate not merely an improvement but also that the logic of the change was sound. That is a special consideration for event tourism, whereas private investors looking to make a profit from events would have a quite different measure, namely:

$$ROI = \frac{\text{gain from investment} - \text{the cost of investment}}{\text{divided by the cost of investment.}}$$

Placing a monetary value on events is one way to establish their 'worth', but it is too narrow an approach to meet responsibility and sustainability criteria. Few events are sold on the open market, but bidding on events does establish a kind of monetary value (i.e., how much did they have to pay, and what other benefits were promised in order to win the event?). In most cases a multi-stakeholder approach will be required to handle the complexities of establishing the worth of an event, in which case one value perspective will be the economic benefits generated. Social, cultural and environmental benefits will also come into play, making it inevitably a political decision. And within a managed portfolio there also has to be consideration of an event's contribution to overall portfolio value, taking a long-term perspective. ROI is an inadequate measure in these instances.

8.2.3 Economic impacts on individuals and families (residents)

There will be no single voice associated with residents; there will always be multiple perspectives to consider, including organized lobby groups. The subject of economic IA might legitimately be 'all residents', or a target group such as families, the poor, minorities, immigrants, children, elderly, etc. The scale is an important variable, as residents of a neighbourhood affected by a new arena or a large festival, for example, will often experience a range of impacts directly, affecting many aspects of their lives. Remember that personal and family impacts of event participation and direct experiences with events are considered in the Social Impact chapter.

Figure 8.3 (A): Economic impacts on individuals and families (residents)

Sample goals for economic impacts on individuals and families (residents)	Sample methods and indicators
Increase personal earning & employment opportunities	Resident surveys and other forms of input to measure the following:
Provide opportunities for family-owned and other small businesses	Utility, or use value: requires data on participation, voluntarism, preferences)
Improve quality of jobs and working conditions	Income and other financial value accruing to workers, volunteers, sponsors, suppliers
Ensure workplace health and safety	
Prevent loss of purchasing power owing to inflation	Perceptions of impacts (positive and negative, strength/importance) and attitudes towards events and tourism
Prevent displacement from affordable housing	
Use events as learning and training opportunities	Measure: trends in employment, income, consumption, working conditions in the events and tourism sectors;
Foster entrepreneurship & innovation in the event sector	

8.2.4 Social and cultural groups

Examples are community associations, leisure and sport clubs, service clubs, churches, parent-teacher associations and groups organized around gender identity, professions, hobbies or other self-defined interests. Some of these groups are frequent participants in the planned-event sector, as co-producers, volunteers, athletes, performers or sponsors, in which case they share economic and financial impacts. Others are impacted by money raised by cause-related events, or the leveraging of event tourism for their economic advantage. It is also possible that some are harmed by grants and sponsorships that are diverted to events.

Figure 8.3 (B): Economic impacts on social & cultural groups

Sample goals for economic impacts on social & cultural groups	Sample methods and indicators
Raise money for charitable causes	Stakeholder consultations and surveys to measure:
Share event revenues with community groups	Amount of money raised
Engage in social marketing and education that benefits community groups	Projects funded
	New events produced
Enable groups to produce events.	Activities of community groups

8.2.5 Events and event organisers

Governments and the tourism industry should have policies and strategies for creating and sustaining financially viable events and event-producing organisations, otherwise event tourism will falter, and the social and cultural losses to the community will be high. That seems obvious, yet the predominant approach around the world appears to be one of *laissez faire*, being an abandonment of planned events to the free marketplace in which the start-ups and failures are not managed. In more progressive jurisdictions one can identify some degree of event portfolio management.

Another challenge is to assess the economic value of events, event-producing organisations, event venues and event portfolios. What is a venue, organization, single event or portfolio of events worth on the open marketplace, or to the city and its tourism/hospitality sectors in terms of current and future benefits? Considering the synergistic and cumulative impacts of event portfolios, what is their long-term value? These are questions currently without firm answers, neither in theory nor methodologically.

Figure 8.3 (C): Events and event organisers

Sample goals for economic impacts on events and event organisers	Sample methods and indicators
Sustain financially viable events, venues, event organisations and event portfolios	Periodic surveys of event-producing organisations, and sharing data and formal benchmarking within event associations to measure:
Train and retain skilled workers	Profit or surplus revenue
Recruit, train and share volunteers	Training and education for event management (numbers engaged, certified)
Maximise the economic value of event venues and managed event portfolios	Ratios: measure financial health of events versus debt; ability to fund growth or give to causes
Generate surplus revenue (or make a profit) for participating groups, community projects and charities	The health of the event population (birth & death rates, growth or decline, resource use & competition)

8.2.6 Community and city

Most major venues and events are located in cities, and most tourism is city-to city in nature. But the potential economic value of events and venues is greater, in relative terms, in small towns and rural areas that lack other options. The 'eventful city' (Richards and Palmer, 2010) in which multiple portfolios of events are managed to meet diverse policy aims, requires both a supportive environment and the full integration of events and tourism within all the policy fields directed at achieving the 'sustainable city' (Getz, 2017).

8.2.7 Businesses

Chalip (2004) advocated the 'leveraging' of events for both business gains and social benefits. He suggested four main ways of maximising trade and revenue from an event in the short term, including increasing visitor spending locally by offering more outlets and enticing tourists to stay longer, and enhancing local business linkages to events and tourism. Business relationships with events should be improved through explicit leveraging strategies and collaborations.

Figure 8.3 (D): Community and city

Sample goals for economic impacts on the community and city	Sample methods and indicators
Establish an eventful city through proactive support of events and the integration of events and tourism within sustainable- city policies	Inter-agency reporting within local government to provide data on:
Ensure that events support economic development and are adapted to individual community/city needs	Tourism and event employment, new businesses and failures
Prevent disruption of established economic activities	Also measure: Self-sufficiency of event portfolios
	Asset value of events, using multiple criteria

Figure 8.3 (E): Economic impacts on businesses

Sample goals for economic impacts on businesses	Sample methods and indicators
Leverage events for the benefit of local businesses (through direct sales and promotions at events, knowledge exchange, fostering trade links, attracting investors, making them export-ready, cultivating backward linkages)	Business associations with events to measure:
	Impacts on sales, profits, competiveness, new business opportunities, (re)distribution of economic activity (seasonally and geographically)
Maximise local income from events and event tourism	
Attract and keep the best workers (training programmes essential)	Survey businesses or interviews to measure:
Avoid or reduce the costs of displacement effects (i.e., the shifting of consumer demand away from established business areas)	Investment, sponsorship, networking and collaboration with events (benefits and costs)
Increase co-branding and investment/ownership opportunities for local businesses partnering with events	
Avoid loss of employees from existing businesses (which can happen with major developments)	Inflation and cost increases attributable to events and tourism

8.2.8 Tourism destinations

There are some unique economic issues that destinations have to evaluate. A sustainable destination has to remain competitive, and that involves keeping up with the competition, and delivering to stakeholders (including residents) the benefits of development and promotion. Temporal and spatial considerations begin this discussion.

Seasonality: this was one of the earliest event-tourism considerations by academics (Ritchie and Beliveau, 1974), with events being examined for their role in overcoming seasonality, or at least extending the established tourist seasons. This remains an important challenge, as many destinations experience 'extreme seasonality' (Getz and Nilsson, 2004). Most destinations and businesses can benefit from extending demand beyond peak seasons, and there is a good argument to be made for spreading demand more evenly related to the avoidance of congestion and consequent environmental problems. It should also be considered that building venues and infrastructure to accommodate a short, peak period of demand is very inefficient – they need all-year use.

Concentration (or clustering) versus dispersal: Over-concentration of people and development in one or a few places poses problems for destination managers and for residents. Events can help spread out demand both temporally and spatially, with a good destination strategy being to foster events across the season and across the area's communities. The risk, and a real management challenge, is that tourism and development might be attracted into sensitive environments or unprepared communities.

Image making: Image, positioning, reputation and brand management all have to be considered together (see section 6.5).

Competitiveness and sustainability: Ritchie and Crouch (2003) argued that a destination has to be economically viable to be sustainable. It has to compete with the rest of the world in a very dynamic environment, and it has to manage its resources for the long term within a sustainability paradigm. Can it do both synergistically? When we look at long-term trends such as demand and supply we might see only ups and downs, surpluses or excesses, but there is much more to consider. Creation and management of event portfolios has entered the competitiveness equation, with new theory and methods needed to support this advancement.

Equity: Equitable destination management has at least two major dimensions, first the distribution of events and business opportunities geographically and by business sector, and second the equitable distribution of benefits and costs within the resident population. Mega events and investment in infrastructure and large venues generates the most equity concerns. It is easy to generate a large debt burden for future generations, but difficult to justify.

The IA questions "what impact do events have on… seasonality, concentration, image, competitiveness or equity?" cannot be answered without a lot of effort and debate. So in this chapter we look at how these gaps can be filled within an IA framework.

8.2.9 Politics and government

Taxes, jobs, efficiency gains and economic growth, these are the highly valued economic benefits desired by politicians and government. In addition, governments want to exploit venues and events for place marketing and sometimes purely political reasons. Although economic considerations are often paramount for politicians, it is increasingly recognised that pursuing economic gains is not always justifiable.

Figure 8.3 (F): Economic impacts on tourism destinations

Sample goals for economic impacts on tourism destinations	Sample methods and indicators
Increase competitive advantages	From regular visitor surveys:
Develop a portfolio of events as attractions, image makers, catalysts, animators	Analyse by visitor segment: motivation, reasons for trip, all expenditures within study area, marketing effectiveness, satisfaction, loyalty
Reduce seasonality of demand	From surveys of events, accommodation and other businesses determine:
	The occupancy-rate and revenue effects of events; monitor trends such as growth in bed nights by season, time of week, and spatially
Spread tourism demand geographically	Diversification of the events and attractions portfolio
Increase visitor yield	Capacity indicators have to be developed (both in terms of supply, and reflecting sustainability policies)
	Forecast, and monitor from impact assessments:
Avoid or reduce mass tourism / over-tourism	The direct economic contribution (DEC) of event tourism (use DEC calculators)
Manage supply and demand for stability	Total number of national and international event tourists
Improve customer satisfaction, word-of-mouth recommendations, and loyalty (employ measures of customer satisfaction and loyalty)	Number and percentage of repeat tourists, both national and foreign visitors
	Per cent of tickets sold to visitors: both from outside the local area and outside the country
Grow the capacity of the area for tourism (measure the numbers and diversity of attractions, venues, events, and services) if appropriate, while meeting all sustainability goals	Average and total visitor expenditure in local area and within country (i.e., The direct economic contribution of event tourists)
	The proportion of event tourists using commercial accommodation
	Average length of stay at the event location and within the country
	Average expenditure breakdown (accommodation, private car, public transport, restaurants, food, tours, purchases on-site, shopping etc.
Attract external funds and sponsorship revenue	Amount of external funds (categorized by grants, sponsorships, investment) generated by the event for the local area and the country
	Total organizational spend of "new money" within the local area and the country (only count the expenditure of funds received from outside the area or country)
Utilise events to develop infrastructure and venues for hosting future events and for the benefit of residents	Number of event jobs and full time equivalent jobs taken by local residents (full time and part time)
	Number of local and national businesses contracted to the event as suppliers
Enhance event and destination marketing through constant innovation and evaluation	Monetary value of goods and services purchased from local/national suppliers (and as a per cent of total purchases)
	Number and percentage of event tourists arriving outside "peak tourist season" (defined locally)
Cultivate support for events and event tourism among residents, politicians, businesses and the media	Number of new business links created by the event
	Trends in exports (trade)
IA should concentrate on a balanced and comprehensive Benefit And Cost Evaluation (BACE)	Displacement effects should be calculated by determining if non-event tourists or tours were replaced by event tourists
	Financial accounting to include details of the sources of all expenditures and revenues

Figure 8.3 (G): Politics and government

Sample goals for economic impacts on politics and government	Sample methods and indicators
Develop strategies for achievement of government goals on employment, skills training, professionalism, entrepreneurship and innovation Pursue sustainable development Justify interventions by demonstrating public good and ensuring equity of the costs and benefits distribution	Public accounts and impact assessments to measure: The full costs and benefits of investment in tourism and events including externalities The availability of resources for government interventions Tax revenue and employment attributable to events and tourism Innovative spin-offs from events (e.g. new events, export potential) Reduction in regional or inter-community disparity

8.2.10: Society as a whole; the nation

Economic growth and development are preoccupations of national governments, and most of them recognize the importance of events and tourism within economic strategies.

National governments must usually provide guarantees when bidding on mega events, and in some countries the construction of major venues for business, culture or sport becomes a matter for investment from the highest levels. Advancing the international appeal of a country's events can be an important source of foreign earnings, and establishing a reputation as a friendly, safe and attractive event host is a vital precondition. In turn, nations want the economic benefits to flow to all regions and residents: high employment, increasing incomes, more choices, entrepreneurship and innovation.

Figure 8.3 (H): Economic impacts on society as a whole, or the nation

Sample goals for economic impacts on society as a whole, or the nation	Sample methods and indicators
Increase satisfaction and well being through gainful employment and productive business Meet migration and demographic goals, as linked to events, tourism and related employment Use events as drivers of innovation, modernization and international competitiveness	Public impact assessments and accounts to measure: Events and tourism contributions to balance of payments and gross national product or gross domestic product (use satellite accounts) Economic patterns (e.g., concentration vs. regional development) National tax revenues Inflation or stagflation Poverty reduction Average incomes Jobs created (& unemployment rates and trends)

8.3 Creating economic value with events and tourism

Understanding how value is created is essential for IA and evaluation, and the following discussion is intended to provide the basics. See Figure 8.4, being an illustration of the process, and Figure 8.5 which compiles the key definitions.

When conducting economic impact assessments a defined area is required, and this determines the benefits and costs that are deemed to be *within-scope*. The impacts of event tourism might occur only within the event itself (although this is unlikely), a city, region, or country. If the whole nation is defined as within scope, only money coming into the country will be counted (e.g., from international tourists, sponsors bringing in new money solely because of the event, or broadcast revenue from international sources), and only money leaving the country will be deducted as *leakage*. By expanding the within-scope area from a city to a region or the whole nation, the economic impacts will be increased.

Economists typically attempt to measure *output impacts* (the total increase in business sales revenue) or *value added*, being the increase in the area's gross regional product. Neither of these can be estimated without a lot of data about the economy in question and econometric models of some type, so they are beyond the ability of most event and tourism professionals – nor is it usually useful for practitioners to know such things.

Economic impact can be classified as direct and indirect, with indirect being divided into secondary and induced. *Direct effects* are the results of the *new money* brought into the area by tourism attributable to an event. Economists use the term *incremental income* when assessing the potential impact of each new monetary unit injected into an area, but that is a technical term for specific applications.

Most new money attributable to events consists of event-tourist spending, augmented by money generated through grants from higher levels of government (e.g., to pay for infrastructure and venues, or security and marketing) and money paid to organisers by sponsors and the media. Some of the inflow and outflow might come before or after the event in the form of capital investments, grants for infrastructure, revenue from media, payments to suppliers, etc., so that the period in which impacts are assessed becomes a key issue. For mega events we could be talking about ten years, but for most events a calendar year probably suffices. Inflow quantification has to be matched by measurement of outflow, because event organisers will often spend a great amount of money outside the area in question. Accordingly, the expenditure of the organisers made outside the area have to be subtracted from the new money brought into the area because of the event.

The secondary effects result from business-to-business transactions, with recipients of the new money (mainly the event organisers, hospitality and retail services) purchasing supplies and labour. These constitute *backward linkages* that create additional value, but we have to consider *leakages* as well. A small area requires imports of goods, workers and services, and these are leakages. They are quite high for small areas like towns and rural regions. If the within-scope area is a large city or country, the leakages will be much less, and the secondary impacts are therefore going to be higher.

Induced effects are the result of increased personal income, including profits for businesses and wages/salaries for workers, because they have more to spend. But the leakages can be very high owing to imports and spending outside the area. This is not to be confused with the concept of *induced demand*, being the additional flow of visitors that can arise as a consequence of an event, usually a mega event, attributable to the publicity it generates.

The economic impacts of many events are small, and for some there can be a negative economic value. That happens when the costs exceed revenues, both for the event organisers and the city or destination. Some arts festivals, for example, attract few tourists and have high production costs. That does not mean they have no value, only that they are not generating a net economic contribution. Within a diverse portfolio they have other potential value, such as image enhancement, and of course for many people they hold intrinsic value.

The direct economic contribution of most small or medium-sized events (especially when they are permanent and require no additional infrastructure or venues) is largely confined to the direct effects of new money from event tourists. The spending of organisers has to be considered, and of course money raised outside the area, but often these are small amounts.

The building of new venues and related infrastructure, which is typical for mega events, can generate much greater direct and indirect effects owing to larger numbers of higher-paid workers, the fact that construction in general has many backward linkages right down to the level of natural resource extraction, and the possibility of attracting investment money to the area.

Figure 8.4 illustrates the above discussion. The process starts with *new money* (or *incremental income*) injected by event tourists, and it has to be determined that they came to the area in hole or part because of the event – that is the *attribution* problem. IA also has to account for the fact that many event tourists will spend money that does not reach (or stay in) the within-scope area, and typically airfares and some or all of the cost of tour packages are to be excluded, as well as tourist spending along the travel route. If event tourists travel specifically because of an event but combine that with expenditure elsewhere, it can be included in a separate estimate for the region or nation.

Outflows have to be carefully documented. Organisers typically spend money outside the area on advertising, fees paid to event owners, prize money that is not kept locally, and goods and services. There might be hidden outflows such as wages being sent abroad by foreign workers. These are all *leakages*, and as the new money circulates within the area there are many other leakages attributable to imports consumed, supplies required, wages and profits exported, and savings that do not circulate locally. The *backward linkages* are critical for creation of the *multiplier effect*, as using local suppliers and workers ensures that money continues to circulate. However, the secondary and induced contributions from most events are much smaller than the original injection of new money, because of leakages.

Figure 8.4: The direct and indirect contribution of event tourism

Figure 8.5: Key definitions for economic IA

New money or incremental income: Money (or equivalent value) brought into the within-scope area because of the event. It can include government grants, sponsorship and media revenue, investment in venues or infrastructure; for most small and medium-sized events tourism expenditure is the biggest source.

Attribution or additionality: The attribution problem is this: what new money can we *attribute* to the event, as opposed to tourism in general or normal inflows? The event has to be the cause, otherwise we are talking about something other than event impacts. For tourists, we need to determine if they came solely or in part for the event, or stayed longer or spent more. See the detailed discussion later in this chapter for relevant methods. In the UK (see the EventImpacts website) where the term *additionality* is used to describe new money attributable to the event.

Direct impacts: Direct impacts are caused by tourist expenditure and other new money generated by events such as grant, sponsorship or media fees. These almost always account for the vast majority of income that can be attributed to events, making the use of multipliers unnecessary.

Secondary or indirect impacts: Businesses and individuals receiving new money spend some of it within-scope, resulting in secondary or indirect income for the area, but there are many leakages that reduce the contribution

Induced spending and induced demand: (a) increased consumer spending as a result of the new money coming into an area; this is considered in income multipliers as a *tertiary* effect

(b) Induced demand can be generated by the publicity surrounding an event

Linkages: Inter-business linkages constitute the event supply chain, and the ideal is to maximise local supply of labour and materials – these are *backward linkages*. For example, where does the food and beverages come from? the equipment? performers? staff?

Leakages: Any imports to the area result in the leakage of money, as does money paid externally to advertisers and workers, prize money taken outside the within-scope area, wages and profits sent away, and savings that do not circulate locally

Income multiplier: For every unit of currency brought into the within-scope area because of the event (i.e., new money attributable to the event), additional value is created by re-spending within the area (backward linkages) and by increased consumer spending owing to higher incomes

Capacity constraints: IA cannot assume that within a given area there is surplus capacity to meet the needs of new development or job creation; new construction and tourism demand from events cause inflation and diversions of materials and workers; importing supplies and workers reduces the economic contribution

Time switchers: Visitors who would have come to the area anyway, but because of the event they changed their schedule. This can be difficult to measure, requiring questions like this: "Would you have come here this year anyway if this event had not been held? What would be your reason for the planned trip?" Not only is it difficult to collect this information, but do people really know if they would have come? And during what time period – a year? It is arbitrary. Time switching exists, but is often ignored.

Casual tourists: These were in the area for other reasons, not the event being assessed, so their spending is not normally attributable to the event. However, they might provide a partial contribution by staying longer and spending more than normal because of the event.

Transferred expenditure: Local resident spending is usually transferred from one spending outlet to the event; it is part of the leisure budget of households. In some cases a major or unique event could stimulate spending above the normal. This is so hard to measure, and such a hypothetical question if put to residents that it is best to ignore local spending when estimating direct economic contribution. It might be a problem if residents change their spending habits in such a way that local businesses are hurt. This can happen when a mega event eats up a big proportion of local leisure budgets. Geographical transfer also occurs, with people attracted to an event and businesses in other areas consequently suffering.

Diverted expenditure: Major events have the effect of diverting money from other projects, this being an opportunity costs or alternative that should be evaluated before decisions are made. Labour and supplies will be diverted for mega construction projects such as new venues, and this can have a deleterious impact on other sectors of the economy.

Retained expenditure: An event might have the effect of keeping people at home who would otherwise spend money outside the local area. This retained expenditure is not new to the area, however, and should not be counted in the direct economic contribution.

An interesting issue does arise, being the competitiveness of destinations through event tourism. If a city has more attractive events, it is likely to retain more resident spending.

Displacement effects: Potential tourists sometimes stay away because of all the hype surrounding events, fearing a lack of accommodation, crowds, higher prices or perhaps crime. A lack of accommodation can be an impediment, and regular business or leisure travellers might be displaced by event tourists, resulting in no net increase in occupancy rates (but possibly an increase in yield). The same goes for residents who flee the city when events are held, because they do not like the atmosphere. This is all difficult to measure, again being somewhat hypothetical in the minds of people.

8.3.1 Maximising local benefits

The larger one delimits the within-scope area, the larger the multipliers can be. This depends mostly on the ability of the economy to provide the necessary inputs of labour, construction material, consumables and other supplies. In economies that rely on imports, as opposed to producing everything they need locally, the income multiplier is always small.

Some cities attract large numbers of day-trippers from surrounding regions for events, and their spending can be defined as being within-scope. It makes little financial difference to the event, or shops and restaurants, as long as its additional money. But remember that real tourists staying in commercial accommodation are the high-yield visitors that destinations want most. Also, if the within-scope area is expanded to include the hinterland of cities, this day-tripper contribution disappears.

If we want to maximise benefits there are several strategies to pursue. First, event organisers should focus on attracting high-yield tourists who come to the area mainly because of the event and spend a lot of money within-scope; usually these are the tourists who stay in commercial accommodation. Overnight visitors are also more likely to spend locally on food, restaurants, shopping and entertainment. Length of stay is important, so one-day events have less potential. Yield per visitor is much more important than the number of event tourists.

The Edinburgh impact study (BOP Consulting, 2016a, p.17) determined that the average number of nights spent in the city in 2015 by dedicated festival-goers (i.e., those whose spending was attributed, or additional) was 3.9, with 1.3 additional nights elsewhere in Scotland. Their average daily expenditure was about £50 per person (so group size matters a lot). Tickets to events accounted for about 19% of total within-city expenditure. Of the non-ticket spending, food and drink accounted for 30%, accommodation 29%, shopping 20%, other entertainment 14% and local transport 8%. This distribution of spending is important, and will vary a lot between events and cities. The longer people stay, the more opportunities there are to leverage the event for other businesses, and to get visitors into cultural attractions.

Performers, media, athletes, officials, sponsors, exhibitors, accompanying family, delegates, volunteers, and any other groups that might generate new money should be given encouragement. Participation events such as sport competitions for amateur athletes often attract large numbers of high-yield tourists plus accompanying family members, and they can be encouraged to stay longer for a holiday. Various studies have shown media personnel to be high in yield.

Developing backward linkages is also a key to maximising local economic benefits, and this is done by employing local workers and using local suppliers as much as possible. Generally a large events sector is needed to ensure the viability of technical suppliers like lighting, staging, audio-visual equipment. Managed portfolios of events therefore have greater potential to increase local economic benefits. Co-ordinating event timing can also help, by spreading demand over the year and spreading it geographically.

To the extent possible, event organisers and the event sector in general (or portfolio managers) will aim to leverage events to enhance economic benefits. Getting businesses involved, both as sponsors and planners, can increase the mount of money spent locally. Linking local businesses to external buyers or partners, through the experiences offered by events, can have longer-term benefits.

Legacy

This term is often used inappropriately to describe the purported long-term or permanent benefits of events and event tourism, whereas its real meaning is either (a) a gift of property, left in a person's legal will or (b) anything handed down from the past, as from an ancestor or predecessor. There is no doubt that people expect the event legacy to be positive, as reflected in efforts to use 'legacy' to justify major investments, but is just as likely to be in the form of debt, 'white-elephant' venues with no practical after-use, and displaced or marginalised groups. Orr and Jarvis (2018) surveyed sport-event organisers and concluded that "there is no universal understanding of legacies as a term or concept; and organizers are biased when asked about legacies, favoring the positive, and ignoring the negative." Reis et al. (2017) examined the literature on sport-event legacies, concluding that the evaluation of legacy seldom occurs. To do that requires the establishment of baseline data and access to consistent and comparable data. A long-term perspective is needed to determine if legacies have been sustained.

Ritchie (2001) discussed Olympic legacies and outlined the strategies and actions needed to ensure a positive event legacy, beginning with the establishment of a long-term vision and planning for realisation of specific legacy targets. Legacy programmes are generally associated with mega events and a number have been documented. Bottero et al. (2012, p. 205) reported on the evaluation of legacy of the Turin Winter Olympics of 2006, with five key themes related to tourism examined:

1   A territory open to external systems (networking and communication infrastructure).

2   A liveable environment (improving the quality of life for residents).

3   The enterprises and development (leveraging, innovating, new development).

4   A new type of tourism (sustainable tourism, geographical spread of benefits).

5   The landscape resource (improving natural and cultural heritage; image).

Bottero et al. concluded the event positively affected the local and regional tourism systems through increased demand and an improved image. Innovative approaches to governance involving local authorities was also a benefit with lasting impact, owing to better decision making.

The so-called *halo effect* describes the desired improvement of a city's or destination's image surrounding the hosting of a mega event. Event portfolio managers can aim for a similar permanent improvement in image through cumulative enhancements. The halo effect supposedly brings more tourists and small events to cities hosting mega events both before and after, and indeed there is some evidence to suggest that Olympic cities do gain this way – for a while.

A *quantum leap* is one way to describe how a destination can make a big leap forward in terms of its attractiveness because of events. Bidding on and hosting a mega event can be accompanied by improved marketing, better organisation and governance (such as through more stakeholder collaboration) and improved infrastructure (including transport, hotels, restaurants, and other services). This is in opposition to the incremental advances that can be realised through portfolio management, however the portfolio is permanent.

Positive economic legacy indicators:

♦   Capacity increased: the number and types of new event venues constructed; gains in marketing effectiveness and efficiency; infrastructure to accommodate increased tourism and trade; additions to the event portfolio attributable to new venues and improved reputation.

♦   Skills improved: number of volunteers and staff trained and future value of their time.

- Growth in size and reach of events; the asset value of each event and total portfolio value.

- Leveraging: the number of new organizations and businesses formed by the event; net increase in local business turnover and profits.

- Innovation fostered: new solutions to technological problems; new products and services created.

Negative economic legacy indicators:

- Gross public debt incurred

- Tax increases for residents and businesses

- Housing displacement (number of people displaced, costs incurred, units removed from supply)

- Jobs lost and businesses displaced

- Social and cultural harm (e.g., increases in crime, exclusion, mistrust)

- Ecological harm (e.g., loss of wildlife habitat; increased pollution)

Taxes

Taxation varies greatly from country to country, but it is true that many cities and destination organisations gain directly from events and event tourism. In North America it is fairly common for DMOs to obtain all or part of their revenue from hotel and/or restaurant taxes, so it obviously pays them to aggressively develop event tourism. Local governments do not always get the taxes from consumption, such as retail sales taxes or value added taxes, but events and tourism generate these in large numbers. Indeed, it is quite possible that the largest single beneficiaries of tourism, in financial terms, are governments and DMOs.

Consumer surplus and subsidies

Why would an IA include a measure of the consumer surplus accruing from an event? By testing 'willingness to pay' it might be found that some event-goers would be willing to pay more than they actually did pay for the experience, but is the difference between what was paid and what hypothetically might have been paid, a benefit?

IF a consumer surplus is created, it is clearly only for a small segment of the population – the ones who not only could afford to pay more, but would have done so in order to attend. But consider this – if the event was deliberately priced low in order to foster equity (as in "we want no-one excluded by price") then the main benefit is social, not economic. If government keeps the price low for social reasons, who is it really benefitting? The rich can afford to go at any price, so they benefit the most in monetary terms. Therefore in this context consumer surplus is an equity issue, not an economic one.

Spatial considerations

Tyrell and Johnston (2001) emphasized the spatial dimension of economic impact assessment for events and argued that regional cooperation could enhance benefits. If only a city is within-scope, the direct economic contribution will be smaller than if a region is studied. Moreover, tourists will often have difficulty knowing where exactly they spent money, as legal boundaries might mean little to them. Where visitors come from, and how their trips take place, are important variables. Day-trippers (not staying overnight) from the suburbs can add considerably to spending at an event, but perhaps no-where else. Account should also be taken of the origins and spending of officials, media, vendors and exhibitors, sponsors and volunteers, all of whom might add to local benefit, but also to leakages.

An important consideration for small towns and rural areas is often the lack of accommodation and other services, resulting in much of the potential economic impact of hosting an event accruing to nearby cities where the services are available. This too is an argument for regional cooperation, and has been studied in the context of 'central place theory' by Daniels (2007).

8.4 Considerations for types of events

Different types and sizes of events present challenges related to how impacts are generated, their goals, and how stakeholders evaluate them. The following sub-sections point to major differences, but this is not intended to be a definitive comparison. Figure 8.6 indicates special considerations and suggested economic impact indicators. Potentially the same type of comparison of event types could be made for social, cultural and environmental impacts, but that is going to require a focused research effort to get valid evidence.

Figure 8.6: Special considerations for types of events and their economic impacts

Types	Special considerations	Suggested key economic impact indicators
Festivals and other cultural celebrations Including parades, Pilgrimages, carnivals, commemorations	Many celebrations are not tourist oriented, are small in scale and generate little economic contribution	Number of tour groups and repeat visitors attracted (a measure of marketing efficiency)
	Hallmark events can be sport or cultural in nature, providing image and branding benefits as well as attracting tourists	Creating brand recognition and value through hallmark events
	Iconic events cater to special interest groups and can be sport or lifestyle oriented	Special-interest segments attracted (e.g., market share, growth potential)
	Many cities have built special festival places	Creating symbolic value through iconic events

Sport events
Single and multi-sport
Amateur and professional
	Spectators and participating athletes are the primary tourist segments; accompanying friends and family can be important
	
	Frequently dependent on special-purpose venues, although multi-purpose are more flexible
	
	International sport competitions can be mega events requiring huge investments
	
	Numerous smaller events are iconic, holding symbolic value for special-interest groups
		Yield per athlete/team/spectator/family group (spending x length of stay)
		
		More efficient use of facilities (revenue or operating costs subsidized)
		
		Enhanced reputation for cities and regions as sport-tourism destinations
		
		Enhanced reputation for organizing events and hosting sport-related visitors
		
		A positive sport legacy to host cities and countries in terms of:
		  New and/or improved sport facilities
		  Assistance to athletes and groups with special needs
		  Generate income for organisers and federations
		  Promote the sport/organization through event media coverage (generating positive image and increased awareness, public and political support)
		  Capacity building: foster learning and competence building with regard to winning and hosting future events
		  Increased sponsorship and improved networking with the corporate world

Business events Meetings Conventions Congresses Exhibitions & world fairs Consumer and trade shows	Association events differ from corporate events in terms of motivation to attend, and who pays Consumer and trade shows differ in terms of purpose and target audiences Special-purpose convention and exhibition centres are found in most cities but other venues are widely used	Yield per visitor (length of stay x spending) The number of accompanying family Potential repeat visits (i.e. the same events held periodically) Number of international attendees International trade links established (e.g., contacts, contracts signed, knowledge transferred) Leveraging effects for local businesses (e.g., new supply opportunities) Sales volumes generated
Entertainment Travelling shows Music concerts Mobile exhibitions (art, etc.)	Usually produced in the private sector within built venues like arenas & theatres; sometimes temporary structures are used Museums and galleries attracting mobile exhibitions usually are not-for-profits	Revenue and publicity gains for public venues Profit and monetary ROI Number of first time and repeat customers (indicating both loyalty and renewal of a customer base)

8.4.1 Sport events

There are many books that cover sport-event and sport-tourism impacts, including: Crompton (1999); Ritchie & Adair (2004); Preuss (2004); Higham (2005); Rosentraub (2009); Weed (2008 a/b); Weed and Bull (2004); Shin (2010); Hinch & Higham (2011); Maennig & Zimbalist (2012); Shipway & Fyall (2012); Masterman (2014); Zimbalist (2015a).

Crompton (1999) revealed the potential significance of amateur, minor sport tournaments in the USA, with economic impacts being related to the length of the event (short ones generate few bednights in commercial accommodation), the number of teams, and whether or not families accompanied participants. Youth events usually had higher impacts because they were family experiences, and this target audience remains an important source of benefit in many cities and towns. Daniels and Norman (2003) concluded that regular sport events maximised their economic benefit if they required little or no bidding, the infrastructure was already in place, there was little or no public subsidy, and residents were not adversely impacted. Gratton, Shibli and Coleman (2005) reported on a UK study, finding that media events with TV audiences can generate long stays and high. Also, events attracting seniors (e.g. Masters games) had high impact owing to the average income levels and daily expenditure of participants, plus their propensity to add holidays.

UK Sport (2004) reported on impact assessments of 16 major sporting events and made the key finding that spectator quantity and spending was the key determinant of economic impact. Over 80% of the impact was attributable to visitor spending, with organisers accounting for 20% or less, on average. Participation events generate considerable tourist expenditure if commercial accommodation is used. For additional insights on this topic re-visit the discussion of forecasting in Chapter 3 and the reference to Ramchandani and Coleman (2012).

Participation sport events depend mostly upon the travel and spending of amateur athletes when it comes to generating economic impacts. Sometimes participants are billeted in homes, or stay with friends and relatives, in which case their spending in an area is greatly reduced. The same issue arises for wilderness events like the TransRockies Run and bicycle events reported by Getz and McConnell (2011, 2014) when participants stay in temporary tent villages. Other distance events go from village to village, using a variety of accommodation, and this model has potentially greater impacts, and on multiple communities.

Potwarka and Snelgrove (2017) summarized the literature on sport-event impacts by noting that economic benefits have received significant attention, but recently a shift has been observed towards more intangible benefits such as social cohesion, urban regeneration and sport participation. More interest in negative impacts has been recorded, including diversion of taxes, congestion, displacement of residents and environmental damage.

In terms of forecasting, the implications are clear: be certain to make reliable predictions of tourist numbers, segments and their average spending. To do this requires detailed knowledge from comparable impact assessments. Most forecasting errors will likely be due to over or underestimating the number of dedicated event tourists who will use commercial accommodation, and their average length of stay. IA also has to include impacts from the sport media (who tend to stay longer and spend more when covering major events), officials, volunteers, sponsors and members of governing bodies. For more detail on all these stakeholders see the *Routledge Handbook of Sports Event Management* (Parent & Chappelet, 2015).

8.4.2 Festivals and other cultural celebrations

This category of planned events is primarily concerned with the arts and social/cultural impacts, nevertheless their economic impacts have been widely studied. Many festivals are required (or feel obliged) to demonstrate economic impacts for funding agencies, and to participate in tourism and place-marketing strategies. Recent books covering festival impacts include Newbold et al. (2015, *Focus On Festivals*), Lundberg et al. (*The Value of Events*, 2017) and Mair (*Routledge Handbook of Festivals*, 2019).

There are a number of challenges somewhat unique to festivals and other celebrations, starting with measuring attendance at open events (Tyrrell and Ismail, 2005). The main problem is that of estimating proportions of residents and other segments versus dedicated festival tourists. Resistance to quantification can be an issue, either on the part of organisers who do not want to 'play the numbers game', stakeholders who value celebrations intrinsically, and perhaps some attendees who are too involved with their experience to participate in data collection. Beyond tourism impact, there are a number of additional benefits related to arts and culture development, some of which are economic in nature and discussed elsewhere in this book.

Multiple festivals have been studied in several cities, reflecting a portfolio approach to impact assessment. BOP Consulting (2011) conducted a study of Edinburgh's twelve major festivals, covering social, cultural, environmental, economic and media impacts. Compared to an earlier, similar study it was found that the overall economic contribution had considerably increased. For the year 2010, the Edinburgh Festivals were estimated to have generated new output of £245m in Edinburgh and £261m in Scotland, £59m in new income in Edinburgh and £82m in Scotland, and supported 5,242 new FTE jobs in Edinburgh and 4,917 in Scotland. Other economic impacts discussed for the Edinburgh festivals were routes to employment and skills provided by festivals, supporting the wider economy in Edinburgh and Scotland, and providing a marketing platform for sponsors and stakeholders.

8.4.3 Entertainment and music events

UK Music conducted a study of music events (Wish You Were Here 2015: Music Tourism's Contribution to the UK Economy), reporting that "...music tourism in the UK increased by 34% between 2011 and 2014, with 9.5 million people travelling to music events in 2014. These music tourists, attending live concerts and festivals in the UK, helped generate £3.1 billion pounds in direct and indirect spend." Music festivals and concerts were also credited with having increased happiness and wellbeing in the country, and generating wealth for many localities. As an export industry, music events were generating increasing numbers of international arrivals, each with an average spend of £751, and this supported 38,238 full time jobs in 2014. The figures are based on attendances at live music events with a capacity limit of at least 1,500, and cultural festivals, arts festivals and musical theatre were excluded.

8.4.4 Business events

Private business meetings and corporate events will have their own ROI and ROE measures of performance, but many business events are considered to be event tourism, important to place marketing, and with additional possible economic benefits related to knowledge, networking and trade.

Dwyer (2002: 21-35) noted the following key facts about conventions, and these can also apply to exhibitions and fairs:

◆ Substantial numbers of people accompany convention-goers (in Australia the accompanying tourists add 15-20% to convention-related expenditures).

◆ Convention tourists are likely to spend more than other types of visitor (in Singapore, about three times as much!).

◆ International convention tourists stay longer and spend more than domestic visitors.

◆ Corporate and medical conferences generate the highest visitor expenditure.

◆ Longer conventions generate more spending in total.

◆ Pre- and post-meeting tours add considerably to the economic impacts (in one study, up to 50% of total spending by international convention-goers was on tours).

◆ Substantial economic benefits can also accrue from spending by organizers, associations and sponsors (if it is 'new money' to the area).

◆ International convention tourists (at least in Australia) spend most of their money in capital cities and tourist 'gateways', while interstate visitors spend equally in urban and non-urban areas.

In 2011 the Convention Industry Council released a study entitled *The Economic Significance of Meetings to the U.S. Economy* (www.MeetingsMeanBusiness. com) and reported that "the U.S. meetings industry directly supports 1.7 million jobs, a $106 billion contribution to GDP, $263 billion in spending, $60 billion in labor revenue, $14.3 billion in federal tax revenue and $11.3 billion in state and local tax revenue". Key impact factors include the fact that the vast majority were held at venues with commercial accommodation, generating 250 million overnight stays, 5 million of these by international tourists. The study also concluded that: "The meetings serve as vehicles for job training and education, generating sales revenue, linking domestic and foreign buyers and developing lasting relationships in personal environments that build trust and unity."

Other impacts can be measured in terms of learning and resultant ROI for businesses or career progression for professionals, fundraising for charities, and image enhancement for destinations.

Mair (2013) tabulated benefits and costs and noted that business-event bidding and venues are very expensive, and spending can be very unequal spatially and by economic sector. Cities compete in different leagues with convention and exhibition centres, their size being one factor in attracting events. A number of books deal with venue and city attractiveness for business events (e.g., Fenich, 2014; Rogers and Davidson (2014); Davidson and Hyde, 2015).

Impact assessment for business events has to start with the different value perspectives of stakeholders: the venues, destinations/cities, corporations, associations and attendees. Each has a set of goals and key impact indicators that shape impact assessment and ultimately the evaluation of outcomes. As distinct from other types of planned events, business events often go unnoticed in cities, being highly targeted or open only to invitees, and held indoors in otherwise busy city centres.

8.4.5 Mega event economic impacts

Mega events are able to cause a shock to the system, and within economic systems this can be achieved through large injections of capital for physical developments and operations, numerous visitors and their spending, and media coverage that influences image, reputation and attractiveness of the city or nation. Economic impacts are felt from the start of bidding, through the event, and potentially for many years afterwards. Mega events can also cause disasters and tragedies (from terrorism to disease), be the catalysts for major urban and environmental change, and create positive or negative legacies that last generations. The study of mega-event impacts includes books by Weed (2008), Maennig & Zimbalist (2012), the UNWTO (2017) and Frawley (2017).

Of all the impacts, none has been more visible and controversial than the enormous expenditure on venues and infrastructure that is required for sports and world's fairs. While convention/exhibition centres and arts/cultural venues have long, active lives, too many purpose-built facilities for sports and World's Fairs have little or no viable after-use. Many sports facilities have fallen into disrepair, while most World's Fair sites have been re-purposed (some leaving iconic structures behind). Although invisible, the debt legacy of many mega events has been substantial, and governments prefer to keep quiet about it.

Many economists and other researchers have been very critical of the purported economic benefits of mega events, relative to costs, and of the neglect of externalities, distributional or equity issues and other negative impacts. Mills and Rosentraub (2012) argued that the financial benefits claimed by mega-event boosters are hardly ever realized, and that overestimation of economic gains is the norm. Mostly held in major urban areas, mega events bring substantial displacement of business and substitution effects (that is, spending patterns are changed). Zimbalist (2015b, p. 35) concluded: "Scholarly evidence suggests that hosting either the IOC's Olympic Games or FIFA's World Cup event is no economic bargain for the host city or country." As to legacy, Zimbalist documented the resulting debt, for example London's 2012 Olympics, and added (p.36): "... the independent scholarship has not corroborated any long-term gains in tourism, trade or foreign investment from hosting".

Other than entertainment and feel-good effects, the literature makes it clear that most of the gains of mega events accrue to special-interest groups, the elites in society, and to politicians who can boast of their triumphs. This is why I always advocate permanent events and managed event portfolios to deliver the real public good.

8.4.6 Hallmark and iconic event impacts

Hallmark events are those with tradition, are periodic, and tend to be permanent institutions (Getz & Andersson, 2008). They are valued by residents and other stakeholders for their contributions across many social, economic and cultural domains. Most occupy public sites and venues. When threatened, they are almost always saved. They solve real problems and deliver high value for little cost. For additional material on the goals, planning and impacts of hallmark events see Getz et al. (2012).

It is almost certain that permanent events (or 'enduring festivals' as defined by Derrett, 2016) have committed stakeholders, including a strong volunteer core, long-term sponsors and political support. In these situations, evaluation and impact assessment will be both routine (for problem solving and decision making) and able to focus on the multiple, public-good outcomes that have been discussed in this book – such as social capital formation, inclusivity, sustainability, image enhancement and tourist attractiveness.

Iconic events are targeted at special interests by providing specific benefits and high symbolic value (Getz, 2013). They can be one-time or periodic, and permanent iconic events are built around a strong brand and in-depth knowledge of the social world or special-interest being attracted. Evaluation will focus on meeting the needs of the customers/guests, and impact assessment on sustaining the long-term value propositions. For many special interests, such as runners and mountain bikers, personal development is the key motivator, but communitas - belonging and sharing within a group – is also important.

Hallmark events can also be iconic, there is no contradiction, because both terms are related to the function of events, not their form (see Getz, 2015b). They can perform as tourist attractions, co-branded with destinations, and bring tourists to areas that might not otherwise be considered attractive. Their long-term value combined with lower costs (compared to bidding on one-time events and start-ups) should make them the central part of event portfolio strategies.

8.5 Methods for economic IA

The standard economic impact assessment model for events and tourism has employed multipliers derived from the input–output (I–O) tables that most countries publish. According to Dwyer, Forsyth & Spurr (2006) I-O modelling has serious limitations, namely fixed technical coefficients, no capacity constraints, and consequently no impact of an event on wages or prices is measured. This means it fails to capture interactive effects and ends up exaggerating the purported economic benefits.

Computable general equilibrium (CGE) models are better able to capture the complex pattern of price changes, feedback effects and resource constraints which exist in all economies following a shock such as the holding of a mega event (Blake 2005; Dwyer, 2015). CGE modelling can incorporate different assumptions about price increases and constraints and recognizes that contractions might occur in economic activity in some sectors or the whole economy. However, it is very expensive to construct a new CGE model.

Most planned events produce little or no 'shock' to the economy and therefore long-term or structural impacts cannot occur; surplus capacity of labour and materials exists in most economies and that surplus absorbs the demand. Events cumulatively can alter the economy of a city or destination, and mega events with high investment costs can exhaust available supply and lead to inflation. What we want for most events, most of the time, is a simple way to indicate their economic contribution. These measures can be compared, when standard methods are used, and changes over time can be monitored leading to improved forecasting capability.

8.5.1 The process of economic impact assessment

The following steps are necessary for reliably forecasting economic impacts and for post-event quantification of the event's 'direct economic contribution'. I consider multipliers and econometric models to be unnecessary and potentially misleading. Standard methods and measures are necessary to permit meta-analysis and improve forecasting, for transparency and accountability. Both the before and after steps are included here, reflecting the principle that if only forecasts of impacts are made, without post-event estimates, we learn nothing and can easily be fooled.

1 *Define 'within-scope'* (most IAs are done for a city or region, but a well-designed IA can provide simultaneous forecasts and estimates for cities, regions and nations).

2 *Profile the event*: based on past experience, benchmarking, and the event's marketing plan, what types and numbers of visitors are expected? (i.e., demand forecasting); careful segmentation of visitors is important, including media, staff and volunteers, participants versus spectators, etc.; it is critical to make realistic forecasts and post-event estimates of the number and types of dedicated event tourists (i.e., the attribution problem), including the proportions of casuals and time switchers.

3 *Forecasts*: make a forecast of 'new money' expected from visitors using a Direct Economic Contribution Calculator (see the Methods section). The accuracy of such forecasts improves through meta analysis.

4 *Assess the event's finances and budget*: what are the planned costs and revenues of the organisers and other stakeholders? Forecast how much new money will be brought into the within-scope area because of the event, and how much direct leakage will occur. Organisers must monitor costs and revenues over the full life cycle of the event. Event organisers will have to provide detailed post-event accounts to measure inflows and outflows.

5 *Prepare a logic model or Theory of Change model.* A simple logic model is appropriate for forecasting and assessing outputs like attendance and direct economic contribution, but for longer-term impacts or legacies a TOC model is better. Both require setting goals and indicators, then determining the actions needed (and related assumptions) to achieve the goals.

6 *Consider costs, externalities and negative impacts*: how will these be identified and mitigated? These are not usually considered in logic and TOC models, but are essential to the comprehensive IA process. Full stakeholder consultations will broaden the scope of economic IA to ensure all issues and costs are identified.

7 *Design research instruments and sampling methods for visitor surveys.* Ideally random samples are desired, and these are feasible at ticketed and gated events. But many events will only be able to obtain a systematic or representative sample of attendees, and from this it is necessary to generate a reliable estimate of tourist numbers, types and spending.

Also make accurate counts or reliable estimates of attendance in various segments (especially isolating the number and expenditure of dedicated event tourists; media, officials, volunteers/staff, exhibitors, suppliers, etc.). When conducting visitor surveys individuals are to be the focus, not groups; make a statistical estimate of sampling errors; compare characteristics of the sample to what is known about the entire visitor population to ensure that the sample is representative.

It is critical to determine the proportion of total visitor spending that is attributable to the event, or 'additional'. Several questions can be asked, and these are from the Edinburgh impact study (BOP Consulting 2016b - Technical Report, p. 3): "How important was the Festival in your decision to visit Scotland?" The possible answers: "My sole reason for coming; a very important reason; a fairly important reason; only a small reason; of no importance at all".

This method assumes the whole Scottish trip is attributed to the festival where the visitor was surveyed. It leads to an estimate of what proportion of the respondent's expenditures can be attributed to that particular event. An alternative is to limit the question to yes or no (Q: "Was this festival the sole reason for your trip") or to ask the respondent to give a percentage (Q: "What percentage of your trip do you attribute to this event?"). Ideally, you want everyone to say it was their sole reason, but realistically that will only account for a portion. The 2015 IA found that "the percentage of people that spent one or more nights in Scotland who reported that the Festival was their 'sole reason' for visiting Scotland has increased from 33.3% in 2010 to 42.9% in 2015" (p.3, Technical Report).

8   *Post-event, estimate average and total tourist expenditures* (broken down by segments, as noted above). Estimates must not include the spending of casual tourists unless it can be determined that they stayed longer or spent more because of the event. Time-switchers are treated in the same way. Both categories should be eliminated from the estimates if such data are not provided (or, estimates might be based on past experience or comparable events).

     ♦   Commercial and other accommodation costs might be aquired from suppliers in order to obtain reliable expenditure estimates.

     ♦   Some data might be acquired from teams or other touring groups in order to obtain reliable estimates of spending (e.g., for group travel, meals and accommodation).

9   *Combine estimated new money from tourists with new money accruing to the event organisation to obtain the direct economic contribution.* Compare post-event estimates with forecasts and consider reasons for any observed differences; large variances are to be expected if forecasts of tourist numbers, types and spending were wrong

10   *Comparing costs and benefits* is the final step, including evaluation of distributional and legacy impacts and related equity issues (see the final chapter).

8.5.2 Estimating the direct economic contribution (DEC)

Otherwise referred to as the direct economic impact, the DEC is the simplest and most reliable tool for economic impact assessors. It measures the new money brought into the within-scope area as a direct result of hosting an event (or events). This is money spent locally by event tourists, money received by event organisers from outside the area, and any other funds coming into the area because of the event, such as local spending by sponsors. No multipliers or econometric models are used.

A DEC calculator is provided at the website EventImpacts.com, and a number of professional associations provide members with these tools. Always evaluate them by asking what evidence has been accumulated and analysed to produce reliable forecasts.

The DEC method is widely recommended, including by Don Schumacher, executive director of the (USA) National Association of Sports Commissions, as quoted in Street and Smith's Sportbusiness Journal, August 4-10, 2014, p. 26:

"The NASC recommends that cities look only at the estimated direct spending from an event to create a fair cost analysis as opposed to a more vague economic impact analysis. The association provides its members with a formula for those calculations. A direct spending analysis is safer, Schumacher said."

And from www.eventimpacts.com:

"There is broad consensus on the standard approach to measuring the economic impact of an event. The spending patterns of event attendees are sampled, averaged and then upscaled to the overall 'event population'. This is typically combined with an assessment of the net spending in the host economy by the event organiser to determine the Direct Economic Impact. This process typically requires some primary research in the form of surveying event attendees to evaluate peoples' spending patterns at the event. Whilst not excessively complex or longitudinal in nature, this research is normally best carried out by a specialist contractor.

Within this basic approach however, there is the potential for diverging results based on different interpretations of the stages within the process. There can be varying approaches to: defining the host economy, surveying and sampling parameters, treatment of local residents, measuring economic flows in and out of the host economy, and the application of multipliers (which is covered in Advanced Economic Impacts). Arguably the biggest scope for error is in upscaling visitor spending patterns to an inaccurate event population - a factor which highlights the importance of securing accurate attendance data."

Dwyer et al. (2010, p. 435) called DEC "direct in-scope expenditure" and stressed its advantages:

♦ "Direct in-scope expenditure measures the level of new funds that are attracted to the region as a result of the event, and which provide the injection for subsequent flow-on impacts in the local economy.

♦ Direct in-scope expenditure can be used to compare quite simply the economic performance of one event with another and thus underpin government decisions as to which events to support as higher priorities.

♦ A further benefit of this approach is that economic impact analysis can be done subsequently if required, given that a direct in-scope expenditure figure is the fundamental starting point for any economic impact study irrespective of which economic model is used.

♦ As long as it is understood to be indicative of the economic significance of the event, the new or inscope expenditure estimate can be a very informative key performance measures."

Davies et al (2013) made the case for using the direct economic contribution "as a pragmatic tool for more routinely held events" and suggested "that it provides industry stakeholders with a method for evaluating event-related economic activity, which retains academic credibility while taking account of limited resources." Those researchers also stressed that it does not consider costs and alternatives.

What data do you need? The EventImpacts site makes it clear that if you enter garbage, that will be the result you get! Entering hypothetical data might be useful as a starting point, like doing sensitivity analysis (e.g., if we get 1,000 international tourists what might the impact be?) but without reliable data from systematic research, calculators that forecast or measure post-event impacts do not produce anything valid or comparable. The accuracy of forecasts and post-event calculations depends upon meta-analysis of similar events using similar methods in the same city or region. EventImpacts considers London and the main regions of the UK.

I have annotated the data categories below, because nothing is ever as simple as a calculator makes it appear. The EventImpacts site provides background material and examples. You MUST read the Guidance Notes (a downloadable PDF). Getting the right data, avoiding invalid assumptions, and knowing how to interpret forecasts and post-event impact assessments is crucial.

Data required to forecast and calculate visitor contribution

Attendance forecasts and counts

♦ Total numbers of spectators, participants, officials, media, sponsors, staff, volunteers, guests

♦ Percentage of residents versus tourists (requires data on home location and where travel began)

♦ Number of dedicated event tourists (requires data on their motivation; cannot include spending of casuals and time switchers)

It is crucial to accurately segment the attendees and participants in order to assign average spending and to estimate new money brought into the country or city. It is also crucial to make estimates on the basis of individuals, as it is individuals that will be sampled. While it is useful to know party size and characteristics (e.g., families, groups of friends, teams), estimates of expenditure, length of stay and use of commercial accommodation must be for individuals. Also, it is necessary to remember that multiple visits are possible, and people must not be sampled twice.

Expenditure

♦   The spending of all visitors (including residents, media, officials) will be important for financial analysis

♦   For dedicated event tourists data are needed on: length of stay in nights; accommodation used; daily average spending by person (requires data on group size and type); breakdown of where money is spent)

♦   Main spending outlets to be included: accommodation; meals in restaurants; food purchase for self-catering; local transport including bus and taxi; petrol/gasoline purchases for private automobiles (separate amounts spent on-site from elsewhere in the within-scope area; usually it is important to cover local, regional and national levels of spending so that money not coming into the country is excluded)

For forecasts, using averages based on past event evaluations is possible, or if comparable data are not available use averages for tourists visiting the country or the area being studied. For post-event evaluations it is best to use data from original research, namely systematic or random sampling of event visitors.

Estimations

Based on samples (random or systematic), overall amounts can be estimated, such as in this example:

Step i) Estimated total number of commercial bed nights =

> Number of dedicated event tourists staying in commercial accommodation
> x average number of nights spent in the host economy ('within-scope')

Step ii) Total amount spend on commercial accommodation =

> Total commercial bed-nights x average cost per bed-night

(Average cost can be estimated from data provided by hotels etc.; otherwise, use spending estimates provided by the tourists.)

Estimates will be more accurate when made for specific segments. For example, make separate estimates for domestic and international tourists, for those staying in commercial accommodation versus those using self-catering, etc.

Note that in the absence of data from an event, it becomes necessary to use averages from general tourist surveys or other, comparable events – those estimates will likely be less accurate.

Data required to forecast and calculate an event organisation's economic contribution

Evaluation and accountability reports from event organisers should routinely include the following information:

♦ Event-specific revenue generated for the organisers by: ticket and package sales; media rights; sponsor fees; grants from governments

♦ Leakages from the within-scope area, such as: advertising; fees paid to event owners; travel connected to bids, planning, operations; prize money taken out of the area

♦ Debt incurred (specifically the cost of repayments) and money spent on capital improvements (i.e., investments)

The aim is to separate event-specific costs and revenues from ongoing financial transactions, and to be able to identify new money and leakages as part of the calculation of the *economic contribution* of an event.

8.6 Presenting the results

The economic impact assessment report can be summarized as illustrated in Figure 8.7.

Standard methods and measures should be used to ensure comparability and permit meta-analysis. Instead of showing hypothetical monetary amounts I have added comments in the cells to emphasize planning, research and analytic issues.

This example is of an amateur football tournament held over three days. The within-scope area for economic contribution is the city. Athletes must register, and therefore the numbers are accurate (unless there are no-shows); spectators get in free, and other important segments are accredited officials, media, sponsors, suppliers and exhibitors (so their numbers are known). Estimating spectator numbers at free events presents a measurement challenge, and for this task advice is available at the EventImpacts website, in the book Event Tourism (Getz, 2013), and an article by Tyrell & Ismail (2005).

Each event will have its own mix of visitor segments, and it is important to record or estimate their numbers, determine what proportion of their spending is attributable to the event (i.e., who are the dedicated event tourists, or the attribution problem), and how much they spend. It is important to also know where they spend their money within-scope. When estimating direct economic contribution the critical variable is the number of dedicated event tourists staying in commercial accommodation as their yield is the highest (i.e., average number of days X average within-scope expenditure). The unit of measurement will be the individual, unless only group data are available.

Figure 8.7: Sample summary of the economic contribution of an event (adapted from EventImpacts (economictoolkit))

Name of event; date; venue(s); description; within-scope area (e.g., 3-day amateur football tournament)

	Participating athletes and their team personnel	Spectators	Officials, media, sponsors, suppliers, exhibitors	Totals
Attendance	Count registered numbers, minus no-shows, for total attendance of athletes and team personnel	Event is free to enter: numbers estimated over 3 days by sampling each day; avoid double-counting as spectators might attend multiple times; report totals for 'through the gate' distinct from number of individuals who attended Separate locals from tourists, athletes/volunteers from others	Accredited numbers should be available, otherwise a survey is needed.	
Number of dedicated event tourists -volunteers from outside the local area that are recruited by organisers are a special case; they might have a significant economic contribution so sample them separately as to trip motive and spending	Count only from outside within-scope area; most visiting athletes/teams are dedicated event tourists, but could have other reasons for the trip, e.g. multiple events; team surveys will confirm travel purpose, team numbers and spending	There are usually friends and relatives accompanying amateur athletes and most will therefore be dedicated event tourists (but they have to be asked!) It is sometimes necessary to estimate the proportion of a visitor's trip that can be attributed to the event Deduct local 'casuals' and 'time switchers'	Separate locals from visitors; most visitors will likely be dedicated event tourists, but they have to be asked.	
Attribution: Calculate the proportion and/or numbers attributed to the event (If multiple reasons for travel, not all within-scope expenditure can be attributed to event)	One of the top reasons for hosting participation events is the high proportion of dedicated event tourists they attract.	Deduct local spectators; Count "day-tripper" visitors from outside the area and their within-scope spending	Attracting external suppliers, etc., might conflict with the aim of leveraging events for local businesses.	
Spending estimates Separate within-scope from external spending, (some trip-related expenses will not impact host area) Report average daily spend per person Accommodation recorded separately, as below Merchandise and food/beverages bought at event Food/beverages bought elsewhere, within-scope Local travel (e.g., taxis, auto expenses) Groceries for self-catering Restaurant meals Entertainment/attractions	There is a choice of diary method or surveys; sometimes team spending has to be covered separately	Accompanying friends and family will likely spend time and money outside the event	A local business survey can reveal if they experienced additional turnover and/or profit as a result of the event; local sponsors and suppliers are backward linkages that enhance the income multiplier	

Number of commercial bed-nights occupied by each segment (av. no. of nights X no. of dedicated event tourists staying overnight) Report av. length of stay in nights, per person	It is possible that the athletes/teams stay for different lengths of time, and in commercial and non-commercial accommodation	Attracting families, especially for multi-day youth sports, is a good way to boost use of local commercial accommodation.	For major events, sponsors and media can be a source of high-yield tourists
Total direct economic contribution by tourists, within-scope In some studies estimates can be provided for local, regional and national levels	Depending on the event, participants or spectators might provide the highest yield		
Organiser contribution -full post-event accounts will be needed -not all their local spending can be counted; leakages (external spending) has to be deducted; do not include grants or other funds that are not linked to the event			
Total direct economic contribution -tourist plus organiser contributions			

The second part of this table presents a summary of the event organiser's contribution. This should be based on post-event accounts that document how much money came into the area because of the event, and how much was outflowing; the net contribution is required. There can be many leakages, including prize money, advertising, pre-event travel by organisers, fees paid to external officials, imports of supplies, labour costs, etc. Inflows might include sponsorship, grants received, and fees paid by participants and vendors.

A Caution

Very few researchers on their own will tackle the challenge of economic impact assessment, but many consulting forms do it regularly. Being informed of the issues and complications is essential to ensure that whoever hires the IA specialists knows exactly what to require of them (i.e., no black-box models! stick to the direct economic contribution method; provide evidence from other reputable studies). Events need to work collaboratively with researchers, professional associations and government agencies to ensure appropriate, standardized methods are used, meta-analysis occurs, and IA continuously improves.

Study questions

1　Discuss the potential economic benefits and costs of bidding on and producing events, with emphasis on equity and distributional impacts.

2　Use your knowledge of how economic benefits are created from events and tourism to recommend a strategy for maximising local income and jobs. Provide a diagram to illustrate the inflows and outflows of money.

3　Describe the steps to be taken when conducting an economic IA, with details provided on how to forecast and, post-event, estimate the direct economic contribution.

Recommended additional readings and sources

EventImpacts (economic toolkit.pdf)

Shipway, R. & Fyall, A. (Eds.)(2012). *International Sports Events: Impacts, Experiences and Identities*. London: Routledge.

Maennig, W. & Zimbalist, A. (Eds.)(2012). *International Handbook on the Economics of Mega Sporting Events*. Edward Elgar Publishing.

Zimbalist, A. (2015). *Circus Maximus: The Economic Gamble Behind Hosting the Olympics and the World Cup*. Washington D.C.: Brookings Institution Press

9 Conclusions

Learning objectives

- ☐ Learn the uses and limitations of traditional cost-benefit analysis (CBA)
- ☐ Be able to evaluate costs and benefits comprehensively using key impact indicators.
- ☐ Understand and be able to apply the BACE model of planning, evaluation and impact assessment to events and tourism.

9.1 Cost-Benefit Analysis (CBA)

The first part of this chapter is devoted to discussing CBA and offering a more comprehensive approach that employs selected Key Impact Indicators presented throughout this book. In the second part the BACE model is presented as a framework for integrating evaluation and impact assessment within a strategic planning process.

Often CBA is done only for the economic dimension, in monetary terms, and as part of forecasting or a feasibility study. The triple-impact-assessment method of Andersson and Lundberg (2013) has been developed to overcome the incommensurability problem (i.e., different measures for different impact objects), but it is not always acceptable to express all costs and benefits in monetary terms. The Event Compass, as discussed in the companion book, follows a goal-attainment approach that does not require comparable measures for each impact dimension.

According to Dwyer et al. (2010: 267) CBA does the following:

- ♦ Assesses all costs and benefits in monetary terms over the expected life of a project.
- ♦ Measures changes in all sources of economic welfare, both increases and decreases.
- ♦ Shows the estimated net effect of welfare changes, including comparing a hypothetical project to not taking any action; alternatives can be compared and ranked.
- ♦ Discounts future costs and benefits.

According to Dwyer et al., for a public-sector capital investment (or programme or policy) to be socially acceptable, the sum of benefits to society (both private and social benefits) must exceed the sum of the costs to society. However, this does not necessarily take into account distributional effects (i.e., equity).

There are eight steps in the CBA process, according to Dwyer et al. (p. 402):

1 Determination of the scope and objectives of the assessment
2 Consideration of alternatives (e.g., alternative events, investments, policies; doing nothing)
3 Identification of likely or realized impacts
4 Valuation of costs and benefits in monetary terms
5 Discounting of future costs and benefits
6 Application of decision rules (i.e., investment criteria can be evaluated using net present value, internal rate of return or benefit-cost ratio)
7 Sensitivity analysis (test for optimistic or pessimistic scenarios, such as attendance forecasts, inflation rates, exchange rates, etc.)
8 Post implementation review

Some risks are known, others cannot be estimated, so forecasts will include uncertainty. Post-event assessments should therefore be compared to forecasts.

Dwyer et al. (2010, p. 452-3) emphasize two major points in calling for improvements in event evaluation. The first is to use a CGE approach to estimating effects on output (GSP or GDP) and employment plus a cost-benefit analysis. There is also a need to consider inter-jurisdictional effects when government support is sought, because costs and benefits do not always respect borders. The second point is the need for a better institutional framework for 'event assessment'. Here they note that event development corporations (and this will include most DMOs) have too great an incentive to oversell and 'win' events. An appropriate body to evaluate bids and plans would have the mandate and means to assess alternative uses of money (i.e., opportunity costs). Evaluations should have to compare economic, social and environmental costs and benefits, plus risks have to be assessed and their management monitored closely.

Full CBA is probably too complex for most professionals considering the impacts of events and tourism, and will likely not be attempted in most event and event-portfolio management situations. A short-form is recommended below, utilizing some of the key impact indicators recommended in this book. From each chapter's lists of objects and subjects KIIs have been selected, but these can be substituted by users, appropiate to circumstances.

Figure 9.1 shows a range of suggested key benefit indicators on the left and key indicators of costs and negative impacts in the right-hand column. They do not match one on one, as benefits do not always offset costs, and vice versa (a discussion of this crucial issue ends the chapter). I have selected only a few indicators from each chapter to illustrate this analytical framework.

Figure 9.1: Sample key impact indicators for the evaluation of benefits and costs

Suggested KIIs: benefits	Suggested KIIs: costs & negative impacts
Social	**Social**
Perceived personal, group and community benefits (e.g., personal development, identity, pride, inclusion)	Perceived personal, group and community harm
Use and option values: more entertainment, educational or leisure opportunities	Displacement: from affordable housing or established neighbourhoods
Non-use values: belief that events/projects are good for everyone or offer more choice	Amenity and health (e.g., noise, crime, congestion, accidents, disease)
Personal & family socializing/networking opportunities	Exclusion (owing to lack of affordability or access)
Real gains in quality of life (owing to economic gains)	Conflict or social disharmony; over-tourism
Social capital formation (trust, volunteering, collaborations)	
Cultural	**Cultural**
Audience development for the arts and cultural events	Loss of traditions or authenticity
Cultural capital formation for individuals and families	Loss of identity (acculturation)
Artistic creativity enhanced	Host-guest friction or unequal relationships
Heritage conservation (built and intangible)	Cultural appropriation
Cultural identity strengthened	Decline in native language, customs, values
Built environment	**Built environment**
Animated spaces for all groups	Costs of mitigating physical damage through over-use
Enhanced liveability (e.g., services, housing, leisure, parks)	Costs of necessary infrastructure improvements to accommodate events and venues
Image or reputation gains	Disruption to residents' lifestyles and daily patterns of movement; congestion
Increased place identity and attachment	
Nature & ecological processes	**Nature & ecological processes**
Reduced carbon emissions and ecological footprint	Damage to wildlife and habitat
Conservation enhancements (e.g., investments made as part of or a result of the event); better access to nature	Erosion and flooding
Enhanced awareness & support for conservation	Pollution (air, water, land, noise)
Efficiency gains for energy, water and other consumables; recycling and re-use	Costs of waste disposal
	Costs of energy consumed
Economic	**Economic**
Employment for residents (numbers, quality, safety)	Capital costs for new/improved venues and infrastructure
Direct economic contribution by event tourists and organisers	Operating costs through entire life-cycle of event
Investment attracted	Marketing costs
Leveraged benefits for local businesses	Opportunity costs (i.e., alternatives foregone)
Future event benefits; growth in tourism	Amenity and productivity losses to residents
Value of media coverage; image enhancements	Economic displacement (visitors, jobs, and businesses lost because of the event)
Increased capacity to attract events (i.e., the future value of venues)	Inflation (increases in costs to residents)
Increased marketing effectiveness	Debt servicing
Increased capacity to accommodate guests (through added rooms)	Costs of mitigating over-tourism
Reduced costs & prices; increased supply & choice	

Any of the KIIs mentioned in this book can be used, or others, and the aim is to come to a rational conclusion – based on evidence – about the wisdom of making a decision (to bid/build or not), or retrospectively about whether an event, policy, portfolio or strategy accomplished its goals (i.e. its merit) and was worthwhile. This approach can also be used in strategic IA, and for portfolios, incorporating indicators of cumulative impacts.

This is a subjective exercise, but utilizes whatever direct and surrogate measures are considered to be important and are available. It is intended to encourage comprehensiveness. Note that some indicators are for outputs, such as direct economic contribution, while others are for longer-term impacts such as social capital or economic growth.

9.2 Benefits And Costs Evaluation (BACE MODEL)

This strategic planning approach brings together evaluation and impact assessment, including both performance measures and impact indicators. Logic models and Theory of Change models can both be utilized. It is compatible with systems like the balanced scorecard and Event Compass. It is not a calculator, and has to be used with available evidence, or with scenarios and forecasts that specify goals and the indicators that will be used as evidence.

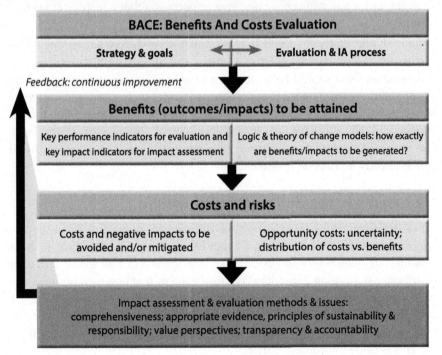

Figure 9.2: The BACE model

Benefits are identified before costs for one main reason, and that relates to the goal-attainment approach taken in this book and in the companion book *Event Evaluation*. It is normal to state goals, things we want to achieve, but then to also evaluate costs, risks and negatives. This approach is embedded in the Event Compass, and in the logic models and theory of change models being recommended.

BACE is a planning process that stresses evaluation. You can do a traditional cost-benefit analysis, or the modified CBA approach suggested above, and use it as one input to evaluation. It is suggested that users start with the notion that the whole process of impact assessment is designed to be part of an evaluation system, and not stand-alone.

Within a sustainability and responsibility paradigm, taking a long-term perspective on planning and impact assessment is essential. Combining the BACE model with a system like the balanced scorecard or Event Compass ensures that it is permanent, reflects diverse value perspectives, and is transparent. Accountability to stakeholders has to be a feature of any evaluation system.

Often the most important issue is not the actual identification and measurement of benefits and costs but their *distribution* – who gains and who pays? There is always a need to consider how disadvantaged and powerless groups will be affected. It is possible that many people gain economically and socially from an event, but a few suffer only negative impacts – is that a justifiable event or project?

There should always be input from all stakeholders before attempting a comprehensive benefit-cost evaluation as there will always be different opinions expressed on what should be evaluated and how. For example, will there be a full accounting of opportunity costs and externalities such as pollution or carbon emissions? Social legacy benefits can be much more important than the so-called legacies of white-elephant venues with no rational after-use. Improved image and increased tourism marketing effectiveness are not needed when 'over-tourism' is already an issue to residents.

9.2.1 Equity issues, and zero-sum situations

Evaluators might be faced with some difficult situations and decisions with regard to impacts. There is often a claim of benefits made, or a goal to create benefits, but evaluators also have to ask: who gains and who loses? This is the distributional question. It is critical because it seems that many events, and tourism in general, create substantial benefits for some, while others pay off the debt or experience some kind of loss. There is a danger in goal-attainment evaluation that the evaluators do not consider this issue, or do not look for externalities at all. That is tunnel-vision evaluation.

In a 'zero-sum game' one side or person wins, and the other loses. No matter how big the gains, they are completely offset by someone else's losses. That applies in sports and gambling, but not in most other human endeavours. By contrast, in a 'win-win' situation everyone gains, and of course we would like to aim for that illusive ideal with our events and other developments. In a 'lose-lose' situation there are no winners, and this is always considered to be a failure unless the stakes are so low that nobody cares.

Refer to Figures 9.3 and 9.4 which can be used in IA and evaluations to anticipate or identify winners and losers. The first table requires the evaluator to list costs and benefits for different stakeholders (there might be more than two groups, and any number of impact objects can be employed). This is a form of BACE evaluation, and the monetary values (usually only the economic domain) will have to be compared with intangibles. So the first question to arise is this: "are economic benefits or costs equivalent in weight to social, cultural and environmental costs and benefits?" This will spark debate.

Figure 9.3: A framework to identify winners and losers

Types of Impact	Examples of stakeholders who win/ benefit (specify the benefits)	Examples of stakeholders who lose or experience negative impacts (specify the costs or losses; consider society, culture and the environment to be stakeholders)
Social	New leisure opportunities in venues and at events, for those who can afford them (both residents and tourists)	Social groups excluded from participation owing to financial, physical or social disadvantage
Cultural	Elite groups benefit from investment in 'high culture' events and venues	Sub-cultures reject mainstream cultural events and institutions and usually fail to secure financial support
Ecological; Nature	Some interventions can restore habitat, clean up polluted areas and contribute to parks and protected areas	Externalities such as pollution (air, water, land, light, noise), greenhouse gas emissions, and impact on wildlife are seldom considered in formal cost-benefit analyses of events and venues
Built environment	Urban renewal, repositioning of cities, improved infrastructure and services can be benefits of major event and venue projects	Some neighbourhoods are likely to suffer increased traffic and noise, disruption of routines, or amenity losses owing to changes in land use
Economic	Tourism & hospitality sectors almost always gain financially from public investments in events, venues & tourism marketing; property owners, builders & suppliers gain from major venue projects	Small businesses might lose custom temporarily because of an event, or permanently from altered shopping and traffic patterns; new employment for some might be matched by redundancies elsewhere

Now evaluate four scenarios (there can be more) that evaluate important issues raised. This exercise can be part of feasibility assessments / forecasting, as well as for post-event, strategic and retrospective assessments. As suggested in the diagram, the only simple decision involves (3), being a lose-lose scenario when there are no benefits or winners identified. Scenario (1) shows up all the time when proponents of events and other investments are quick to identify purported benefits, but ignore or downplay the costs, negatives and equity issues. Scenario (2) is very difficult to evaluate because of different value perspectives; those suffering social or cultural costs will unlikely accept an argument that economic gains outweigh or balance their perceived losses. And, finally, scenario (4) seems improbable for most big investments or interventions – how many events or venues will generate only winners and positive impacts? In all three scenarios where decision-making is complex, opportunity costs should be factored into the equation.

Figure 9.4: Four scenarios to evaluate impacts

(1) Benefits exceed costs/losses	(2) Benefits = costs/losses
This is the usual basis upon which interventions are justified, by demonstrating substantial benefits. But can decision-makers justify the intervention knowing that some people lose, suffer negative impacts or pay more in order that others gain? This is a fundamental equity issue and it always has to be asked: "Do substantial gains for some justify making others pay?"	Analysis reveals that there are both benefits and costs, and/or negative and positive impacts, but they appear to offset each other. This might encourage some proponents to recommend intervention, but there is a serious issue: are all the domains being compared equal in the minds of the stakeholders? Can economic benefits/negatives be assigned the same 'weight' or value as social and cultural gains or losses? It is highly unlikely that stakeholders will accept equivalence across all impact 'objects'.
(3) There are only losses or negative impacts; all stakeholders lose	(4) There are only benefits and winners
Obviously this is a bad idea. Who proposed it, and why? Will they believe the evidence? There must be some hidden agenda.	This scenario seems very unlikely, except for small projects or investments; the bigger the intervention the more likely there are winners and losers. Opportunity costs might be the important issue.

Final words

Congratulations if you now understand all the issues, and can utilise all the theories, concepts, and methods inherent in impact assessment and evaluation! You are now qualified to be a life-long learner! The two companion books provide the foundation for professionalism, but it should also be clear that there is much more to study, and learning through experience will be the best teacher of all. I have always argued for a certification process for professional event evaluators, and that includes impact assessment, but so far this has been an unrealized hope. Perhaps these books will stimulate one or more professional associations or educational institutions to take up the challenge. I also hope that some students will be motivated to pursue evaluation and IA careers, and that some practitioners will contribute to the discourse on evaluation and impact assessment by documenting real-world experiences and contributing to formal learning.

Final study questions

These are essay-style questions covering the entire content of *Event Impact Assessment*, with reference as well to *Event Evaluation*.

1 You are assigned responsibility for forecasting the benefits of a major event that city council wants to bid on. How would you go about the project? Are there any ethical issues to consider?

2 Why does the complexity model claim that assessing the cumulative impacts of a portfolio of events within the sustainability paradigm is the most complex task of all? Discuss the complexity of this challenge in terms of theory, politics and methodology.

3 Of the main impact 'objects' (social, cultural, ecological, built environment, economic) which do you think presents the greatest challenge for impact assessment AND evaluation? Explain your reasoning.

4 Compare and contrast the five objects of IA in terms theory, methodology and the nature of appropriate evidence.

5 Theory of Change models are tools for strategic planning, impact assessment and evaluation. Explain how they work, and illustrate one graphically in the context of an impact assessment project where the event is conceived as an instrument of social marketing.

6 What, in your opinion, are the most important impacts on residents to consider when it comes to events and tourism as agents of change? Consider both benefits and costs/negatives. Where do externalities come into the picture?

References

Aicher, T., Karadakis, K., & Eddosary, M. (2015). Comparison of sport tourists' and locals' motivation to participate in a running event. *International Journal of Event and Festival Management, 6*(3), 215 - 234.

Andersson, T. & Lundberg, E. (2013). Commensurability and sustainability: Triple impact assessments of a tourism event. *Tourism Management, 37* (4), 99-109.

Andersson, T., Armbrecht, J. & Lundberg, E. (2012). Estimating use and non-use values of a music festival. *Scandinavian Journal of Hospitality and Tourism, 12* (3), 215-231.

Andersson, T., Armbrecht, J. & Lundberg, E. (2017). The use and non-use values of events: A conceptual framework. In, Lundberg, E. et al (Eds.), *The Value of Events* (pp. 89-104). London: Routledge.

Andersson, T., Getz, D., & Mykletun, R. (2013). Sustainable festival populations: An application of organizational ecology. *Tourism Analysis, 18* (6), 621-634.

Andersson, T. & Getz, D. (2016). Analyzing whole populations of festivals and events: An application of organizational ecology. *Journal of Policy Research In Tourism, Leisure & Events, 8* (3), 249-273.

Andersson, T., Getz, D., Gration, D. & Raciti, M. (2017). Event portfolios: Asset value, risk and returns. *International Journal of Event and Festival Management, 8* (3), 226-243.

Andersson, T., Jutbring, H. & Lundberg, E. (2013). When a music festival goes veggie: Communication and environmental impacts of an innovative food strategy. *International Journal of Event and Festival Management, 4* (3), 224-235.

Andreasen, A. (1994). Social marketing: Its definition and domain. *Journal of Public Policy & Marketing, 13* (1), 108-114.

Arai, S. & Pedlar, A. (2003). Moving beyond individualism in leisure theory: A critical analysis of concepts of community and social engagement. *Leisure Studies, 22*, 185–202.

Arcodia, C. & Whitford, M. (2006). Festival attendance and the development of social capital. *Journal of Convention & Event Tourism, 8* (2), 1-18.

Armbrecht, J., & Andersson, T. (2016) Subjects and objects of event impact analysis. *Scandinavian Journal of Hospitality and Tourism, 16* (2), 111-114.

Becker, H. & Vanclay, F. (2003). *The International Handbook of Social Impact Assessment: Conceptual and Methodological Advances.* Cheltenham: Edward Elgar.

Benckendorff, P. & Pearce, P. (2012). The psychology of events. In, Page, S. & Connell, J. (Eds.) *Routledge Handbook of Events*, pp. 165–185. London: Routledge.

Blake, A. (2005). *The Economic Impact of the London 2012 Olympics.* Research Report 2005/5, Christel DeHaan Tourism and Travel Research Institute, Nottingham University Business School.

Blakley, J., Duinker, P., Grieg, L., Hegmann, G. & Noble, B. (2017) Cumulative Eff ects Assessment, http://www.iaia.org/uploads/pdf/Fastips_16%20Cumulative%20 Effects%20Assessment_1.pdf

BOP Consulting (2011a). *Edinburgh Festivals Impact Study - Research and Knowledge Exchange in the Creative Economy: Impact and Effect.* Prepared for Festivals Edinburgh.

BOP Consulting (2011b). *Edinburgh Festivals Impact Study.* Prepared for Festivals Edinburgh.

BOP Consulting (2016a). *Edinburgh Festivals 2015 Impact Study Final Report.* Prepared for Festivals Edinburgh.

BOP Consulting (2016b). *Edinburgh Festivals 2015 Impact Study Technical Report.* Prepared for Festivals Edinburgh.

BOP Consulting (2018). *The Network Effect: The Role of the Edinburgh Festivals in the National Culture and Events Sectors.* Prepared for Festivals Edinburgh.

Bottero, M., Sacerdotti, S. & Mauro, S. (2012). Turin 2006 Olympic Winter Games: impacts and legacies from a tourism perspective. *Journal of Tourism and Cultural Change, 10* (2), 202-217.

Bourdieu, P. (1972). *Outline of a Theory of Practice.* Cambridge: Cambridge University Press.

Bourdieu, P. (1986). The forms of capital. In, J. Richardson (ed.), *Handbook of Theory and Research in the Sociology of Education.* New York: Greenwald Press.

Bourdieu, P. & and Passeron J. (1977). *Reproduction in Education, Society and Culture* (1990 edition translated from French by Richard Nice), London: Sage.)

Brouder, P., Anton Clave, S. Gill, A. & Ioannides, D. (2017). Why is tourism not an evolutionary science? Understanding the past, present and future of destination evolution, in *Tourist Destination Evolution,* Brouder, P., Anton Clave, S., Gill, A. and Ioannides, D. (Eds.). New York: Routledge.

Brown, K. (2016). *Resilience, Development and Global Change.* NY: Routledge.

Brown, S., Getz, D., Pettersson, R., & Wallstam, M. (2015). Event evaluation: Definitions, concepts and a state of the art review. *International Journal of Event and Festival Management, 6* (2), 135-157.

Buning, R., & Gibson, H. (2015). The evolution of active-sport-event travel careers. *Journal of Sport Management, 29,* 555-569.

Buning, R., & Gibson, H. (2016). Exploring the trajectory of active-sport-event travel careers: A social worlds perspective. *Journal of Sport Management, 30,* 265-281.

Burns, J., Hatch, J. & Mules, T. (Eds.) (1986). *The Adelaide Grand Prix: The Impact of a Special Event.* Adelaide: The Centre for South Australian Economic Studies.

Butler, R. (1980). The concept of a tourist area cycle of evolution: Implications for management of resources. *The Canadian Geographer, 24* (1), 5-12.

Butler, R. (2006a). *The Tourism Area Life Cycle: Applications and Modifications. Volume 1.* Clevedon: Channel View Publications.

Butler, R. (2006b). *The Tourism Area Life Cycle: Conceptual and Theoretical Issues. Volume 2.* Clevedon: Channel View Publications.

Carlsen, J., Andersson, T., Ali-Knight, J., Jaeger, K. and Taylor, R. (2010). Festival management innovation and failure. *International Journal of Event and Festival Management, 1* (2), 120-131.

Case, R. (2013). *Events and the Environment.* London: Routledge.

Centre of the Theory of Change (n.d.) What is Theory of Change? http://www.theoryofchange.org/what-is-theory-of-change/

Chalip, L. (2004). Beyond impact: A general model for sport event leverage. In, B.W. Ritchie & D. Adair (Eds.), *Sport tourism: Interrelationships, impacts and issues* (pp. 226– 252). Clevedon: Channel View.

Chalip, L. (2006). Towards social leverage of sport events. *Journal of Sport and Tourism, 11* (2), 109–127.

Chambers, J., Mullick, S. & Smith, D. *How to Choose the Right Forecasting Technique*. Harvard Business Review, Forecasting, https://hbr.org/1971/07/how-to-choose-the-right-forecasting-technique.

Cheer, J. & Lew, A. (Eds.)(2017). *Tourism, Resilience and Sustainability: Adapting to Social, Political and Economic Change*. London: Routledge.

Childers, M. (2012). *Colorado Powder Keg: Ski Resorts and the Environmental Movement*. Lawrence, Kansas: University of Kansas Press.

Cohen, E. (1988). Authenticity and commoditization in tourism. *Annals of Tourism Research, 15* (3), 371-386

Coleman, J. (1988). Social capital in the creation of human capital. *American Journal of Sociology, 94*, S95–S120.

Coleman, J. (1990). *Foundations of Social Theory*. Cambridge MA: Belknap Press of Harvard University Press.

Collins, A., & Flynn, A. (2008). Measuring the environmental sustainability of a major sporting event: A case study of the FA Cup Final. *Tourism Economics, 14*(4), 751–768.

Collins, A., Flynn, A., Mundy M. & Roberts, A. (2005). Exploring the environmental consequences of major sporting events: The 2003/04 FA Cup Final. *Urban Studies, 44* (3), 457–476.

Colombo, A. (2016). How to evaluate cultural impacts of events? A model and methodology proposal. *Scandinavian Journal of Hospitality and Tourism 16* (4), 500-511.

Convention Industry Council (2011). The Economic Significance of Meetings to the U.S. Economy, www.MeetingsMeanBusiness.com.

Crompton, J. (1999). *Measuring The Economic Impact Of Visitors To Sports Tournaments And Special Events*. Ashburn, Va.: Division of Professional Services, National Recreation and Park Association.

Crompton, J. (2006). Economic Impact Studies: Instruments for Political Shenanigans? *Journal of Travel Research, 45*, 67 - 82.

Crompton, J., and McKay, S. (1994). Measuring the economic impact of festivals and events: Some myths, misapplications and ethical dilemmas. *Festival Management and Event Tourism, 2* (1), 33–43.

Cultural Development Net (2015) *Outcomes of urban place-making projects: a holistic assessment*, http://www.culturaldevelopment.net.au/outcome

Daniels, M. (2007). Central place theory and sport tourism impacts. *Annals of Tourism Research, 34* (2), 332-347.

Daniels, M., and Norman, W. (2003): Estimating the economic impacts of seven regular sport tourism events. *Journal of Sport and Tourism, 8* (4): 214-222.

Davidson, R. & Hyde, A. (2015). *Winning Meetings and Events for Your Venue*. Oxford: Goodfellow Publishers.

Davies, L., Coleman, R. & Ramchandani, G. (2013). Evaluating event economic impact: Rigour versus reality? *International Journal of Event and Festival Management, 4* (1), 31-42.

Dawson, J. & Jöns, H. (2018). Unravelling legacy: A triadic actor- network theory approach to understanding the outcomes of mega events. *Journal of Sport & Tourism, 22* (1), 43-65.

Deery, M. & Jago, L. (2010). Social impacts of events and the role of anti-social behavior. *International Journal of Event and Festival Management, 1* (1), 8-28.

Delamere, T. (1997). Development of scale items to measure the social impact of community festivals. *Journal of Applied Recreation Research, 22* (4), 293–315.

Delamere, T. (2001). Development of scale to measure resident attitudes toward the social impacts of community festivals, Part II: Verification of the scale. *Event Management, 7* (1), 25–38.

Delamere, T. A., & Hinch, T. (1994). Community festivals. Celebration or sell out. *Recreation Canada, 52*(1), 26–29.

Delamere, T., Wankel, L., & Hinch, T. (2001). Development of a scale to measure resident attitudes toward the social impacts of community festivals, Part I: Item generation and purification of the measure. *Event Management, 7,* 11–24.

Derrett, R. (2003). Making sense of how festivals demonstrate a community's sense of place. *Event Management, 8* (1), 49-58.

Derrett, R. (2016). *The Complete Guide to Creating Enduring Festivals.* Wiley: Hoboken NJ.

du Cros, H. & McKercher (2014, 2d.ed.) *Cultural Tourism.* London: Routledge

Duignan, P. (2009). Using outcomes theory to solve important conceptual and practical problems in evaluation, monitoring and performance management systems. *American Evaluation Association Conference*, Orlando, Florida.

Dwyer, L. (2002). Economic contribution of convention tourism: Conceptual and empirical issues. In, K. Weber & K. Chon (Eds.), *Convention Tourism: International Research and Industry Perspectives*, pp. 21-35. Binghamton NY: Haworth Press.

Dwyer, L. (2015). Computable general equilibrium modelling: An important tool for tourism policy analysis. *Tourism & Hospitality Management, 21* (2), 111-126.

Dwyer, L., Forsyth, P. and Spurr, R. (2006). Assessing the economic impacts of events: A computable general equilibrium approach. Journal of Travel Research, 45 (1): 59-66.

Dwyer, L. & Forsyth, P. (2017). Event evaluation: Approaches and new challenges. In, Lundberg, E., Armbrecht, J., Andersson, T. & Getz, D. (Eds.). *The Value of Events*, pp.105-123. London: Routledge.

Dwyer, L. & and Jago, L. (2014). Economic evaluation of special events: Challenges for the future. In, Yeoman, M. Robertson, U. McMahon-Beattie, E. Backer & K. Smith (Eds.), *The Future of Events and Festivals*, pp. 99-114. London: Routledge.

Edinburgh Festival City (n.d.) https://www.edinburghfestivalcity.com/

Essex, S. & Chalkley, B. (1998). Olympic Games: Catalyst of urban change. *Leisure Studies, 17* (3), 187-206.

Esteves, A., Franks, D. & Vanclay F. (2012) Social impact assessment: The state of the art. *Impact Assessment and Project Appraisal, 30* (1), 34-42.

European Parliament (2011) Directive 2011/92/EU, http://ec.europa.eu/environment/eia/pdf/EIA_Directive_informal.pdf.

EventImpacts (n.d.) Economic Impact Calculator, http://www.eventimpacts.com/Calculator

EventImpacts (n.d.) Environmental impacts, http://www.eventimpacts.com/impact-types/environmental

Falassi, A. (ed.) (1987). *Time Out of Time: Essays on the Festival*. Albuquerque: University of New Mexico Press.

Fenich, G. (2014). *Meetings, Expositions, Events and Conventions: An Introduction to the Industry*, 4th ed. Upper Saddle River NJ: Pearson.

Fennell, D. (2014). Exploring the precautionary principle in an environment and tourism context. In, A. Lew, M. Hall, and A. Williams (Eds.), *The Wiley Blackwell Companion to Tourism*, pp. 513-523. Chichester, UK: Wiley.

Financial Times (n.d.) Definition of Corporate Social Responsibility, http://lexicon.ft.com/Term?term=corporate-social-responsibility--(CSR).

Fox, D., Gouthro, M., Morakabati, Y. & and Brackstone, J. (2014). *Doing Events Research: From theory to practice*. London: Routledge.

Frawley, S. (ed.)(2017). *Managing Sport Mega-Events*. London: Routledge.

Fredline, E., Jago, L., & Deery, M. (2003). The development of a generic scale to measure the social impacts of events. *Event Management, 8* (1), 23–37.

Frost, W. & Laing, J. (2013). *Commemorative Events: Memory, Identities, Conflict*. London: Routledge.

Garcia, I. (2012). *The Olympic Games and Cultural Policy*. London: Routledge.

Getz, D. (2009). Policy for sustainable and responsible festivals and events: Institutionalization of a new paradigm. *Journal of Policy Research in Tourism, Leisure and Events, 1* (1), 61-78.

Getz, D. (2013). *Event Tourism: Concepts, International Case Studies, and Research*. New York: Cognizant Communications.

Getz, D. (2015a). *Draft guidelines for event evaluation and impact forecasting/assessment. Report for RF (Riksidrotts- förbundet — The Swedish Sport Confederation)*. www.svenskidrott.se/globalassets/svenskidrott/doku ment/undersidor/centrum-for-idrottsevenemang/guide line-for-sport-event-evaluation-in-sweden.pdf

Getz, D. (2015b). The forms and functions of planned events: Past and future. In. I. Yeoman, M. Robertson, U. McMahon-Beattie, E. Backer & K. Smith (Eds.), *The Future of Events and Festivals*, pp. 20-35. London: Routledge.

Getz, D. (2017). Developing a framework for sustainable event cities. *Event Management, 21* (5), 575-591.

Getz, D. (2018). *Event Evaluation: Theory and Methods for Event Management and Tourism*. Oxford: Goodfellow Publishers.

Getz, D., & Andersson, T. (2008). Sustainable festivals: On becoming an institution. *Event Management, 12* (1), 1-17.

Getz, D., & Andersson, T. (2010). The event-tourist career trajectory: A study of high-involvement amateur distance runners. *Scandinavian Journal of Tourism and Hospitality, 19* (4), 468-491.

Getz, D. & Andersson, T. (2016). Analyzing whole populations of festivals and events: An application of organizational ecology. *Journal of Policy Research in Tourism, Leisure and Events, 8* (3), 249-273.

Getz, D., Robinson, R., Andersson, T. & Vujicic, S. (2014). *Foodies and Food Tourism*. Oxford: Goodfellow Publishers.

Getz, D., & McConnell, A. (2011). Serious sport tourism and event travel careers. *Journal of Sport Management, 25* (4), 326-338.

Getz, D., & McConnell, A. (2014). Comparing runners and mountain bikers on involvement and event-travel careers. *Journal of Convention and Event Tourism, 15* (1), 69-100.

Getz, D. & Nilsson, P. (2004). Responses of family businesses to extreme seasonality in demand: The case of Bornholm, Denmark. *Tourism Management 25*, 17-30.

Getz, D. & Page, S. (2016). *Event Studies: Theory, Research and Policy for Planned Events.* London: Routledge.

Getz, D., Svensson, B., Pettersson, R. and Gunnerval, A. (2012). Hallmark events: definition, goals and planning process. *International Journal of Event Management Research, 7* (1/2), 47-67.

Gilmore, J. & Pine, J. (2007). *Authenticity: What consumers really want.* Boston: Harvard Business School Press.

Goffman, E. (1959). *The Presentation of Self in Everyday Life.* Garden City NJ: Doubleday.

Goodwin, H. (2012, 2d. ed). *Responsible Tourism: Using Tourism for Sustainable Development.* Oxford: Goodfellow Publishers.

Gration, D., Raciti, M., Getz, D., & Andersson, T. (2016). Resident valuation of planned events: an event portfolio pilot study. *Event Management, 20*, 607–622.

Gratton, C., Shibli, S. & Coleman, R. (2005). The economics of sport tourism at major sports events. In, J. Higham (Ed.). *Sport Tourism Destinations: Issues, Opportunities And Analysis,* pp. 233-247. London: Routledge.

Green, C., & Chalip, L. (1998). Sport tourism as the celebration of subculture. *Annals of Tourism Research, 25* (2), 275-291.

Green, C., & Jones, I. (2005). Serious leisure, social identity and sport tourism. *Sport in Society, 8* (2), 164-181.

Green Event Book (n.d.) Carbon Footprints, www.greeneventbook.com/event-carbon-footprint-possible/

Greenwood, D. (1972). Tourism as an agent of change: A Spanish Basque case study. *Ethnology,* 11 (1), 80–91.

Greenwood, D. (1989). Culture by the pound: An anthropological perspective on tourism as cultural commodification. In, V. Smith (ed.), *Hosts and Guests: The Anthropology of Tourism* (2nd edn.), pp. 171–185. Philadelphia: University of Pennsylvania Press.

Gursoy, D., Kim, K., and Uysal, M. (2004). Perceived impacts of festivals and special events by organizers: An extension and validation. *Tourism Management, 25* (2): 171-182.

Hall, C.M. (2012). Sustainable mega-events: beyond the myth of balanced approaches to mega-event sustainability. *Event Management, 16* (2), 119-131.

Hall, C., Gossling, and Scott (2015)(Eds.). *Routledge Handbook of Tourism and Sustsainability.* London: Routledge.

Hall, C.M. & Lew, A. (2009). *Understanding and Managing Tourism Impacts: An Integrated Approach.* London: Routledge.

Hartmann, R. (2006). Downstream and down-valley: Essential components and directions of growth and change in the sprawling resort landscapes of the rocky mountain west. In Clark, Gill and Hartmann (Eds.) *Mountain Resort Planning and Development in an Era of Globalization,* pp. 278 – 293. NY: Cognizant.

Hartmann, R. (2017a). The world alpine ski championships 1989, 1999 and 2015 in Vail, Colorado: Impacts, issues and the quest for sustainable resort development. *International Journal of Research in Tourism and Hospitality, 3* (3), 43-53.

Hartmann, R. (2017b). Vail's story retold: Applications of John Steinbeck's realistic prose to reconstructing growth and change of a Colorado high mountain town. *Journalism and Mass Communication, 7* (9), September, 481-496.

Higham, J. (Ed.). (2005). *Sport Tourism Destinations: Issues, Opportunities And Analysis.* London: Routledge.

Hinch, T. & Higham, J. (2011) *Sport Tourism Development,* 2nd ed. Bristol: Channel View.

Holmes, K., Hughes, M., Mair, J., & Carlsen, J. (2015). *Events and Sustainability.* London: Routledge.

Hover, P., Dijk, B., Breedveld, K., van Eekeren, F. & Slender, H. (2016*). Creating Social Impact With Sport Events*. Mulier Institute & Utrecht University. https://www. kennisbanksportenbewegen.nl/?file=7147&m=1469436781&action=file.download

International Association for Community Development (n.d.), www.iacdglobal.org

International Association for Impact Assessment (2015), Social Impact Assessment. http://www.iaia.org, http://www.iaia.org/uploads/pdf/SIA_Guidance_ Document_IAIA.pdf

International Organisation for Standardisation, ISO 20121 (2012), https://www.iso. org/standard/54552.html

Jepson, A. & Stadler, R. (2017). Conceptualising the impact of festival and event attendance upon family quality of life (QOL). *Event Management, 21* (1), 47-60.

Jones, M. (2018, 3d. ed.). *Sustainable Event Management A Practical Guide.* London: Earthscan.

Jones, R., Pilgrim, A., Thompson, G. & MacGregor, C. (2008). *Assessing the Environmental Impacts of Special Events: Examination of nine special events in Western Australia.* Report. Australia: CRC for Sustainable Tourism.

Jones, B., Scott, D., and Khaled, H. (2006). Implications of climate change for outdoor event planning: A case of three special events in Canada's National Capital Region. *Event Management, 10* (1): 63-76.

Jutbring, H. (2017). *Social Marketing through Events.* University of Gothenburg, School of Business Economics and Law. Dissertation for the degree of Doctor of Business Administration.

Kania, L. (2013). Social capital in the metropolis BrabantStad: Exploring the role of a community event in developing social capital. In, G. Richards, M. de Brito, & L. Wilks, (Eds.), *Exploring the Social Impacts of Event,* pp. 45-56. London: Routledge.

Kim, H., Borges, M., and Chon, J. (2006). Impacts of environmental values on tourism motivation: The case of FICA, Brazil. *Tourism Management, 27,* 957–967.

Kotler, P. and Zaltman, G. (1971). Social marketing: An approach to planned social change. *Journal of Marketing, 35* (3), 3-12.

Kyle, G., Absher, J., Norman, W., Hammitt, W., & Jodice, L. (2007). A Modified Involvement Scale, *Leisure Studies, 26* (4), 399-427.

Laing, J. & Mair, J. (2015). Music festivals and social inclusion – the festival organizers' perspective. *Leisure Sciences, 37,* 252–268.

Lamont, M., Kennelly, M., & Wilson, E. (2012). Competing priorities as con-straints in event travel careers. *Tourism Management, 33* (5), 1068-1079.

Larson, M. (2009). Joint event production in the jungle, the park and the garden: Metaphors of event networks. *Tourism Management, 30* (3), 393-399.

Larson, M. & Wikstrom, E. (2001). Organising events: Managing conflict and consensus in a political market square. *Event Management, 7* (1), 51-65.

Larson, M., Getz, D. & Pastras, P. (2015). The legitimacy of festivals and their stakeholders: Concepts and propositions. *Event Management, 19*, 159–174.

Lask, T. (2011). Cognitive maps: A sustainable tool for impact evaluation. *Journal of Policy Research in Tourism, Leisure and Events, 3* (1), 44-62.

Leopold, L., Clarke, F., Hanshaw, B., & Balsley, J. (1971). *A Procedure for Evaluating Environmental Impact.* Geological Survey Circular 645. Washington: U.S. Geological Survey.

Levy, S., Getz, D. & Hudson, S. (2011). A field experimental investigation of managerially facilitated consumer-to-consumer interaction. *Journal of Travel & Tourism Marketing, 28* (6), 656-674.

Lew, A. and Cheer, J. (Eds.)(2017). *Tourism Resilience and Adaptation to Environmental Change*: Definitions and Frameworks. New York: Routledge.

London Healthy Urban Development Unit of the National Health Service (2013). Rapid Health Impact Assessment Tool. https://www.healthyurbandevelopment. nhs.uk/wp-content/uploads/2013/12/HUDU-Rapid-HIA-Tool-Jan-2013-Final.pdf.

Lundberg, E., Armbrecht, J., Andersson, T. & Getz, D. (eds.). (2017). *The Value of Events.* London: Routledge.

MacCannell, D. (1973). Staged authenticity: Arrangements of social space in tourist settings. *American Journal of Sociology, 79* (3), 589-603.

MacCannell, D. (1976). *The Tourist: A New Theory of the Leisure Class.* NY: Schocken Books.

McCool, S. (2013). Limits of acceptable change and tourism. In Holden, A. and Fennel, D. (Eds.), *Routledge Handbook of Tourism and the Environment*, pp. 285-298. London: Routledge.

McGillivray, D. & Turner, D. (2018). *Event Bidding: Politics, Persuasion and Resistance.* London: Routledge.

McPherson, G., Misener, L., McGillivray, D. & and Legg, D. (2017). Creating public value through parasport events. *Event Management, 21*, 185–199.

Maennig, W. & Zimbalist, A. (2012). *International Handbook on the Economics of Mega Sporting Events.* Edward Elgar Publishing.

Mair, J. (2013). *Conferences and Conventions: A Research Perspective.* London: Routledge.

Mair, J. (Ed.)(2019). *Routledge Handbook of Festivals.* London: Routledge.

Malek, K., Tanford, S. & Baloglu, S. (2018). Evaluating event effectiveness across alternate platforms. *Event Management, 22* (2), 135-151.

Masterman, G. (2014) *Strategic Sport Management*, 3rd ed. London: Routledge.

Matheson, V. (2002). Upon further review: An examination of sporting event economic impact studies. *The Sport Journal, 5* (1), 1-3.

Matheson, V. (2006). *Megaevents: The effect of the world's biggest sporting events on local, regional and national economies* (Paper No. 06-10). College of the Holy Cross, Department of Economics Faculty Research Press, Worcester, MA.

Matheson, V. & Baade, R. (2003). Bidding for the Olympics: Fools gold? In, C. Baros, M. Ibrahim & S. Szymanski (Eds.), *Transatlantic Sport.* London: Edward Elgar.

Meyrick, J. (2015). Numbers, schnumbers: Total cultural value and talking about everything that we do, even culture. *International Journal of Event and Festival Management, 6* (2), 99-110.

Mayfield, T. & J. Crompton (1995). Development of an instrument for identifying community reasons for staging a festival. *Journal of Travel Research, 33* (3), 37-44.

Mihalik, B. (1994). Mega-event legacies of the 1996 Atlanta Olympics. In, P. Murphy (Ed.), *Quality Management in Urban Tourism: Balancing Business and Environment,* Proceedings, pp. 151-162. University of Victoria.

Mihalik, B. (2000). Host population perceptions of the 1996 Atlanta Olympics: Support, benefits and liabilities. *Tourism Analysis, 5* (1), 49–53.

Miller, S. & Fredericks, M. (2003). The nature of 'evidence' in qualitative research methods. *International Journal of Qualitative Methods, 2* (1).

Mills, B. and Rosentraub, M. (2012). Hosting mega-events: A guide to the evaluation of development effects in integrated metropolitan regions. *Tourism Management, 34,* 238-246.

Misener, L. & Schulenkorf, N. (2016). Rethinking the social value of sport events through an asset-based community development (ABCD) perspective. *Journal of Sport Management, 30,* 329-340.

Moscardo, G. (2007). Analyzing the role of festivals and events in regional development. *Event Management, 11* (1/2): 23-32.

Mules, T. (1993). A special event as part of an urban renewal strategy. *Festival Management and Event Tourism, 1* (2): 65–67.

Newbold, C., Maughan, C., Jordan, J. & Bianchini, F. (2015). *Focus on Festivals: Contemporary European case studies and perspectives.* Oxford: Goodfellow Publishers.

Nordvall, A. (2015). Organizing periodic events: A case study of a failed Christmas market. *Scandinavian Journal of Hospitality and Tourism, 16* (4), 442-460.

Nordvall, A. & Heldt, T. (2017). Understanding hallmark event failure: A case study of a Swedish music festival. *International Journal of Event and Festival Management, 8* (2), 172-185.

Nunez, T. (1989). Touristic studies an anthropological perspective. In, V. Smith (Ed.). *Hosts and Guests: The anthropology of tourism* (2nd ed.). Philadelphia: University of Pennsylvania Press.

Orr, M. & Jarvis, N. (2018). Blinded by gold: Toronto sports community ignores negative legacies of 2015 Pan Am Games. *Event Management, 22* (3), 367-378.

O'Sullivan, D., and Jackson, M. (2002). Festival tourism: A contributor to sustainable local economic development? *Journal of Sustainable Tourism, 10* (4), 325-342.

Pacione, M. (2012). The role of events in urban regeneration. In, S. Page, & J. Connell (Eds.), *Routledge Handbook of Events,* pp. 385- 400. London: Routledge.

Pappas, N. (2014). Hosting mega events: Londoners' support of the 2012 Olympics. *Journal of Hospitality & Tourism Management, 21,* 10–17.

Pappas, N. (2017). Pre- and post-evaluation of residents' participation and support of the 2012 London Olympics. *Event Management, 21,* (6), 747-770.

Parent, M. & Chappelet, J-L. (Eds.)(2015). *Routledge Handbook of Sports Event Management.* London: Routledge.

Parent, M. & Séguin, B. (2007). Factors that led to the drowning of a world championship organizing committee: A stakeholder approach. *European Sport Management Quarterly, 7* (2), 187-212.

Patterson, I. & Getz, D. (2013). At the nexus of leisure and event studies. *Event Management, 17*, 227–240.

Pearce, P., Moscardo, G. & Ross, G. (1996). *Tourism Community Relationships.* Oxford: Pergamon.

Potwarka, L. & Snelgrove, R. (2917). Introduction—managing sport events for beneficial outcomes: Theoretical and practical insights. *Event Management, 21*, 135–137.

Preuss, H. (2004). *The Economics of Staging the Olympics. A Comparison of the Games 1972-2008.* Cheltenham: Edward Elgar Publishing.

Preuss, H. (2007). The conceptualisation and measurement of mega sport event legacies. *Journal of Sport & Tourism, 12* (3-4), 207–228.

Preuss, H. (2013). Are investments in mega-sport events useful and efficient? In, D. Getz, *Event Tourism,* 374-376. NY: Cognizant.

Putnam, R. (1995). Tuning in, tuning out: The strange disappearance of social capital in America. *Political Science and Politics, 28*, 664–683.

Putnam, R. (2001). *Bowling Alone: The Collapse and Revival of American Community,* New York: Simon & Schuster.

Putnam, R. (2004). *Democracies in Flux: The Evolution of Social Capital in Contemporary Society.* New York: Oxford University Press.

Quinn, B. (2006). Problematising 'festival tourism': Arts festivals and sustainable development in Ireland. *Journal of Sustainable Tourism, 14* (3), 288-306.

Quinn, B. (2013). *Key Concepts in Event Management.* London: Sage.

Ramchandani, G. & Coleman, R. (2012).Testing the accuracy of event economic impact forecasts. *International Journal of Event and Festival Management, 3* (2), 188-200.

Ramchandani, G., Coleman, R., Davies, L., Shibli, S. & Bingham, J. (2017). Valuing the inspirational impacts of major sports events. In, Lundberg, E., Armbrecht, J., Andersson, T. & Getz, D. (eds.), *The Value of Events,* pp. 136-158. London: Routledge.

Reid, S. (2007). Identifying social consequences of rural events. *Event Management, 11* (1/2): 89-98.

Reis, A., Frawley, S., Hodgetts, D., Thomson, A. & Hughes, K. (2017). Sport participation legacy and the Olympic Games: The case of Sydney 2000, London 2012, and Rio 2016. *Event Management, 21*, 139–158.

Rethinkurban.com (n.d.) Placemaking, http://rethinkurban.com/placemaking/

Richards, G. (Ed.)(2007a). *Cultural Tourism Global and Local Perspectives.* NY: Haworth Press.

Richards, G. (2007b). Culture and authenticity in a traditional event: The views of producers, residents, and visitors in Barcelona. *Event Management, 11* (1/2), 33-44.

Richards, G. (2017). From place branding to placemaking: The role of events. *International Journal of Event and Festival Management, 8* (1), 8-23.

Richards, G., de Brito, M. & Wilks, L. (Eds.)(2013). *Exploring the Social Impacts of Events.* London: Routledge.

Richards, G. & Palmer, R. (2010). *Eventful Cities: Cultural Management and Urban Revitalisation.* London: Routledge.

Ritchie, B.W. & Adair, D. (Eds.)(2004). *Sport Tourism: Interrelationships, Impacts and Issues.* Clevedon: Channel View.

Ritchie, J.R.B. (2001). Turning 16 days into 16 years through Olympic legacies. *Event Management, 6*, pp. 155–165,

Ritchie, J.R.B. & Beliveau, D. (1974). Hallmark events: An evaluation of a strategic response to seasonality in the travel market. *Journal of Travel Research, 14*, 14-20.

Ritchie, J.R.B. & Crouch, G. (2003). *The Competitive Destination: A Sustainable Tourism Perspective.* Wallingford, UK: CABI.

Ritchie, J.R.B. & Smith, B. (1991). The impact of a mega-event on host-region awareness: A longitudinal study. *Journal of Travel Research, 30* (1), 3-10

Robinson, R.N.S., & Getz, D. (2016). Food enthusiasts and tourism: Exploring involvement dimensions. *Journal of Hospitality and Tourism Research, 40* (4), 432-455.

Rogers, T. & Davidson, R. (2015). *Marketing Destinations and Venues for Conferences, Conventions and Business Events.* London: Routledge.

Rogerson, R. (2016). Re-defining temporal notions of event legacy: Lessons from Glasgow's Commonwealth Games. *Annals of Leisure Research, 19* (4), 497-518.

Rosall Remmen and Cares (1989). *The World Alpine Ski Championships Post-Events Evaluation.* Boulder, Colorado.

Rosentraub, M. (2009). *Major League Winners: Using Sports and Cultural Centers as Tools for Economic Development.* American Society for Public Administration.

Sadd, D. (2012). What is event-led regeneration? Are we confusing terminology or will London 2012 be the first games to truly benefit the local existing population? *Event Management, 13*, 265–275

Sagnia, K. (2004). *Framework For Cultural Impact Assessment Project.* Dakar: International Network for Cultural Diversity (INCD).

Santa-Ibanez, C., Wilson, J. & Anton Clave, S. (2017). Moments as catalysts for change in tourism evolutionary paths. In, Brouder, P., Anton Clave, S., Gill, A. & Ioannides, D. (Eds.), *Tourism Destination Evolution*, pp. 81-102. NY: Routledge.

Scotinform Ltd. (1991). *Edinburgh Festivals Study 1990-91: Visitor Survey and Economic Impact Assessment, Final Report.* Edinburgh: Scottish Tourist Board.

Scotsman, The (May 10, 2018). Public Fury at Edinburgh Festival Impact Reaches an All-Time Peak, By Brian Ferguson. https://www.scotsman.com/lifestyle/public-fury-at-edinburgh-festival-impact-reaches-an-all-time-peak-1-4737466.

Schlenker, K., Foley, C. & Getz, D. (2005). *Encore: Event Evaluation Kit -Review and Redevelopment.* Sustainable Tourism Cooperative Research Centre, Griffith University, Gold Coast, Queensland.

Schulenkorf, S. & Schlenker, K. (2017). Leveraging sport events to maximize community benefits in low-and middle-income countries. *Event Management, 21*, 217–231.

Sharpley, R. & Stone, P. (2012). Socio-cultural impacts of events: Meanings, authorized transgression and social capital. In, S. Page and J. Connell (Eds.), *The Routledge Handbook of Events*, pp. 347-361. London: Routledge.

Shaw, G. & Williams, A. (2004). *Tourism and Tourism Spaces.* London: Sage.

Shin, H. (2010). *The Economic Impact of Sporting Event: How to Measure the Local Economic Impact of Sporting Event by Input Output Analysis.* VDM Verlag Dr. Müller.

Shipway, R. & Fyall, A. (Eds.)(2012). *International Sports Events: Impacts, Experiences and Identities.* London: Routledge.

Small, K. (2007). Social dimensions of community festivals: An application of factor analysis in the development of the Social Impact Perception (SIP) scale. *Event Management, 11* (1–2), 45–55.

Small, K., Edwards, D. & Sheridan, L. (2005). A flexible framework for evaluating the socio-cultural impacts of a small festival. *International Journal of Event Management Research 1* (1), 66-76.

Smith, A. (2012) *Events and Urban Regeneration: The Strategic Use of Events to Revitalise Cities.* London: Routledge.

Smith, A. (2016). *Events in the City: Using public spaces as event venues.* Abingdon, UK: Routledge.

Smith, A. (2017). Animation or denigration? Using urban public spaces as event venues, *Event Management, 21,* 609–619.

Smith, V. (ed.) (1989) *Hosts and Guests: The anthropology of tourism* (2nd ed.). Philadelphia: University of Pennsylvania Press.

Social Capital Research (n.d.) https://www.socialcapitalresearch.com/measure-social-capital/

SQW Economic Development Consultants (2005). *Edinburgh's Year Round Festivals 2004-2005 Economic Impact Study, Final Report to: The City of Edinburgh Council, Scottish Enterprise, Edinburgh and Lothian, EventScotland & VisitScotland. Edinburgh.*

Stadler, R. and Jepson, A. (2017). Understanding the value of events for families, and the impact upon their quality of life. In, Lundberg, E., Armbrecht, J., Andersson, T. & Getz, D. (eds.), *The Value of Events,* pp. 159-177. London: Routledge.

Stankey, G., Cole, D., Lucas, R., Petersen, M. & Frissell, S. (1985). *The Limits of Acceptable Change (LAC) System for Wilderness Planning.* United States Department of Agriculture Forest Service Intermountain Forest and Range Experiment Station Ogden, UT.

Stebbins, R. (1992). *Amateurs, Professionals, and Serious Leisure.* Montréal, Québec:Mc-Gill-Queen's University Press.

Stebbins, R. (2001). Serious leisure. *Society, 38* (4), 53-57.

Study.com (n.d.) Social integration: Definition & theory, https://study.com/academy/lesson/social-integration-definition-theory.html

Taks, M., Green, B., Misener, L. & Chalip, L. (2014). Evaluating sport development outcomes: The case of a medium sized international sport event. *European Sport Management Quarterly, 14* (3), 213-237.

Tanner, M., Künzi, A., Friedli, T. & Müller, H. (2018). Event performance index: A holistic valuation tool. *International Journal of Event and Festival Management, 9* (2), 166-182.

Timothy, D. (2011). *Cultural Heritage and Tourism: An Introduction.* Bristol: Channel View.

Torres-Delgado, A. & Palomeque, F. (2014). Measuring sustainable tourism at the municipal level. *Annals of Tourism Research, 49,* 122–137.

Turner, V. (1969). *The Ritual Process: Structure and Anti-Structure.* New York: Aldine de Gruyter.

Tyrell, B., and Ismail, J. (2005). A methodology for estimating the attendance and economic impact of an open-gate festival. *Event Management, 9* (3), 111-118.

Tyrrell, T., and Johnston, R. (2001). A framework for assessing direct economic impacts of tourist events: Distinguishing origins, destinations, and causes of expenditures. *Journal of Travel Research, 40,* 94-100.

UK Music (2011; 2017). Destination Music: The contribution of music festivals and major concerts to tourism in the UK. https://www.ukmusic.org/assets/general/Measuring_Music_2017_Final.pdf.

UK National Health Service (2017). Healthy Urban Development. https://www.healthyurbandevelopment.nhs.uk/wp-content/uploads/2017/05/HUDU-Rapid-HIA-Tool-3rd-edition-April-2017.pdf

UK Sport (2004). *Measuring Success 2: The economic impact of major sports events.* London.

UNESCO (n.d.) What is Intangible Cultural Heritage? https://ich.unesco.org/en/what-is-intangible-heritage-00003.

United States Council on Environmental Quality (CEQ) (1980). *Regulations for Implementing the Procedural Provisions of the National Environmental Policy Act (CEQ Regulations)*, 40 CFR Parts1500 - 1508.

Unruh, D. (1980). The nature of social worlds. *Pacific Sociological Review, 23* (3), 271-296.

UNWTO (United Nations World Tourism Organisation) (2017). *Maximizing the Benefits of Mega Events for Tourism Development.* UNWTO: Madrid.

Van Aalst, I. & van Melik, R. (2012). City festivals and urban development: Does place matter? *European Urban and Regional Studies, 19* (2), 195.

Vanclay, F. (2003). International principles for social impact assessment. *Impact Assessment & Project Appraisal 21* (1), 5-11.

Vanclay, F.(Ed.). (2014) *Developments in Social Impact Assessment.* Cheltenham: Edward Elgar.

Vanclay, F. & Esteves, A. (Eds.) (2011). *New Directions in Social Impact Assessment: Conceptual and Methodological Advances.* Cheltenham: Edward Elgar.

van Gennep, A. (1909). *The Rites of Passage* (1960 translation by M. Vizedom and G. Coffee). London: Routledge and Kegan Paul.

Vaughan, R. (1979). *Does A Festival Pay? A Case Study Of The Edinburgh Festival In 1976.* Tourism Recreation Research Unit, Working Paper 5, University of Edinburgh.

Veal, A. & Burton, C. (2014). *Research Methods for Arts and Event Management.* Upper Saddle River NJ: Pearson.

Wackernagel, M., Schulz,N.B., Deumling, D., Callejas Linares, A., Jenkins, M., Kapos, V. Monfreda, C. Loh, J., Myers, N. Norgaard, R. & Randers, J. (2002). Tracking the ecological overshoot of the human economy. *Proceedings of the National Academy of Sciences of the United States of America, 99* (14).

Weed, M. (2008a). *Olympic Tourism.* Oxford: Butterworth-Heinemann.

Weed, M. (Ed.) (2008b). *Sport Tourism: A Reader.* London: Routledge.

Weed, M. & Bull, C. (2004). *Sports Tourism: Participants, Policy and Providers.* Oxford: Elsevier.

Weiss, C. (1972). *Evaluation Research. Methods for Assessing Program Effectiveness.* Prentice-Hall, Inc., Englewood Cliffs, New Jersey

Weiss, C. (1995). Nothing as practical as good theory: Exploring theory-based evaluation for comprehensive community initiatives for children and families. In, Connell, J, Kubisch, A, Schorr, L, and Weiss, C. (Eds.), *New Approaches to Evaluating Community Initiatives.* Washington, DC: Aspen Institute.

Whitford, M. & Ruhanen, L. (2013). Indigenous festivals and community development: A sociocultural analysis of an Australian indigenous festival. *Event Management, 17* (1), 49-61.

Wikipedia articles: cascade effect; ecological footprint; heuristic; outcomes theory; precautionary principle; strategic impact assessment; validity

Wilks, L. (2011). Bridging and bonding: Social capital at music festivals. *Journal of Policy Research in Tourism, Leisure and Events, 3* (3), 281-297.

Wood, E. (2006). Measuring the social impacts of local authority events: A pilot study for a civic pride scale. *International Journal of Nonprofit and Voluntary Sector Marketing, 11* (3), 165–179.

Woosnam, K., Van Winkle, C. & An, S. (2013). Confirming the festival social impact attitude scale in the context of a rural Texas cultural festival. *Event Management, 17,* 257–270.

Xie, P. & Gu, K. (2015). The changing urban morphology: Waterfront redevelopment and event tourism in New Zealand. *Tourism Management Perspectives 15,* 105–114.

Xie, P. & Smith, S. (2000). Improving forecasts for world's fair attendance: Incorporating income effects. *Event Management, 6* (1), 15-23.

Yeoman, I., Robertson, M., McMahon-Beattie, U., Backer, E. & Smith, K. (Eds.). *The Future of Events and Festivals.* London: Routledge.

Ziakas, V. (2013). A multi-dimensional investigation of a regional event portfolio: Advancing theory and praxis. *Event Management, 17* (1), 27-48.

Ziakas, V. (2014). *Event Portfolio Planning and Management: A holistic approach.* Abingdon: Routledge.

Ziakas, V. (2018). Issues, patterns and strategies in the development of event portfolios: Configuring models, design and policy. *Journal of Policy Research in Tourism, Leisure and Events.* Published online: doi.org/10.1080/19407963.2018.147 1481.

Zimbalist, A. (2015a). *Circus Maximus: The Economic Gamble Behind Hosting the Olympics and the World Cup.* Washington D.C.: Brookings Institution Press.

Zimbalist, A. (2015b). The illusory economic gains from hosting the Olympics and World Cup. *World Economics, 16* (1), 35–42.

Index